The Charismatic Movement

The Charismatic Movement

I. All About Tongues--Scriptural or Fraud?
II. Divine Healing & Healers. Some Healed, Many Not.

by Dr. John R. Rice

SWORD OF THE LORD PUBLISHERS
Murfreesboro, Tennessee 37130

Printed and bound in the United States of America

Table of Contents

Acknowledgments

The author has done extensive research and thorough study in the preparation of this volume. He wishes to acknowledge with sincere gratitude the kind cooperation of the following publishers and authors for granting permission to quote from the books indicated:

Miraculous Healing by Henry W. Frost, published by Fleming H. Revell Company;

They Speak With Other Tongues by John L. Sherrill, copyright 1964 by John L. Sherrill, published by McGraw-Hill Book Company;

HEALING: A Doctor in Search of a Miracle by William A. Nolen. Copyright © 1974 by William A. Nolen, M.D. Published by Random House, Inc.;

Tongues in Biblical Perspective by Charles Smith, published by The Brethren Missionary Herald Books;

These Are Not Drunken As Ye Suppose by Howard M. Ervin, published by Logos International;

The Baptism of the Holy Spirit and the Value of Speaking in Tongues Today by Oral Roberts;

New Testament Teaching on Tongues by Merrill F. Unger, published by Kregel Publications; and

The Mission of the Holy Spirit by H. A. Ironside, published by Loizeaux Brothers, Inc.

PART I:

All About Tongues— Scriptural or Fraud?

Non-Christian Religions and in Secular Non-Christian Literature
2. Mistakenly, Christian Scholars, Sometimes Not Very Spiritual, Have Read This Heathen Meaning of Tongues Into the Bible
3. In Bible Cases Where Tongues Are Mentioned, It Referred to Literal Foreign Languages

CHAPTER III—THE LANGUAGES (TONGUES) AT PENTECOST

I. WE ARE TOLD EXACTLY WHAT HAPPENED AT PENTECOST
II. THE BIBLE GIFT OF TONGUES—MIRACULOUS POWER TO SPEAK TO OTHERS IN THEIR OWN KNOWN LANGUAGE IN ORDER TO GET THEM THE GOSPEL
III. MIRACULOUS LANGUAGES AT PENTECOST ONLY ONE OF THREE INCIDENTAL MIRACLES, ACTS 2:1-4 TELLS US
IV. MIRACULOUS FOREIGN LANGUAGES NOT "INITIAL EVIDENCE OF BAPTISM OF HOLY SPIRIT," AS SOME CLAIM

CHAPTER IV—BAPTISM OF HOLY SPIRIT MEANS ENDUEMENT OF POWER

I. MISTAKEN SCOFIELD BIBLE AND PLYMOUTH BRETHREN TEACHING
1. First Corinthians 12:13 Does Not Refer to Pentecost
2. Sealed With the Spirit Comes at Salvation
II. OBVIOUS INTENT OF SCRIPTURES SEEMS TO BE THAT "BAPTIZED OF THE HOLY GHOST" MEANS "ENDUED WITH POWER FROM ON HIGH"
1. They Were to Tarry for Enduement of Power
2. John the Baptist Must Have Referred to Enduement of Power
3. Indwelling Holy Spirit Given Before Pentecost
III. TESTIMONY OF BEST SOUL WINNERS OF AGES IS THAT SOUL-WINNING POWER IS ITSELF EVIDENCE OF FULLNESS OF SPIRIT
IV. SEVERAL TERMS—"BAPTIZED," "FILLED," "THE GIFT OF THE HOLY GHOST," "ANOINTED"—MEAN "ENDUED WITH POWER FROM ON HIGH"
V. "BAPTIZED IN THE HOLY GHOST" ONLY ONE OF FOUR FIGURATIVE USES OF "BAPTIZED" IN NEW TESTAMENT

SINGLE BIBLE STATEMENT TO VERIFY IT
II. NO OTHER BIBLE DOCTRINE ACCEPTED IN HISTORIC CHRISTIANITY IS EVER BELIEVED ON SOME IMPLICATION AND WITHOUT CLEAR STATEMENT IN BIBLE
III. BIBLE EXAMPLES SHOW TO BE FILLED WITH SPIRIT OR BAPTIZED WITH SPIRIT NEED NOT INVOLVE TALKING IN A FOREIGN LANGUAGE
1. Jesus Did Not Speak in Foreign Languages
2. Spirit-Filled John the Baptist Never Spoke in a Miraculous Language
3. Samaritan Converts, First Filled With Spirit, Had No Language Evidence
4. Paul, First Filled With Spirit, Did Not Speak in Foreign Languages
IV. BIBLE HAS CLEAR COMMANDS, PROMISES ABOUT BEING FILLED WITH SPIRIT THAT DO NOT INVOLVE SPEAKING IN FOREIGN LANGUAGES OR TONGUES
V. THROUGH THE CENTURIES, GREATEST CHRISTIANS, GREATEST SOUL WINNERS, FILLED WITH SPIRIT, HAVE NOT TALKED IN TONGUES OR FOREIGN LANGUAGES
1. Would You Deny Spurgeon Had God's Mighty Power?
2. John Wesley
3. John Knox, George Whitefield
4. Charles G. Finney Won Hundreds of Thousands
5. D. L. Moody, "Baptized With Holy Ghost," Did Not Talk in Tongues
6. Other Mighty Soul Winners Did Not Talk in Tongues

CHAPTER VIII—REAL PURPOSE AND EVIDENCE OF HOLY SPIRIT BAPTISM OR FULLNESS

I. MANY SCRIPTURES DECLARE THAT FULLNESS OR BAPTISM OF SPIRIT IS FOR SOUL-WINNING POWER
1. Prophecy of Joel in Acts 2:14-21 Shows Meaning of Pentecost Beyond Doubt
2. Luke 24:46-49 Teaches They Were Waiting for Power to Win Souls
3. In Acts 1:8 Jesus Told Them the Results They Should Seek and Expect

II. BIBLE EXAMPLES ALSO SHOW WHAT IS BIBLE EVIDENCE OF FULLNESS OF SPIRIT

1. John the Baptist Saw Multitudes Saved
2. Disciples, Again Filled With Holy Spirit After Pentecost, Saw Many Saved
3. Spirit-Filled Stephen Won Paul
4. Samaritan Converts, Spirit-Filled, Did Not Speak in Foreign Languages
5. Paul, Filled With Spirit, "Straightway" Won Souls

III. GREATEST SOUL WINNERS WHO CLAIMED TO HAVE BEEN FILLED OR BAPTIZED WITH HOLY SPIRIT, WON THOUSANDS, DID NOT TALK IN TONGUES

1. Charles G. Finney
2. Evangelist A. B. Earle Won 150,000 With No Tongues
3. Billy Sunday Used to Win Perhaps a Million Souls; No Tongues!

IV. THOSE WHO PUT MOST EMPHASIS ON "SPEAKING IN TONGUES" PUT LESS EMPHASIS ON SOUL-WINNING POWER

CHAPTER IX—FOREIGN LANGUAGES IN I CORINTHIANS 13 AND 14

I. TONGUES IN I CORINTHIANS 13

1. Tongues of Angels
2. When Will "Tongues" Pass Away?

II. PAUL WRITES TO CORINTHIAN CHRISTIANS AS CARNAL BABES IN CHRIST

1. Division and Strife Prove Them Carnal
2. Fornication Accepted, Defended by These Worldly Christians
3. Led Astray About Meats Offered Idols
4. Like Israel's Rebellion and Sin in Wilderness
5. Drunkenness at the Lord's Table; Many Die Because of This

III. ALL DISCUSSION IN CHAPTER 14 ABOUT FOREIGN LANGUAGES

IV. WHOLE CHAPTER ABOUT PUBLIC SERVICES, NOT PRIVATE PRAYER

1. Paul Insists He Must Use His Mind, His Understanding When He Speaks
2. All This Chapter Discusses Public Services, Not Private Worship
3. All This Is "to the Edifying of the Church," Not Private Enjoyment

V. WHOLE DISCUSSION ABOUT FOREIGN

II. EVANGELIST ORAL ROBERTS SPEAKS ABOUT THIS DOCTRINE
   1. He Thought Mark 16:17 Taught Continual Miracles for All Christians
   2. Evangelist Roberts Supposed Jesus Had Promised "Tongues" for Everyone
   3. Perverts the Reference in I Corinthians 14
   4. Pentecostal People Do Not Notice That All 120 at Pentecost Prophesied, Witnessed, Preached
   5. Peter Addressed Jerusalem Jews, Others Addressed Jews "Out of Every Nation Under Heaven"
   6. Bible Never Hints That Praying Should Be in an "UnknownTongue"

III. FOLLY OF THIS PENTECOSTAL TEACHING
   1. Gift of Tongues Never Given to Many
   2. None of the Other Miraculous Gifts or Works of Holy Spirit Left to Choice of Every Christian
   3. Gifts of Spirit Were Each Single, Separate Gifts
   4. Is "Praying in the Spirit" Talking in Tongues? So Mr. Roberts and So Other Pentecostal Teachers Say

CHAPTER XII—WHAT REALLY HAPPENS WHEN PEOPLE TALK IN TONGUES?

I. HAPPINESS, DEVOTION, SINCERITY DO NOT NECESSARILY PROVE PEOPLE RIGHT IN RELIGION

II. SPEAKING IN TONGUES NOT NECESSARILY CHRISTIAN: WIDESPREAD IN HEATHEN RELIGIONS

III. FALSE PROPHETS, EVIL SPIRITS CONTINUALLY TRY TO MISLEAD GOD'S PEOPLE

IV. HOW EXPLAIN TONGUES?
   1. When Miraculously Useful in Winning Souls Like at Pentecost, It May Be Counted of God
   2. If It Is Like the Carnal, Worldly Group at Corinth Who Used Foreign Languages Unknown to the Unlearned Present, and to Make a Show, Then That Is Probably Wrong, Worldly
   3. If It Is Carefully Worked Up, With Explicit Instructions How to Empty the Mind, Say Syllable After Syllable, and Continue Until You Fall Into Some Pattern and Practice, Until You Become Fluent in Tongues—Then That Is Probably Some Kind of Self-Hypnotism
   4. Talking in Tongues Is Often Deliberate Fraud

Introduction

We are told that 4,000 Catholics met at Notre Dame University to talk in tongues and to meet with leaders of the charismatic movement.

In *The Baptist Bulletin*, for November, 1975, Ralph G. Colas says on this matter:

> A Roman Catholic Jesuit priest, Father Donald Gelpi of Berkeley, California, has called on Roman Catholic charismatics to "beware of fundamentalists who are filled with anger, fire and brimstone." He declared that the fundamentalists "are preoccupied with rigid interpretations of Scripture." Gelpi, who spoke at a Catholic Charismatic Renewal Conference in San Diego which drew 3,500 people from 20 states and 5 foreign countries, said "those in the charismatic renewal are being called by God to renew the Roman Catholic Church."
>
> Meanwhile, in Minneapolis the Fourth International Lutheran Conference on the Holy Spirit, sponsored by the Lutheran Charismatic Renewal Services, attracted more than 20,000 persons.

The radio and TV ministry of Evangelist Oral Roberts, of Kathryn Kuhlman, of Jimmy Swaggart and movie star Pat Boone, along with the nationwide radio broadcast of Dr. C. M. Ward of the Assemblies of God, have spread the charismatic movement very widely.

The term "charismatic" comes from the Greek word *charisma* which means "gift," and the usual emphasis is on the "gift of tongues" instead of on the other gifts of the Spirit discussed in I Corinthians 12.

So many well-meaning Christians have gone into the charismatic movement that it deserves attention and an earnest investigation. And it deserves a kindly examination, too, because it is in the main a movement of godly people who claim we should go back to the New Testament, with all the power and joy and miraculous gifts of New Testament Christians.

We should go into this study as brother Christians, dealing with others whom we recognize as earnest Christians who seek to have the New Testament Christianity in its fullness.

(We do not here address Catholics or modernists or false cultists who talk in tongues, but the main groups of earnest Christians who talk in tongues and claim all should be able to talk in tongues, and with gifts of the Spirit. We have in mind those good Christians who believe it is God's will to heal everyone and who sometimes claim what seems to be spurious miracles.)

However widespread and prospering the glossolalia movement is (from the Greek word *glossa* for tongues or language and *laleo*, to speak), that does not prove it correct on the controversial doctrine. Catholicism has been more widespread than any Protestant movement: does that prove Catholicism is right in selling masses for souls, as a sacrifice of Christ anew to get people out of purgatory? Is it right to have prayers to Mary and teach that priests can forgive sins? Is the pope really in effect God on earth? No. Just because millions believe these heresies does not make them right. Jehovah's Witnesses, Christian Scientists, followers of Herbert Armstrong and the Mormons have spread amazingly. But that does not make their particular doctrines scriptural or right. So we do not need to accept the tongues heresy (we regard it as heresy) as correct because many Christians believe it. It still must stand or fall on the scriptural evidences.

I. WE RECOGNIZE GENERALLY PENTECOSTAL·PEOPLE AS FUNDAMENTAL, BIBLE-BELIEVING CHRISTIANS

I rejoice to say I have found no modernists among Pentecostal people, those who deny the deity of Christ, the inspiration of the Bible and salvation by the atoning death of Christ. As far as I know, they have escaped the plague of modernism much better than the major denominations. There may be, and doubtless are, Pentecostal people who deny some of these great fundamentals. Since the tongues teaching includes unconverted Catholics, and since it is approved by some liberals, we might expect some unsaved and liberals among them. (John Sherrill, Pentecostal editor of *Guideposts*, the Norman Vincent Peale magazine, quotes favorably the late Dr. Henry Van Dusen and other liberals.) But the movement is carried on, in the main, as a movement of Bible believers, usually very devoted Christians.

1. We Seek Christian Fellowship With Godly, Saved, Bible Believers

In major citywide campaigns I was glad to welcome Pentecostal people in cooperation. We had it understood there would be no talking in tongues nor teaching about tongues nor entire sanctification in the inquiry room, and no division and strife over these matters, but all would help to win souls, bless Christians and build up good churches. I would not go into a cooperative meeting where these heresies, as I see them, are taught, but I would gladly have fellowship with them on undisputed grounds.

Romans 14:1 says, "Him that is weak in the faith receive ye, but not to doubtful disputations." That teaching is repeated in Psalm 119:63, "I am a companion of all them that fear thee, and of them that keep thy precepts." Godly Christians should give some latitude and have charity in lesser and incidental doctrines, but should be united on the great fundamentals of the Faith.

In the early years of the National Association of Evangelicals, when Dr. H. A. Ironside, Dr. Bob Jones, Sr., and I were active in it, we had fellowship with Dr. Flowers, who was then, I believe, the General Superintendent of the Assemblies of God. On the Board of Bob Jones University I had fellowship with a prominent and godly Pentecostal pastor. Dr. Gaulke, president of the Gulf-Coast Bible College of Houston, a Church of God school, is a friend whom I love. I was glad to accept his invitation to speak there at chapel. In the big four-pole circus tent in my citywide campaign in Springfield, Missouri, one night twenty-six Assembly of God pastors sat on the platform. I spoke in devotions at their printing plant. I have published in THE SWORD OF THE LORD two or three good sermons by Dr. C. M. Ward, nationwide radio preacher of the Assemblies of God.

I say, I am glad to have fellowship with Pentecostal people where I can do it without strife or compromise and without being misunderstood. I will not have fellowship even with a Baptist who denies some of the great essentials, but I hold out my hand of friendship to every born-again, godly, Bible-believing, soul-winning Christian. Even so, I must be true to them and to Christ and the Bible in trying to show them where I think they are wrong and unscriptural.

2. We Honor Pentecostal Insistence on New Testament Power

I must say also that I honor the Pentecostal insistence that we should have the fullness of the Spirit and the gifts of the Spirit as God gave them severally as He would in Bible times and as He may do so now. I think we should have the refreshing and joy of Bible Christianity. I do not believe the gifts are passed away. I do not believe the days of miracles are past. But, I do not think Pentecostal people are right in their idea of the gift of tongues, as in *unknown* tongues, unknown to them or anyone else. I do not think God intended everybody to talk in tongues. I do not think that anyone in New Testament times ever spoke in any language that was totally unknown to him and to others nor spoke in any kind of tongue for his own enjoyment and pleasure.

But I am glad they want the Holy Spirit of God upon them and in the New Testament fashion. The fact that I do not agree with their opinion about what it all means, does not change the fact that they are right in wanting what

Christians had in Bible times. In fact, the Pentecostal person who has Holy Spirit power and who wins souls, as some of them do, pleases God, I think, better than a Baptist or Presbyterian or Methodist who does not have Holy Spirit power and does not win souls. In other words, I think that the Great Commission of getting the Gospel to all the world and winning souls is more important by far than talking in tongues, and it is worse to be wrong on the Great Commission than to be wrong on the lesser matter of tongues.

As far as I am able, I intend to be fair and honest as I study this matter and have Christian love toward all who truly love and trust the Lord Jesus Christ. Those of like brotherly disposition surely should read with the same fairness and charity, and with holy concern to know the very will of God.

II. HOW THOROUGHLY, HOW PATIENTLY WE HAVE SOUGHT GOD'S WILL IN THIS MATTER OF HOLY SPIRIT POWER AND GIFTS OF THE SPIRIT!

First, all who have known well this editor and author in fifty-four years of ministry, know that I do not seek to propagate a denominational viewpoint. Most denominational leaders and, as far as I know, all denominational colleges and seminaries in the great Southern Baptist denomination in which I grew up and was trained and began my ministry, were post-millennial or amillennial. But earnestly following the Bible, I came to believe in the premillennial return of Christ and associate doctrines. I take the Bible literally where they often did not.

1. Our Sincerity Proved at Great Sacrifice

Because of increasing modernism that could not be corrected, I felt I must not give support to open unbelief in the seminaries and colleges and denominational leadership and Sunday School Board literature, so I left the Southern

Baptist Convention. That cost the loss of friends of a lifetime and necessarily many heartaches and tears. But as God is my witness, my aim was then and is now to find the will of God and do it and to be true to Him at any cost.

With the same devotion to Christ and the Bible, I felt I must withdraw from the National Association of Evangelicals which I had helped to build, along with other fundamentalists. And I have been as earnest in exposing modernism and liberalism among Baptists as among Methodists and Presbyterians and others.

So I do not approach this matter to bring a Baptist viewpoint. The simple truth is, I suspect Baptists generally will not agree with my teaching here. They do not believe in tongues, but most of them think perhaps the day of miracles is past and the gift of tongues is no longer available, and they do not thoroughly understand what is involved in the question. So I am not speaking from a denominational viewpoint.

2. With Holy Concern We Seek Holy Spirit's Enduement of Power

Again, I must say that this was the matter of the most earnest concern because my heart was set on soul winning. With God as my helper, I undertook to bring back mass evangelism in America when it had ebbed and almost gone. And to win many, many souls, I knew I must have the power of God, and with all my heart I have sought to have upon me the Holy Spirit power which other godly evangelists have had and which Bible Christians had. I studied so much on this matter of the Holy Spirit power and preached so often about it, that good friends were troubled and warned me I would become a fanatic, would be rolling on the floor or talking in tongues if I persisted in waiting on God and pleading for His power. I told my friends then that I did not think so, but that I must find what the Bible itself clearly taught on this matter, and I must pay whatever price there was to pay to have the power of God.

But I would not settle this on the matter of experience, or how I felt, or what somebody else had done, but only on the clear Word of God. I said then and I say now, if it took talking in tongues to have the power of God, then I would want the tongues as well as the power. I did not find that in the Bible, of course. I found the fullness or baptism of the Spirit but no encouragement to "talk in tongues."

I worked on this matter so thoroughly that my book, *The Power of Pentecost*, was about seventeen years in the writing. First, I worked and worked until I had prepared the book nearly completely in manuscript form. Then I said by God's grace I would set out to prove it. So I laid it aside until God blessed in great citywide campaigns. And then, with my teaching proven by actual experience, and thousands saved, I brought out *The Power of Pentecost*. That not only represents long hours on my knees and much study and searching every Scripture, but great citywide campaigns in Buffalo, Cleveland, Chicago, Miami, San Pedro, Seattle, Oakland, Winston-Salem, and elsewhere. I am poor and weak, but I thank God that He has put His blessed power on this poor man and poor speaker, and God has given the evidence.

Does somebody who talks in tongues say, "You say you prayed about power?" Yes. You may have prayed more for tongues, but you didn't pray more than I for the power of God.

A Holiness woman preacher said, "Brother Rice, I am praying that you will be filled with the Holy Ghost." I replied, "I am glad you are. Keep on praying for that. As God is my witness, I pray more for the power of the Holy Spirit than for anything else." But I told her, as I tell you, that I was not seeking what would meet her standards but what would meet the Bible standards in the power of God and souls saved.

3. Who Has More Carefully Studied the Best Pentecostal Writers?

Again, it is only fair to remind you that I have gone into

all the writings and teachings of the best of Pentecostal people. Years ago I had the books of Donald Gee, one of the most outstanding Pentecostal writers. I noted that he said there is no clear statement in the Bible that being filled with the Spirit meant one must talk in tongues. I read what Evangelist Wigglesworth had to say.

I have consulted in the last few weeks about thirty books of the principal Pentecostal writers that I have assembled and read through the years. That includes two or three by Kathryn Kuhlman; one on *The Baptism With the Holy Spirit and the Value of Speaking in Tongues Today* by Oral Roberts. I have *Speaking in Tongues and Its Significance for the Church* by Laurence Christenson; *These Are Not Drunken As Ye Suppose* by Howard M. Ervin, a scholarly teacher in Oral Roberts University in Tulsa; *They Speak With Other Tongues* by John L. Sherrill, editor of *Guideposts* magazine.

I have also *Have You Received the Holy Spirit?* by A. G. Dornfeld who says that through THE SWORD OF THE LORD and our conference on revival and soul winning at Winona Lake, Indiana, in 1945, "That conference revolutionized my ministry. We were convinced that we must hold evangelistic services in our churches." But then he got under the influence of healer Jack Coe and others and became Pentecostal.

I have the pamphlet, *Baptists and the Baptism of the Holy Spirit*, published by the Full Gospel Business Men's Fellowship International, compiled by Jerry Jensen. He was the one who ignorantly and foolishly claimed that "Dwight L. Moody, Charles G. Finney, and others testified of speaking in other tongues. . . ," which they never did.

I have *The Acts of the Holy Spirit Among the Baptists Today,* also put out by the Full Gospel Business Men's Fellowship International; the large, very full *With Signs Following*, by the famous Stanley H. Frodsham, published by the Gospel Publishing House in Springfield, Missouri; *The Last Chapter,* by A. W. Rasmussen, overseer of the Independent Assemblies of God International; *Baptism in the Holy Spirit: Command or Option?* by Bob Campbell; the pamphlet where Johnnie Barnes tells why he, as a Methodist minister, took up tongues. I have two pamphlets by Gordon Lindsay, *How to Receive the Holy Spirit Baptism* and *All About the GIFTS of the Spirit*; also, *What Is the Good of Speaking With Tongues?* by Harold Horton; the book by the late T. J. McCrossan dated 1927, *Speaking With Other Tongues Sign or Gift, Which?* published by Christian Alliance Publishing Company.

I think I may say that if ever a man honestly went thoroughly into a subject to know the truth of it and get the evidence, I have done so about speaking in tongues.

Let no one say that I have not investigated this question earnestly and carefully and with a brotherly heart. My kindly attitude has been well known as I have had friendship with Pentecostal people and treated them kindly.

4. What Part Is From God? What Part From Satan?

Somebody asks, "Is this tongues heresy of God, or of the Devil?" Well, let us speak humbly and charitably. All error is from Satan, and so that means that everybody who is not perfect on everything is therefore somewhat influenced by evil.

When a Baptist, for example, is a hyper-Calvinist and does not win souls, his heresy is from the Devil. When a Methodist or Presbyterian sprinkles babies and calls that baptism, that is unscriptural and that heresy is not of God. And so when a Pentecostal man insists that speaking with tongues is for everybody and in the modern sense, that is not of God.

That does not mean that Pentecostal people are of the Devil any more than are Baptists and Methodists and Presbyterians and others. We are all poor, frail beings with a carnal nature as well as a new nature, if we have been born again, and so everyone has to try and measure himself by the Bible.

I think the tongues matter is wrong. That does not mean that in other matters Pentecostal people are necessarily wrong. Often a Pentecostal man or woman is a better Christian than a Baptist or a Methodist who does not love God as much, does not pray as much, and does not care as much about souls.

5. This Question Must Be Settled by the Scriptures, Not Experience or Feeling

Someone may say, "You can't know anything about this because you yourself have never talked in tongues." No, and I have never been drunk, but I already know drunkenness is wrong. No, I have never married two wives as the Mormons often do, but I already know that is wrong. I have not yet had the glorious experience of the rapture when the Lord Jesus will come to receive His saints in the air, but that does not keep me from knowing that what the Bible says on that matter is true. So, this is not to be settled by my feelings, by my impressions, by my experiences; it is to be settled by the Word of God.

In his book, *They Speak With Other Tongues,* Mr. John Sherrill tells how this editor of *Guideposts* magazine set out to study the tongues business and how at long last he himself spoke in tongues. But you will note that his approach was not my approach. I was not seeking to talk in tongues; I was seeking to have the power of God to win souls. He got the tongues and did not win souls. I got the power of God and by His loving mercy and with the help of many, have won some tens of thousands of souls.

Those who are seeking for an ecstatic experience and are conditioned to it may seek and find tongues. But those who come to face, as I do, the great need for the power of God to help win souls and have New Testament Christianity in its fullness, need the power of God and they do not need to talk in tongues and will not, unless they are so taught or unless they give way to their own subjective feelings and so may be misled. So I understand the Scriptures.

And now I beg that you will read carefully this which

constitutes years of study of the Scriptures, a holy devotion to it, and a literal viewpoint and interpretation.

John R. Rice

1976

CHAPTER I

The One Promise of Tongues or Foreign Languages

It seems wise to go through the New Testament and carefully examine every Scripture that discusses the matter of tongues. The first of these is found, along with the Great Commission, in Mark 16:15-18:

"And he said unto them, Go ye into all the world, and preach the gospel to every creature. He that believeth and is baptized shall be saved; but he that believeth not shall be damned. And these signs shall follow them that believe; In my name shall they cast out devils; they shall speak with new tongues; They shall take up serpents; and if they drink any deadly thing, it shall not hurt them; they shall lay hands on the sick, and they shall recover."

I. THE GREAT COMMISSION

The primary teaching here is the Great Commission. The Great Commission is given by the Lord Jesus at least five times in those forty days after His resurrection and before His ascension, in Matthew 28:18-20; Mark 16:15-18; Luke 24:46-49; John 20:21-23 and in Acts 1:8.

Let us say, then, that clearly this is the all-inclusive command that Jesus left the apostles and every Christian. Those saved were to be baptized, then they were to be taught to observe all that the apostles were commanded, as you see in Matthew 28:19,20. This was to continue literally "to all the world." The command is to reach every creature.

We remember that it was to save sinners that Christ came into the world. "This is a faithful saying, and worthy of all acceptation, that Christ Jesus came into the world to save sinners; of whom I am chief" (I Tim. 1:15). Keeping people out of Hell is the one great goal of Christ's incarnation, His crucifixion and His resurrection. It is the one great thing commanded to every Christian in this Great Commission. The other things connected with it are incidental corollaries to this great command and duty. All who trust in Christ are saved and born again according to John 3:16 and many other Scriptures. Here we see those who believe and are baptized are saved, but those who do not believe are lost. As John 3:16 and other Scriptures tell us, the believer is already saved. Being baptized, as they were at once in Bible times, they are still saved, of course.

II. CERTAIN SIGNS WERE TO FOLLOW

Some scholars have doubted that the last few verses in Mark really belong there. A Scofield note on this passage says:

> The passage from verse 9 to the end is not found in the two most ancient manuscripts, the Sinaitic and Vatican, and others have it with partial omissions and variations. But it is quoted by Irenaeus and Hippolytus in the second or third century.

We believe all of it is the Word of God although some copyists may have omitted it in copying the Scriptures. It is easy to believe that this is the Word of God because the things promised here followed the apostles, as Jesus said they should.

Notice that whatever is promised here, were to "follow them that believe"—obviously, we are to understand here, to follow soul-winning Christians who are carrying out this command. The promise is not said to be for those who do not win souls.

It has always been true that in great times of revival blessing when multitudes are saved, God did some wonderful things in answer to prayer. Oh, I have seen it, thank God, many times—the healing of the sick, the control of the weather, even sometimes the taking out of the way by death men who oppose the work of God. I do not believe God ever intended wonderful, amazing answers to prayer and manifestations of God's power to go with nonchalant, lukewarm, halfhearted Christians. These blessings follow those that obey the Great Commission. It would not be right to teach that the coldhearted, the unfaithful, the backslidden Christian could have the same kind of blessings as those believers who are in the will of God and have the power of God to win souls.

III. THESE SIGNS FOLLOW ONLY AS CHRISTIANS BELIEVE

It would be rather foolish to suppose that one who believes for salvation and gets saved automatically gets everything else mentioned here. No, those who believe for salvation get salvation. Those who believe for other things get the things they trust the Lord for.

For example, in the matter of the healing of the sick, the Scripture says, "The prayer of faith shall save the sick" (Jas. 5:15). The Scripture certainly does not mean that one who trusts Christ for salvation automatically can get any sick person well that he wants to get well. No, particular faith for particular things gets the blessings named.

Many, many Christians have never cast out devils. That is only given those to whom God gives faith to miraculously cast out devils. Many, many Christians, of course, cannot take up serpents and be safe from their bite. Paul the apostle, on the Island of Melita in the rain and cold, helped to build a fire for the shipwrecked people. Then we read how this promise was fulfilled for him.

"And when Paul had gathered a bundle of sticks, and laid them on the fire, there came a viper out of the heat, and fastened on his hand. And when the barbarians saw the venomous beast hang on his hand, they said among themselves, No doubt this man is a murderer, whom, though he hath escaped the sea, yet vengeance suffereth not to live. And he shook off the beast into the fire, and felt no harm."—Acts 28:3-5.

Paul did not seek to be bitten, nor do that to show off his great faith. In God's loving mercy he was protected. In that particular case he no doubt was given faith and so was kept from harm. Other Christians who trusted Christ have likewise found themselves delivered. And sensible Christians ought never pretend that it means every

Christian should go about picking up snakes and trying to prove how much faith he has.

The Scripture says, "If they [those who are given faith for the occasion] drink any deadly thing, it shall not hurt them." We do not have Bible examples given, so that certainly would be very rare.

In Fort Worth, Texas, I was called to the hospital to see a woman about to die. Her home was broken and so to commit suicide she swallowed four bichloride of mercury tablets. She was expected to die soon. Now she was penitent over her sins and her attempted suicide. I prayed that God would raise her up. The nurse at her bedside simply said, "She cannot get well. Even if the poison does not kill her, the lining of her stomach is destroyed and she can never digest food. She cannot live!"

But a few days later when I came back to inquire, she had been restored. She was up and had gone back to Oklahoma with her family and was in good health again!

I do not pretend that every Christian who takes poison can be delivered. It was a very foolish thing she did, and God was under no obligation, but in this case the prayer of faith saved the sick.

IV. "THEY SHALL SPEAK WITH NEW TONGUES"

Who shall speak with new tongues? Those who believe for that blessing.

"Tongues" in the Bible always means languages, if not the physical tongue in a mouth. And since it is plural—"tongues"—it means other languages than one's own, that is, foreign languages. Remember, "tongues" means natural foreign languages.

No doubt this was fulfilled at Pentecost. These who naturally spoke the Aramaic tongue and, perhaps, Koine Greek, now talked to those from some sixteen different nationalities (Acts, chap. 2). And they heard "every man in our own tongue" in which he was born. That was a particular miracle for a particular case and given in answer to a particular faith. These Christians spoke in "new tongues," that is, foreign languages. New to them.

Is every Christian supposed to cast out devils? Obviously not. Should every Christian expect to drink poison and then be healed? Obviously not. Should every Christian expect to lay hands on the sick and see them recover? Obviously not. Then, should every Christian expect to talk in a foreign language, miraculously given? Certainly not. These are special signs or wonders given, as needed, in answer to particular faith in each case.

Notice also that the matter of tongues here simply means "languages." It never means anything else but the literal, physical tongue in one's mouth or a natural language. At Pentecost it refers simply to those foreign languages that would be necessary to get the Gospel to people who were present that day.

On this matter, Paul said in I Corinthians 14:10, "There are, it may be, so many kinds of voices in the world, and none of them is without signification." There is no such thing as an "unknown tongue," except that one may not be familiar with a particular foreign language. There is no heavenly tongue. No jabber without a human meaning to somebody is ever given by the Holy Spirit. This is a promise just exactly like God fulfilled it at Pentecost, that people who had faith for it, when there was a need for it, would be given the power to speak in a language new to them.

And, that would be rarely necessary. Just at God does not expect every Christian to drink poison and be healed, so God does not expect every Christian to talk in tongues. It would be foolish to presumptuously make an occasion by willfully drinking poison and expect God to heal. And so it would be also presumptuous to try to make an occasion for tongues when there is no natural need or occasion for it.

CHAPTER II

Bible "Tongues" Literal, Natural Foreign Languages

Pentecostal writers insist that their modern type "tongues" are not necessarily an ecstatic utterance. It sometimes is that—the manifestation of a great emotional upheaval—but they insist that that is not always true, and perhaps not usually true. But they do hold that the tongues are not usually natural languages but a heavenly language known only to God.

So they interpret falsely I Corinthians 14:2, "For he that speaketh in an unknown tongue speaketh not unto men, but unto God." The inspired apostle, rebuking them for testifying in church in foreign languages unknown to some brethren, said that hearers would not understand, though God would. Pentecostal people prefer to have that mean that these people at Corinth were speaking in some heavenly language known to God but not known to any men. That is not the meaning of the Scripture, as we will see further.

I. SPEAKING IN AN ECSTASY IN UNINTELLIGIBLE WORDS, OR IN LANGUAGES KNOWN ONLY TO GOD, CAME FROM HEATHEN WORLD

The idea that "speaking in tongues" meant some ecstatic jumble of words, not a regular language, or whether in ecstasy or not, a language known only to God—that idea came from secular literature based on the tongues of almost all heathen religions! That idea is not ever taught in the Bible.

1. This Kind of Tongues Appeared Nearly Everywhere in Non-Christian Religions and in Secular Non-Christian Literature

In the book, *Tongues in Biblical Perspective,* Dr. Charles R. Smith says on pages 20 and 21:

> In non-Christian religions.—Tongues occupied a significant place in ancient Greek religion. The seeress at Delphi, not far from Corinth, spoke in tongues. According to Plutarch (A.D. 44-117), interpreters were kept in attendance to explain her incoherent utterances. Many scholars have stated that tongues were experienced in the mystery religions (Osiris, Mithra, Eleusinian, Dionysian, and Orphic cults). Some have concluded that the unintelligible lists of "words" in the "magical papyri" and in certain Gnostic "prayers" are records of ecstatic utterances. About A.D. 180 Celsus reported ecstatic utterances among the Gnostics. Lucian of Samosata (A.D. 120-198) described tongues speaking as it was practiced by the devotees of the Syrian goddess, Juno.

> Today shamans (witch doctors, priests, or medicine men) in Haiti, Greenland, Micronesia, and countries of Africa, Australia, Asia, and North and South America speak in tongues. Several groups use drugs to aid in inducing the ecstatic state and utterances. Voodoo practitioners speak in tongues. Buddhist and Shinto priests have been heard speaking in tongues. Moslems have spoken in tongues, and an ancient tradition even reports that Mohammed himself spoke in tongues. According to his own account, after his ecstatic experiences he found it difficult to return to "logical and intelligible speech" (Kelsey, p. 143).

Dr. Smith does not overstate the case. He gave more detail on pages 15 and 16 of the same book:

> Extrabiblical records are quite explicit with regard to unintelligible ecstatic utterances prior to the Christian era. As early as 1100 B.C. an Egyptian, Wen-Amon, recorded an incident when a young man in Canaan, seemingly "inspired" by his god, behaved strangely and spoke ecstatically all one night (Pritchard, pp. 25-29).

> In three of Plato's dialogues he makes references to religious ecstatic speech. He discusses prophetic

"madness" as a departure from one's normal senses. He cites the utterances of the prophetess at Delphi, the priestess at Dodona, and the Sibyl as examples of such madness or ecstasy. Only when those women were "out of their senses," that is, when their speech was unintelligible, were their utterances considered significant. He also describes the incomprehensible speech of certain diviners whose utterances were expounded by an attendant prophet or interpreter (Hutchins, vol. 7).

In the *Aeneid* Virgil describes the sibylline priestess on the island of Delos who, in an ecstatic state, spoke obscurely and unintelligibly. Such utterances were considered the result of some type of divine inspiration, and when "interpreted" by a priest or prophet they were considered divine oracles (Hutchins, vol. 13, bk. 6).

It is apparent that tongues speaking occurred in pagan cultures prior to the day of Pentecost. Martin concludes that tongues have appeared in varying circumstances, among different peoples, and in various periods of history. They have even appeared "outside the area of strictly religious phenomenon," and therefore "no claim may be made for glossolalia as an exclusively Christian demonstration" (Martin, p. 13).

Dr. Smith shows that "tongues speaking occurs among anti-Christian spiritistic mediums" (p. 21).

Then Dr. Smith shows how this worldwide usage in heathen religions and in non-Christian religion prevailed and so made the meaning of "tongues" in the non-Christian viewpoint to mean "unintelligible ecstatic utterances." He says on page 28:

Because the Greek word *glossa* ("tongue") sometimes means "language," some have argued that in tongues passages this must be its meaning. It is striking, however, that *every* Greek lexicon, or dictionary, states that the word is also used for unintelligible ecstatic utterances. All of the standard lexical authorities have so understood tongues. It just is not true that when the word does not refer to the physical organ it must refer to a language spoken by some group of individuals.

He speaks of the word in a nonbiblical sense. That is not true of the Bible use of the word "tongue." He is mistaken, as we will show you.

2. Mistakenly, Christian Scholars, Sometimes Not Very Spiritual, Have Read This Heathen Meaning of Tongues Into the Bible

In his book, *The History of the Christian Church*, Dr. Philip Schaff is said to have explained tongues this way: as an ecstatic language not known to any on earth, unintelligible. He got this idea from Greek literature, of course, and from "tongues" in heathen religion, not from the Bible.

Dr. A. T. Robertson, regarded by many as the most eminent Greek scholar, in his extensive set of volumes, *Word Pictures in the New Testament*, has comments on this I Corinthians, chapter 14. Note how he takes for granted that which is not in the Scripture itself, on this matter. On I Corinthians 14:14 he says, *"But my understanding is unfruitful (ho de nous mou akarpos).* My intellect *(nous)* gets no benefit (*akarpos*, without fruit) from rhapsodical praying that may even move my spirit (*pneuma*)."

Note the term "from rhapsodical praying." However, the Bible says nothing like that. It does not mention praying in a rhapsody. He simply takes for granted the use of the word "tongues" as it is in the heathen religions and literature.

Then on verse 15 he says, "There was ecstatic singing like the rhapsody of some prayers without intelligent words." And he says that Paul is rebuking that. However, though Paul is rebuking what they did, it was not "ecstatic singing." There is nothing in the Scripture like that. At Corinth it was singing or praying in a foreign language, unknown to those present, to make an impression. These carnal and baby Christians at Corinth were doing wrong, but they were not talking in the heathen kind of ecstatic language or singing in rhapsody some unintelligible words, as was common in heathen religions.

Note how this scholar takes for granted the heathen meaning of tongues.

In verses 18 and 19 of this chapter Paul was inspired to

write:

"I thank my God, I speak with tongues more than ye all: Yet in the church I had rather speak five words with my understanding, that by my voice I might teach others also, than ten thousand words in an unknown tongue."

He talked in foreign languages more than all of them. He preached continually in the Koine Greek as well as the Aramaic and Hebrew. But in the church there was no use in speaking in foreign languages that no people could understand.

However, on verse 19 Dr. Robertson comments, "Private ecstasy is one thing (cf. II Cor. 12:1-9) but not in church worship." However, Paul was not talking about "private ecstasy"; he is talking about the carnal putting on of a show by speaking in the church services foreign languages some people could not understand.

In his scholarly book, *New Testament Teaching on Tongues*, Dr. Merrill F. Unger takes for granted and accepts this general meaning of tongues and interprets it as a special, wonderful sign at Pentecost, and with Cornelius, and in Acts 19, a heavenly language simply to mark a new age. He does not regard the gift of tongues, as we think it is and as it certainly was at Pentecost, as a practical matter of giving people power to speak to others in their own language in an emergency and so to preach them the Gospel. He says on page 23:

It is in connection with the commencement of a new economy in Goa's dealing that the supernatural phenomena of fire, wind, and the languages of Pentecost are to be seen in their real significance. They were the outward visible signals that the new age was being inaugurated.

And so he proceeds that on that basis tongues are passed away. The simple truth is that there never was any such thing as tongues given simply as a sign without any real meaning or any practical use.

Dr. Charles Smith, in the book, *Tongues in Biblical Perspective*, holds to this position using the classical meaning of non-Christian literature and religions, and says on page 38:

> In extrabiblical literature this word was used to describe the "inspired" utterances of diviners. Moulton and Milligan cite three occurrences of the word in Vettius Valens where it designates irrational or unintelligible speech. It is stated that the speakers' minds had "fallen away," they were overcome with "madness," and they spoke in "ecstasy" (p. 72). *Apoptheggomai* was almost a technical term for describing the speech of oracle-givers, diviners, prophets, exorcists, ecstatics, and other "inspired" persons (Kittel, I, 447; Arndt and Gingrich, p. 101). The basic idea is "an unusual utterance by virtue of inspiration." Though the word obviously cannot be limited to unintelligible speech, it is certainly appropriate for such. Its usage in Greek literature, in fact, definitely suggests a connection with ecstatic, often unintelligible, utterances.

But, since these good men believe there was not any practical usefulness in a gift of tongues to speak to people in their own language so they could hear the Gospel, they think that the matter of tongues passed away, and they go into great detail to show that after the Bible was completed and the apostolic age was over, there should be no speaking in tongues. The trouble is they have in mind the wrong kind of tongues.

3. In Bible Cases Where Tongues Are Mentioned, It Referred to Literal Foreign Languages

There can be no question about the use of tongues at Pentecost. Acts 2:6-11 says:

"Now when this was noised abroad, the multitude came together, and were confounded, because that every man heard them speak in his own language. And they were all amazed and marvelled, saying one to another, Behold, are not all these which speak Galileans? And how hear we every man in our own tongue, wherein we were born? Parthians, and Medes, and Elamites, and the dwellers in Mesopotamia, and in Judaea, and Cappadocia, in Pontus, and Asia, Phrygia, and Pamphylia, in Egypt, and in the parts of Libya about Cyrene, and strangers of Rome, Jews and proselytes, Cretes and Arabians, we do hear them speak in our tongues the wonderful works of God."

They heard the Gospel in their own language in which they were born. And we remember that Peter was addressing, when he preached, only "Ye men of Judaea, and all ye that dwell at Jerusalem" (Acts 2:14). He spoke to Jerusalem Jews in their common Aramaic language. But these who spoke in the various languages with the gift of tongues spoke to these fourteen or sixteen nationalities of Jews represented here. Tongues there meant literal foreign languages.

Was there a different kind of tongues or a different purpose in the case of Cornelius the centurion in Acts, chapter 10? Why should there be? Acts 10:44-47 says:

"While Peter yet spoke these words, the Holy Ghost fell on all them which heard the word. And they of the circumcision which believed were astonished, as many as came with Peter, because that on the Gentiles also was poured out the gift of the Holy Ghost. For they heard them speak with tongues, and magnify God. Then answered Peter, Can any man forbid water, that these should not be baptized, which have received the Holy Ghost as well as we?"

They were filled with the Spirit. This crowd, some of them from Rome who would naturally speak Latin, and others, no doubt, who spoke Koine Greek, as most cultured people did, and the servants and friends who were Jews spoke Aramaic, when they were filled with the Spirit, then the Jews who came along "heard them speak with tongues [foreign languages], and magnify God."

How did they know they were magnifying God? Because they heard them and understood them. And note that this is the same blessing that came at Pentecost, not another one. They spoke in foreign languages. Whether the languages here were miraculously given or the languages they regularly spoke, the Bible doesn't say. The important thing is they were filled with the Spirit and praised God in languages that could be understood. "Tongues" in the Bible mean literal foreign languages.

And in Acts 19, there were some believers in Ephesus who did not understand about the fullness of the Spirit, so in verse 6 we are told, "And when Paul had laid his hands upon them, the Holy Ghost came on them; and they spake with tongues, and prophesied." Now why make this something different from the other uses in the Scriptures of the word "tongues"? They spoke in foreign languages. Ephesus was a city of many races, many people, many languages. They may have spoken several languages praising God naturally. Or God could have given them the miraculous use of some foreign languages, only the Bible doesn't say so and we do not know more than the Scripture says. At any rate, they praised God and the fullness of the Spirit that came on them meant the same as it means everywhere else in the New Testament, "an enduement of power from on high," enabling them to be "witnesses."

Then the use of tongues in I Corinthians 14 refers to natural foreign languages. Verse 10 says, "There are, it may be, so many kinds of voices in the world, and none of them is without signification." All the languages have meaning, and he is talking about the languages used at Corinth. And in verse 16 he says that if one prays in a foreign language that those present do not understand, "how shall he that occupieth the room of the *unlearned* say Amen at thy giving of thanks, seeing he understandeth not what thou sayest?" He is talking about natural languages that can be learned, and "unlearned" people present would not understand.

The Lord repeats the same thought in I Corinthians 14:23,24:

"*If therefore the whole church be come together into one place, and all speak with tongues, and there come in those that are UNLEARNED, or unbelievers, will they not say that ye are mad? But if all prophesy, and there come in one that believeth not, or one UNLEARNED, he is convinced of all, he is judged of all.*"

The languages discussed were foreign languages that could be learned.

If everybody speaks in foreign languages not understood by those present, then "those that are unlearned" will think you are crazy. But if one prophesies or witnesses in the power of the Lord in the language they can understand, then the unlearned "is convinced of all, he is judged of all."

It is wrong to put the heathen interpretation on the term "tongues" in the Bible. When a Delphi oracle in Greece talked in tongues, or when Mohammed, founder of the Muslim religion, talked in tongues, or when a witch doctor talks in tongues, that is not what God gave in Bible times and it is not what even these backslidden carnal Christians at Corinth had. They had natural languages, although they were trying to put on a show and imitate the gift of tongues, and they are reproved.

Tongues in the Bible always refers to natural languages. And no one can come to the right understanding of the term if he takes it with the heathen background and not take what the Scripture itself says literally.

CHAPTER III

The Languages (Tongues) at Pentecost

The most important Scripture, the definitive basic Scripture on the miraculous speaking in tongues in all the Bible is in the second chapter of Acts, the account of what happened at Pentecost.

"*And when the day of Pentecost was fully come, they were all with one accord in one place. And suddenly there came a sound from heaven as of a rushing mighty wind, and it filled all the house where they were sitting. And there appeared unto them cloven tongues like as of fire, and it sat upon each of them. And they were all filled with the Holy Ghost, and began to speak with other tongues, as the Spirit gave them utterance. And there were dwelling at Jerusalem Jews, devout men, out of every nation under heaven. Now when this was noised abroad, the multitude came together, and were confounded, because that every man heard them speak in his own language. And they were all amazed and marvelled, saying one to another, Behold, are not all these which speak Galileans? And how hear we every man in our own tongue, wherein we were born? Parthians, and Medes, and Elamites, and the dwellers in Mesopotamia, and in Judaea, and Cappadocia, in Pontus, and Asia, Phrygia, and Pamphylia, in Egypt, and in the parts of Libya about Cyrene, and strangers of Rome, Jews and proselytes, Cretes and Arabians, we do hear them speak in our tongues the wonderful works of God.*"—Acts 2:1-11.

It will be simpler and more true to the Scriptures and the plain intent of the Bible if, when we speak of tongues, we mean simply foreign languages. That is what they meant in the Bible in all the Scriptures referring to a gift of tongues.

Sometimes the Bible speaks of tongues or languages that were *miraculously* given. That was clearly the case in Acts

2:4 when they spake every man "as the Spirit gave them utterance." *That is not expressly said* in Acts, chapter 10, in the case of Cornelius and his family, nor in Acts 19 with the dozen men filled with the Spirit there. So they might have been foreign languages which they already knew. The Scripture *never indicates* that the languages which they used in Corinth and rebuked so soundly in chapter 14 *were miraculous languages.* No, they were foreign languages, evidently the languages people used in human pride, these carnal Christians at Corinth, but not miraculously given.

So when Paul said, "I would that ye all spake with tongues" (I Cor. 14:5), he was saying, and it would be an exact translation, "I wish you all spoke in foreign languages." When Paul said, "I speak with tongues more than ye all" (I Cor. 14:18), he simply meant, "I speak more in foreign languages than any of you." When Paul said, "Forbid not to speak with tongues," it would be an exact translation to say, "Don't forbid people to speak in foreign languages." Only, if they did it before others in church, they should have somebody to translate it.

The word "tongues" in all these Scriptures refers to foreign languages. So at Pentecost they were natural, foreign languages, given miraculously so people could preach the Gospel in those languages.

I. WE ARE TOLD EXACTLY WHAT HAPPENED AT PENTECOST

1. The disciples had waited to be endued with power from on High with a promise that they should have power to witness and win souls. The Holy Ghost came upon them (Luke 23:46-49; Acts 1:8). They were to obey the Great Commission. They were to get people saved, get them baptized, then to win souls. Everything else in the whole passage and as far as that is concerned, in the whole book of Acts, is around carrying out the Great Commission, getting people saved.

2. The so-called "tongues" were natural languages of the Parthians, Medes, Elamites, those in Mesopotamia, in Judaea, Cappadocia, in Pontus, Asia, Phrygia, Pamphylia,

in Egypt, and in Libya, and of Rome and the Cretes and Arabians. Nothing here is said about some heavenly language, about some language not known and used regularly. They were simply foreign languages.

And the purpose is clear. God gave the Christians power to speak to these in their own language so they could hear the Gospel and be saved.

3. It is clear that the disciples were not waiting for any gift of tongues, had not prayed for the gift of tongues, and these languages were given them miraculously, only as an incidental way in getting out the Gospel.

4. And the great theme of Pentecost is that now that the power of God is come, three thousand people were won to Christ in that day! The scriptural emphasis is on getting people saved, not on languages.

5. The essential thing is that these people "prophesied," that is, witnessed for God in the power of the Holy Spirit, in whatever language was needed. It was made clear in Joel's prophecy which was plainly referred to this time as part of the whole New Testament age, "the last days."

"And it shall come to pass in the last days, saith God, I will pour out of my Spirit upon all flesh: and your sons and your daughters shall prophesy, and your young men shall see visions, and your old men shall dream dreams: And on my servants and on my handmaidens I will pour out in those days of my Spirit; and they shall prophesy. . .and whosoever shall call on the name of the Lord shall be saved."—Acts 2:17-21.

The speaking in tongues was incidental. The important thing is that they were witnessing for God in the power of the Holy Spirit and all those present could say, "We do hear them speak in our tongues the wonderful works of God."

Note here that the speaking in tongues was not something separate and different from witnessing or prophesying. Joel foretold that the disciples would "prophesy," and they did in whatever language was used. Those who spoke to their own Jerusalem Jews in the Aramaic language, witnessing about Christ, and those who spoke to others from other countries in their language, were all witnessing for Christ and it resulted in many being saved.

Some have thought that those who talked in tongues were simply having some spiritual enjoyment of praise but that only Peter preached the Gospel. No, Peter's message was addressed to "Ye men of Judaea, and all ye that dwell at Jerusalem" (Acts 2:14). But those who spoke in other languages spoke to "devout men, out of every nation under heaven" (vs. 5). The tongues were languages and those who spoke "prophesied" we are told, that is, they witnessed, in the power of God and got people saved.

II. THE BIBLE GIFT OF TONGUES—MIRACULOUS POWER TO SPEAK TO OTHERS IN THEIR OWN KNOWN LANGUAGE IN ORDER TO GET THEM THE GOSPEL

Someone asks, "Is the gift of tongues for our day?" I answer very plainly. First, if you mean what the Bible means, then if there be an occasion and the need for it, then God could and would give this gift to some as He did at Pentecost. It was a very rare and unusual thing in Bible times, and very rarely needed. It would be rare now. It never was for anybody except as an occasion like this demanded it and people had faith for it, to get out the Gospel.

But if you mean the gift of tongues in the modern sense of a jabber that nobody understands and which people do for their own enjoyment, or claim that they thus have evidence of the "baptism of the Holy Ghost," then that not only is not for today, but it was not even in Bible times. That is a wholly human invention and not the Bible gift of tongues.

If someone finds a Chinaman or someone from a heathen tribe in Borneo who cannot speak English and doesn't understand it, and if one cannot understand his language and begs God for some way to speak to the man in his own language and tell him how to be saved, and if God does it, then that is miraculous and is the Bible gift of tongues. And if you bring him to me, I will be glad to help see that he gets baptized and recognized as a Christian.

There is logic and reason in everything God does. Dr. Bob Jones, Sr., said, "If it hasn't any sense in it, then God isn't in it." God had a reason, very clearly shown, for giving some people at Pentecost the power to speak to others in their own language in which they were born so they might be saved.

G. Campbell Morgan of England, following some of the ancient church fathers, says that speaking in tongues is "a language of ecstasy." He didn't get that from the Bible. There is nothing like that in the Word of God. He got it, as did Dr. Schaff in *History of the Christian Church*, from heathen religions that talk in a jabber. Latin, as these people at Pentecost spoke to the people from Rome, is not a "language of ecstasy." Arabic, which they spoke to others from Arabia, is not a "language of ecstasy." These were natural languages and that is the kind the Holy Spirit used then and might use now if necessary.

We are reminded again of I Corinthians 14:10, "There are, it may be, so many kinds of voices in the world, and none of them is without signification." So all the languages spoken were natural, foreign languages, for the purpose of "prophesying" or witnessing, as Acts 1:8 had foretold.

First Corinthians 13:1 says, "Though I speak with the tongues of men and of angels, and have not charity, I am become as sounding brass, or a tinkling cymbal." Then is the gift of tongues some special angelic language? No. When angels talk to men they always talk in the natural language of these men. The Bible never hints that angels have some special kind of heavenly language. "Tongues of angels" simply means that angels know all languages, and if a man knew all the languages in the world as really nobody but an angel would know them, it still would be without value unless he had Christian love. So the word "tongue" means "language," and always means the natural language, a foreign language.

In I Corinthians 14, we find the term *"an unknown*

tongue" in verses 4, 13, and 19, but in every case "unknown" is in italics, which means that it was not in the original manuscript but was inserted by the translators, hoping to make the meaning clearer. The languages mentioned will be unknown to those who do not know that language, but the Scripture does not mean that there is any language unknown to everybody.

The languages and the gift of tongues are always natural, foreign languages given for a purpose, to help people get out the Gospel to those who otherwise could not understand the speaker.

III. MIRACULOUS LANGUAGES AT PENTECOST ONLY ONE OF THREE INCIDENTAL MIRACLES, ACTS 2:1-4 TELLS US

At Pentecost there was the sound of *"a rushing mighty wind, and it filled all the house."*

There were *"tongues like as of fire, and it sat upon each"* of the people.

Speakers were given the power to speak miraculously in foreign languages they did not know, in order to get out the Gospel.

None of these miracles were promised. They were incidental. They were not what the disciples waited and prayed for. They tarried to be "endued with power from on high" (Luke 24:49). They waited for the power so they might be witnesses and win souls and carry out the Great Commission.

No one has a right to put a special meaning in the cyclonic wind beyond what is naturally inferred. The truth is, one Greek word *pneuma*, for wind and for Spirit, is the same and one Hebrew word, *ruach* sometimes may mean either. So symbolically we suppose that kind of incidental miracle was fitting with the mighty pouring out of the Holy Spirit. But it was incidental.

Tongues like as a fire sitting on the people may be a symbol of the mighty power of God in the Gospel. Of the Gospel, when preached in Holy Spirit power, it is said, "Is not my word like as a fire? . . . and like a hammer that breaketh the rock in pieces?" (Jer. 23:29). It was said of John the Baptist that "he was a burning and shining light. . ." (John 5:35). So we think it perfectly fitting that at such a wondrous occasion of preaching the Gospel in power, there should be some colorful and sweet picture of it in the accompanying miracles. But it was incidental. The purpose of Pentecost was to preach the Gospel and get people saved.

But the gift of foreign languages here is also incidental. It was given for a purpose. It was not promised. No one was taught to pray for it. These incidental miracles were never mentioned as the evidence of Holy Spirit baptism or power.

A man said to me, "Brother Rice, have you been filled with the Holy Ghost like at Pentecost?"

I replied that in God's loving mercy there had been some sweet enduement of power enabling me to win thousands of souls, and if he meant that, then I had been filled with the Spirit like those at Pentecost.

But he asked, "Well, did you speak in tongues like they did at Pentecost?"

I told him, "No, I spoke in an English tongue so people could hear me and understand, just as back there they spoke in regular languages so people would hear and understand and be saved."

"Ah," he said, "but you didn't get it like at Pentecost. You didn't speak in tongues."

I asked him, "Were you filled with the Holy Spirit just like at Pentecost?"

"Oh, yes!" he said proudly. "I was filled with the Spirit. I spoke in tongues."

"But was there a sign of a rushing mighty wind that filled all the house like at Pentecost?"

He answered somewhat surprised, "No, I didn't hear any."

"Were there tongues like as of fire on people's head and shoulders, visible to all?"

He was in more trouble. "No, I didn't see anything like that," he answered.

I declared, "You didn't get it like at Pentecost if you are talking about the incidental surroundings. You may have been filled with the Spirit if you got the power to win souls. You did not get the outward incidentals as they did at Pentecost."

No one has a right to make an issue of the tongues where it is not needed, anymore than make an issue of a rushing mighty wind, or the visible tongues like as of fire.

If one must speak in tongues the first time he is filled with the Holy Spirit, as at Pentecost, must he have an earthquake the second time he is filled, as the disciples had at their second filling in Acts 4:31? Why manufacture a doctrine when God does not?

If God had meant the tongues to have a special universal meaning He would have said so. He did not. Then no one else has a right to put that meaning to it.

IV. MIRACULOUS FOREIGN LANGUAGES NOT "INITIAL EVIDENCE OF BAPTISM OF HOLY SPIRIT," AS SOME CLAIM

In a following chapter I feel we should go into the whole matter of the baptism of the Holy Spirit and misunderstandings and false claims about it. But here, as we consider the pouring out of the Spirit at Pentecost, we see there is not a shred of evidence that the disciples regarded speaking in foreign tongues as the "initial evidence of the baptism of the Holy Ghost." It was never promised; it was never described that way on the occasion itself. Paul said nothing like that when he discussed the tongues later with the people at Corinth. That is a human, unjustified fabrication.

Someone asked me, "Then how did Peter know they were filled with the Holy Spirit, if they did not know because they spoke in tongues?"

I answered perhaps a little facetiously, but I think nevertheless it is an adequate answer: "When they lined up the converts and found there were 2,095; 2,096; 2,097; 2,098;

2,099; 3,000! I think Peter may have said, 'Glory to God! this is it!' "

One who has the anointing of the power of God and sees people wonderfully saved and changed will know that is the power of God. When many are saved through Holy Spirit power, then why seek some sign? Soul winning is itself the evidence of Holy Spirit power, and the disciples in Bible times needed no further evidence, nor do we. In fact, it is a kind of a perversion, a carnal mind seeking for fleshly things, not to want to primarily win souls and not to be satisfied when God gives soul-winning power.

CHAPTER IV

Baptism of Holy Spirit Means Enduement of Power

The term "baptized with the Holy Ghost" has been often misused by people claiming entire sanctification, even sinless perfection, and those to whom it simply meant a jabber in tongues, so that there is an odium on the term. However, it is a Bible term, if properly used.

I. MISTAKEN SCOFIELD BIBLE AND PLYMOUTH BRETHREN TEACHING

1. First Corinthians 12:13 Does Not Refer to Pentecost

Not only have Holiness people and the tongues people misused the term, but Plymouth Brethren and those who follow Plymouth Brethren and the Scofield Bible notes have misunderstood the meaning and, in many cases, missed the power and blessing of seeking and finding the enduement of power from on High for soul winning.

Now, the matter is so important that we think it ought to be dealt with very carefully, looking at every Scripture involved and taking the Scripture at face value.

It is a modern fad to teach that baptism of the Holy Ghost refers simply to a new dispensation, the origin of the church. And so Dr. Scofield, following Plymouth Brethren, in his notes on Acts 2:4 says,

> The Spirit forms the church (Mt. 16.18; Heb. 12.23, note) by baptizing all believers into the body of Christ. . . .

He says "by baptism of the Spirit, the Christians were formed into a church." The Bible says nothing like that. That is simply inferred from a misunderstanding of I Corinthians 12:13, which says, "For by one Spirit are we all baptized into one body." But the Christians addressed in that letter to Corinth were not present at Pentecost and were not then baptized into the body. The Corinthian Christians were no more involved at Pentecost than were Old Testament Christians, whom Dr. Scofield leaves out. That happens to each individual as he is buried in, submerged in, made a part of that group which will be called out at the rapture. That is, they are made a part now of that great "general assembly and church of the firstborn" (Heb. 12:23) which will be called out at Christ's coming to meet us in the air.

2. Sealed With the Spirit Comes at Salvation

Dr. Scofield's note on Acts 2:4 says,

> Every believer is born of the Spirit (John 3.3,6; 1 John 5.1), indwelt by the Spirit, whose presence makes the believer's body a temple (1 Cor. 6.19; Rom. 8.9-15; 1 John 2.27; Gal. 4.6), and baptized by the Spirit (1 Cor. 12.12,13; 1 John 2.20,27), thus sealing him for God (Eph. 1.13; 4.30).

Dr. Scofield seems to have understood that at Pentecost people were baptized with the Spirit, they were "sealed by the Spirit." Now he thinks every believer was potentially "baptized into one body" by the Spirit.

However, in Ephesians 1:13 and 14 we see that when one is saved he is then sealed with the Spirit, that is, the Holy Spirit Himself is the seal and comes in at salvation: "In whom ye also trusted, after that ye heard the word of truth, the gospel of your salvation: in whom also after that ye believed, ye were sealed with that holy Spirit of promise, Which is the earnest of our inheritance until the redemption of the purchased possession, unto the praise of his glory."

The Holy Spirit Himself is indwelling every Christian. That happens when he is saved. And Ephesians 4:30 says, "And grieve not the holy Spirit of God, whereby ye are sealed unto the day of redemption." But that sealing took place at salvation, when the Holy Spirit came in.

However, in the case of the disciples, the Holy Spirit (His indwelling) was given them when Jesus arose from the dead

(John 20:19-21). There Jesus breathed on them and said, "Receive ye the Holy Ghost," and they did. That means they were sealed in the Spirit and did not have to wait for Pentecost.

It is not true to Scripture, we think, to teach that the baptism of the Holy Ghost which was promised at Pentecost and came was simply a dispensational matter of this so-called "origin of the church."

II. OBVIOUS INTENT OF SCRIPTURES SEEMS TO BE THAT "BAPTIZED OF THE HOLY GHOST" MEANS "ENDUED WITH POWER FROM ON HIGH"

In reading the closing chapters of the Gospels, it is obvious that the main thing on Jesus' heart was the Great Commission, that is, getting the Gospel out and getting people saved. Already before He was crucified, He reminded the disciples, "Ye are the light of the world" (Matt. 5:14). In John 8:12 He had said, "I am the light of the world." In John 9:5 He said, "As long as I am in the world, I am the light of the world." Obviously, then, He intended that we Christians should take His place and that we are to be the light of the world now that He is taken away. So we are to do the work of Christ. If the Lord Jesus had an enduement of power, as Luke 3:22; 4:18-21 and Acts 10:37,38 say He did, and He did not talk in tongues, we certainly need not.

In His high priestly prayer, Jesus said, "As thou hast sent me into the world, even so have I also sent them into the world" (John 17:18).

And now forty days after His resurrection He appeared to the disciples again and again. What was the principal theme on which He spoke to them? The Great Commission! He may have mentioned the matter fifty times or more, but that Great Commission is recorded at least five times: in Matthew 28:19,20; in Mark 16:15,16; in Luke 24:46-49; in John 20:21,22; and in Acts 1:8.

Surely that was the main thing He had on His heart and the main thing He laid on the hearts of His disciples.

1. They Were to Tarry for Enduement of Power

When Jesus commanded the disciples to tarry in the city of Jerusalem to be endued with power from on High, He said:

"Thus it is written, and thus it behoved Christ to suffer, and to rise from the dead the third day: And that repentance and remission of sins should be preached in his name among all nations, beginning at Jerusalem. And ye are witnesses of these things. And, behold, I send the promise of my Father upon you: but tarry ye in the city of Jerusalem, until ye be endued with power from on high."—Luke 24:46-49.

You see, the tarrying was for power to do what He had been commanding them to do. They were to wait for enduement of power for soul winning, to get the Gospel out.

So what are they to expect at Pentecost? Foreign languages? No. That is incidental. Power to speak in the foreign languages will come if needed, but that is not what they are waiting for.

Was it for a new dispensation and the founding of the church and such matters? Those were not even mentioned in the commands of Jesus to the disciples. If anybody suspected there would be some dispensational change at Pentecost, it was not because anything like that had been foretold, nor because they were commanded to expect it. No, they had one great thing in mind—they were to wait for enduement of power! They had an overwhelming duty to go out and make black hearts white, to make infidels into saints, to make heathen into Christians, to make harlot women into pure women, and to take this life-changing Gospel to all the world. So they were to wait for power to do that. Surely that was the intent of all the teaching Jesus gave them in those forty days after His resurrection.

Again, let us consider that last promise and command in Luke 24:46-49, with Acts 2:4,5.

The book of Acts starts out with a reference to "the former treatise have I made, O Theophilus, of all that Jesus began both to do and teach, Until the day in which he was taken up, after that he through the Holy Ghost had given commandments unto the apostles whom he had chosen."

Luke explicitly says he is recounting again the closing things of his Gospel in Luke. He is telling the same story again.

Jesus said, "Tarry ye in the city of Jerusalem, until. . . ," in Luke 24:49. And here, in slightly different words of Jesus (for He probably said it several ways), "And, being assembled together with them, commanded them that they should not depart from Jerusalem, but wait for the promise of the Father, which, saith he, ye have heard of me." That is a restatement of Luke 24:49.

And they were to tarry until they were to be "endued with power from on high." But the restatement here, in other words of Jesus, is "ye shall be baptized with the Holy Ghost not many days hence."

Now it seems that the obvious intent of the Scripture as on the very face of it is that the first few verses in the book of Acts recount the last part of the book of Luke and are telling about the same thing. They were waiting for an enduement of power from on High. So, baptized with the Holy Ghost must mean endued with power from on High.

Again, consider the passage in Acts 1:4-8. Let us look over it again.

"And, being assembled together with them, commanded them that they should not depart from Jerusalem, but wait for the promise of the Father, which, saith he, ye have heard of me. For John truly baptized with water; but ye shall be baptized with the Holy Ghost not many days hence. When they therefore were come together, they asked of him, saying, Lord, wilt thou at this time restore again the kingdom to Israel? And he said unto them, It is not for you to know the times or the seasons, which the Father hath put in his own power. But ye shall receive power, after that the Holy Ghost is come upon you: and ye shall be witnesses unto me both in Jerusalem, and in all Judaea, and in Samaria, and unto the uttermost part of the earth."

It is a wonderful promise Jesus gave them, but what does it mean? They asked Him, "Do You mean that now You are about to set up the kingdom of David on earth and start the millennial reign? Will You regather Israel now? Is that what You mean?"

Jesus answered that was not what He meant. They are not supposed to know prophetic matters about the future and dates and times; that is kept in the Father's power.

"Well, what did You mean, Jesus?"

He explains: "Ye shall receive power, after that the Holy Ghost is come upon you: and ye shall be witnesses unto me both in Jerusalem, and in all Judaea, and in Samaria, and unto the uttermost part of the earth."

No one has a right to disassociate verses 4 and 5 from verse 8. To be baptized with the Holy Ghost means that they should receive power and be witnesses, as verse 8 says. I think that the openhearted, honest approach to this passage shows that verse 8 explains verse 5. Jesus did not mean the restoration of Israel; He meant the enduement of power for soul winning. So He explained. No one has a right to split this passage and make verse 5 mean something different from what Jesus Himself explained that He meant.

2. John the Baptist Must Have Referred to Enduement of Power

Again, remember that John the Baptist had foretold Pentecost and it is mentioned in all four of the Gospels that although John baptized with water, he was baptizing Jesus and ". . . he shall baptize you with the Holy Ghost" (Matt. 3:11; Mark 1:8; Luke 3:16; John 1:33). We know that John was "filled with the Holy Ghost, even from his mother's womb." We know he was a great gospel preacher and that through his preaching thousands repented and were saved. It was foretold about him:

"For he shall be great in the sight of the Lord, and shall drink neither wine nor strong drink; and he shall be filled with the Holy Ghost, even from his mother's womb. And many of the children of Israel shall he turn to the Lord their God."—Luke 1:15, 16.

John worked no miracles. He foretold no future events except that Jesus would baptize people with the Holy Ghost. And what did John have on his heart? Of course it was soul winning. And what did Jesus have on His heart? Getting people to win souls, of course.

It is fair for us to believe that John the Baptist had in mind a special enduement of power like he himself had (filled with the Spirit and winning many souls). It is farfetched to suppose that John the Baptist was foretelling the origin of a church or a new dispensation. When John said that Jesus would "baptize with the Holy Ghost," no doubt he meant the same thing as Peter meant when he explained the coming of Holy Spirit power at Pentecost in Acts 2:33: "Therefore being by the right hand of God exalted, and having received of the Father the promise of the Holy Ghost, he hath shed forth this, which ye now see and hear."

3. Indwelling Holy Spirit Given Before Pentecost

What happened at Pentecost? Read over the whole passage, in Acts, chapter 2, and see if the Bible gives any intimation that there was some dispensational change. I do not think so.

Some people speak of "the descent of the Holy Ghost at Pentecost." But I think it is fair to remind you that the Holy Spirit was given to the disciples to dwell in their bodies the day Jesus rose from the dead when in John 20:21,22 we read, "Then said Jesus to them again, Peace be unto you: as my Father hath sent me, even so send I you. And when he had said this, he breathed on them, and saith unto them, Receive ye the Holy Ghost."

He said to the disciples, "Receive ye the Holy Ghost." Surely they did receive the Holy Ghost, that is, to move into their bodies and live in their bodies. The indwelling of the Holy Spirit began everywhere for Christians the day of the resurrection of Jesus, not at Pentecost.

Of course this was expected. In John 7:37,39 we read, "In the last day, that great day of the feast, Jesus stood and cried, saying, If any man thirst, let him come unto me, and drink. . . .for the Holy Ghost was not yet given; because that Jesus was not yet glorified.)"

Notice the indwelling of the Holy Spirit as given into the bodies of Christians waited for the glorification of Jesus, that is, for His resurrection. How else can you explain the day of the resurrection when Jesus said to the disciples, "Receive ye the Holy Ghost," and "he breathed on them"?

We remember that Jesus was glorified at His resurrection. In John 17:1 Jesus prayed to the Father, "Father, the hour is come; glorify thy Son, that thy Son also may glorify thee." As I understand it, the Lord could not give the Holy Spirit's indwelling until Jesus was glorified. When He arose from the dead with a glorified body, then He was ready to give the Holy Spirit to dwell in the bodies of Christians. So, as I understand the Scriptures, the day Jesus rose from the dead the Holy Spirit moved into the body of every Christian. That is the only dispensational change I know of between the Old and the New Testaments, except that of the ceremonial law. Now it is fulfilled and every Christian has the Holy Spirit dwelling within (I Cor. 6:19,20; Rom. 8:9,10). Christians before Pentecost had the Holy Spirit within but not the enduement of power they waited for. It came at Pentecost.

Come back and read the story of Pentecost again. What a marvel! Here these Galilean fishermen and others, "unlearned and ignorant men," were all filled with the Spirit of God and so spoke mightily. The promise was fulfilled, "Ye shall receive power, after that the Holy Ghost is come upon you: and ye shall be witnesses unto me. . . ." They spoke with such power that they had 3,000 people saved in a day!

When I was fifteen years old, I first came face to face with this marvelous chapter. Perhaps I had read it before, but I remember I was so charmed and enthralled with the idea that the power of God could come so that 3,000 people could be saved in a day! I still feel the marvel of this chapter and of what happened at Pentecost. The disciples were endued with power from on High. I soon won my first soul, and these long years there has been a glow in my heart to think what God did at Pentecost, and what He promises, He can do again!

So baptized with the Holy Ghost, as Jesus promised in Acts 1:5, was not a new dispensation, was not the origin of a church, was not any difference in the plan of salvation. It was simply endued with the mighty power of God. As D. L. Moody said, it was a "specimen day." And there was one day in that period which Joel called "the last days," the whole New Testament age, going down to "the great and the terrible day of the Lord" when Christ returns to reign.

So baptized with the Holy Spirit seems obviously from the context to mean endued with power from on High, like filled with the Spirit and such terms.

Beware of any Bible teaching that is more interested in the "origin of the church" or in tongues than in getting people saved, when they think of Pentecost. Why not center here on what God centers on in all the Scriptures about Pentecost?

What is the evidence of the fullness of the Spirit? We find that again in the case of Barnabas. In Acts 11:24 it is said about Barnabas, "For he was a good man, and full of the Holy Ghost and of faith: and much people was added unto the Lord." The results were clearly stated: much people were saved, and that was because this Barnabas was filled with the Holy Ghost and faith.

We have no indication that Barnabas ever talked in tongues, or that he ever had a flame of fire sitting on him, or that he ever heard the sound of a rushing mighty wind. Whether he did or not doesn't matter. What matters is that he had the power of God to win souls when he was filled with the Holy Spirit.

The testimony of all the cases in the Bible when people were filled with the Holy Spirit is that the purpose is witnessing in the power of God and winning souls, and that in itself is the evidence, and all the evidence we need.

III. TESTIMONY OF BEST SOUL WINNERS OF AGES IS THAT SOUL-WINNING POWER IS ITSELF EVIDENCE OF FULLNESS OF SPIRIT

In the book, *The Life of D. L. Moody by His Son*, on pages 146 and 147 Mr. Moody says:

> "Ever since that night of the great fire I have determined as long as God spares my life to make more of Christ than in the past. I thank God that He is a thousand times more to me today than He was twenty-two years ago. I am not what I wish I was, but I am a good deal better than I was when Chicago was on fire."

The year 1871 was a critical one in Mr. Moody's career. He realized more and more how little he was fitted by personal acquirements for his work. An intense hunger and thirst for spiritual power were aroused in him by two women who used to attend the meetings and sit on the front seat. He could see by the expression on their faces that they were praying. At the close of services they would say to him:

"We have been praying for you."

"Why don't you pray for the people?" Mr. Moody would ask.

"Because you need the power of the Spirit," they would say.

"I need the power! Why," said Mr. Moody, in relating the incident years after, "I thought I had power. I had the largest congregations in Chicago, and there were many conversions. I was in a sense satisfied. But right along those two godly women kept praying for me, and their earnest talk about anointing for special service set me to thinking. I asked them to come and talk with me, and they poured out their hearts in prayer that I might receive the filling of the Holy Spirit. There came a great hunger into my soul. I did not know what it was. I began to cry out as I never did before. I really felt that I did not want to live if I could not have this power for service."

Later Moody went to New York City to get money for the poor of Chicago, impoverished by a great fire, and to rebuild his Sunday school tabernacle.

On page 149 he tells the rest of the story. His son writes,

> During this Eastern visit the hunger for more spiritual power was still upon Mr. Moody.

"My heart was not in the work of begging," he said. "I could not appeal. I was crying all the time that God would fill me with His Spirit. Well, one day, in the city of New York—oh, what a day!—I cannot describe it. I seldom refer to it; it is almost too sacred an experience to name. Paul had an experience of which he never spoke for fourteen years. I can only say that God revealed Himself to me, and I had such an experience of His love that I had to ask Him to stay His hand. I went to preaching again. The sermons were not different; I did not present any new truths, and yet hundreds were converted. I would not now be placed back where I was before that blessed experience if you should give me all the world—it would be as the small dust of the balance."

Elsewhere he tells us that soon thereafter he preached, using the same sermon notes he had used before. Before he had seven or eight saved; now he had some two hundred saved with the same message but with new power.

Notice that Moody never claimed that there was any talking in a foreign language, nor did he seek it, nor did he teach that anyone ought to seek that. What he claimed was that the power of God came in answer to prayer and that was the fullness of the Spirit.

May I ask every honest Christian, Would not you rather have what D. L. Moody got than some jabber in a foreign language that doesn't do anybody any good but simply show how pious you are?

IV. SEVERAL TERMS—"BAPTIZED," "FILLED," "THE GIFT OF THE HOLY GHOST," "ANOINTED"—MEAN "ENDUED WITH POWER FROM ON HIGH"

In Luke 24:49 this Holy Spirit gift is called "endued with power from on high." Elsewhere in the Bible, "anointed" is used to mean the same enduement of power. The more frequently used term is "filled with the Holy Spirit" (like Acts 4:8; 4:31; Luke 1:15; Acts 11:24; Acts 6:3). So the term I most often use for this enduement of power is "filled with the Spirit."

You need not be surprised if God uses a number of terms for this wonderful matter of enduement of power. In the same way, there are many names for Jesus. He is the Messiah, the Christ, the Son of God, Son of man, Son of David, Son of Abraham. He is the Saviour, Redeemer. He is the Head of the church. He is our High Priest. He is Alpha and Omega, the Beginning and the End, and many more wonderful things. All the names do not describe Him too well.

Then there are a number of names for getting saved. One is saved, or redeemed or born again or converted or has everlasting life, etc. Also several terms are used for how to be saved: repent, believe, come to Christ, obey the Gospel, take the cup of salvation, etc. Those do not mean different happenings; these are just different names for the same wonderful thing.

So here God uses a number of terms. One may be baptized (overwhelmed, covered, surrounded), in the power of God. He may be *filled with the Spirit*, or he might say that God *poured the Holy Spirit upon him*, or that he was *anointed with the Holy Spirit*, or he has *the gift of the Holy Ghost*. All these surely, in these first two chapters of Acts, refer to the same enduement of power from on High.

V. "BAPTIZED IN THE HOLY GHOST" ONLY ONE OF FOUR FIGURATIVE USES OF "BAPTIZED" IN NEW TESTAMENT

Baptism in the Bible means *literally* the physical immersion of a believer in water and always it has that literal meaning unless the context shows differently. But there are four times in the Bible that the term baptism is used in the FIGURATIVE sense.

1. Israel Crossing Red Sea Said to Be "Baptized"

The Children of Israel were "baptized unto Moses in the cloud and in the sea" (I Cor. 10:2). With the Red Sea walled up on each side and the clouds covering and giving darkness behind and light ahead, they were simply buried, immersed, covered, and so in a figurative sense it was a baptism. Not literal baptism in water, but a picture of it.

2. Christ Overwhelmed in Suffering, a "Baptism"

Christ said, "I have a baptism to be baptized with; and how am I straitened till it be accomplished!" (Luke 12:50). He simply meant that He was coming to a time when He would be overwhelmed, buried, covered in suffering in trouble at Gethsemane and Calvary. That is a figurative use of the word, not a literal, physical baptism.

3. Each New Convert Received Into Body of Christ

In I Corinthians 12:13 we find that when one is saved he is put into the body of Christ and submerged there becoming a part of the body of Christ, with everlasting life, waiting for the rapture. So the Scripture says we "as lively stones, are built up a spiritual house" (I Pet. 2:5), and that group "groweth unto an holy temple in the Lord" (Eph. 2:21) as converts are added day by day.

Jesus said in Matthew 16:18, "Upon this rock I will build my church." But more literally, "I will *be building*" or "I will continue to build" my church. It is a continued action, the Greek shows, not the origin of the church but the continued building of the church. Every time one is saved he is built into that body. So that is figuratively "baptized into one body" (II Cor. 12:13). It is a figurative use of the term "baptized."

4. Baptized in Holy Ghost Similar Figure of Speech for Buried, Surrounded in Holy Spirit Power

Thus the term "baptized with the Holy Ghost" is likewise a figurative use of the term "baptized." It is like the other three mentioned figurative uses, and simply meant covered, surrounded with the Holy Spirit, in an enduement of power, as promised.

VI. THE CHURCH WHICH IS HIS BODY, ALL THE SAVED, DID NOT BEGIN AT PENTECOST

But the church which is His body did not begin at Pentecost. The Bible never says so and no one else has the right to say so, if he intends to preach what the Bible teaches.

The word "church" in the New Testament is the little Greek word *ecclesia* meaning "a called-out assembly."

It is used in Acts 7:38 about Israel called out of Egypt to Mount Sinai, called "the church in the wilderness."

The same Greek word *ecclesia*, meaning church, is used three times in Acts, chapter 19, only there it is translated "assembly." It refers to that mob of idol worshipers who wanted to lynch the missionaries. They were a "called-out assembly," not Christians, but still the Greek word *ecclesia* is used. It was a church.

The word "church" is used about ninety times in the Bible about a local congregation of Christians and that is the way we are most familiar with the term, such as the "church of God at Corinth," the "church at Rome," the "seven churches of Asia," the "churches of Galatia," etc. These were called-out assemblies but, in these cases, local groups of Christians.

But "church" is also used about the greatest called-out assembly that will ever happen and that will be at the rapture. So, Hebrews 12:22-24 says, speaking not of the Children of Israel assembled at Mount Sinai but of Christians who will be assembled at the Heavenly Zion:

"But ye are come unto mount Sion, and unto the city of the living God, the heavenly Jerusalem, and to an innumerable company of angels, To the general assembly and church of the firstborn, which are written in heaven, and to God the Judge of all, and to the spirits of just men made perfect, And to Jesus the mediator of the new covenant, and to the blood of sprinkling, that speaketh better things than that of Abel."

And that great called-out "general assembly and church of the firstborn, which are written in heaven" to be with Jesus and "the spirits of just men made perfect" has to be that group of all Christians of all ages who will be caught up at the rapture.

As I Thessalonians 4:16,17 says:

"For the Lord himself shall descend from heaven with a shout, with the

*voice of the archangel, and with the trump of God: and the dead in Christ
shall rise first: Then we which are alive and remain shall be caught up
together with them in the clouds, to meet the Lord in the air: and so shall
we ever be with the Lord."*

That called-out assembly is called "the church which is
his body" (Eph. 1:22,23). Colossians 1:18 says, "And he is
the head of the body, the church: who is the beginning, the
firstborn from the dead: that in all things he might have
the preeminence." That is the church which Christ loved
"and gave himself for it" (Eph. 5:25). But surely Abraham
and righteous Abel and all Old Testament saints are
among "the dead in Christ," so will be in that assembly.

The term never refers to a denomination nor to a group
of denominations. It does not refer to New Testament
Christians as being different from Old Testament
Christians. Everybody who will be caught up at the rapture
will be a part of that great assembly or church. That
certainly did not begin at Pentecost. So "baptized by the
Holy Ghost" could not refer to the origin of the church.

Dr. Scofield mistakenly says in his notes on Ephesians
3:6:

> That the Gentiles were to be saved was no mystery (Rom.
> 9.24-33; 10.19-21). The mystery "hid in God" was the divine
> purpose to make of Jew and Gentile a wholly new thing—"the
> church, which is his [Christ's] body," formed by the baptism
> with the Holy Spirit. . . .

But the Scripture does not say the church is "a wholly
new thing." Dr. Scofield should have read more carefully
the verse upon which he was commenting. Ephesians 3:6
says that the mystery is "that the Gentiles should be
fellowheirs, and of the same body, and partakers of his
promise in Christ by the gospel." The mystery was not that
there would be a church body but that both Jews and
Gentiles would be united in the body, the middle-wall
partition being broken down.

That does not seem of any importance to us but it
certainly did to the Jewish converts. The greatest called-
out assembly that this world will ever see will be at that

"general assembly and church of the firstborn, which are written in heaven." Old Testament saints will be raised up at that time when ". . . then Christ shall rise first: Then we which are alive and remain shall be caught up together with them in the clouds, to meet the Lord in the air."

Our Plymouth Brethren friends and those who followed their fad about the Holy Spirit, including Dr. Scofield and the Bible institutes, have been carried away by over-dispensationalism. Dr. Scofield thought that converts of John the Baptist were simply unsaved Jewish proselytes (see his note on Acts 19:2). Many have thought that there was even a different plan of salvation in the Old Testament than in the New Testament, disregarding the plain statement of Acts 10:43. Only one who has a theory to uphold, a new dispensation to provide for, or a tradition firmly established by his schools or denominations, would come to the conclusion from simply reading the first two chapters of Acts that "the baptism of the Spirit" meant the formation of the church. It did not. It meant the disciples were "endued with power from on high" and 3,000 people were saved.

VII. CORNELIUS WAS "BAPTIZED WITH THE HOLY GHOST": WAS THAT ALSO ORIGIN OF CHURCH?

Many say with Scofield, Walvoord and Ironside that the church was formed at Pentecost and that the baptism of the Spirit meant that God's people united with Him in a body, and that was the origin of the church.

In his book, *The Mission of the Holy Spirit*, pages 31 and 32, Dr. Ironside says:

> But on that memorable day He did a new work. He took up one hundred and twenty units (all born of God), and He baptized them into one body, thus forming the Church of the new dispensation. By this act He established them into the Christ, making them one body with their glorified Head, and linking them one with another in a union as close as members in the human body. The baptism of the Spirit is therefore collective, and, as I have remarked, dispensational. It is not

something to be sought or prayed for, nor yet tarried for, since the body has already been formed.

Get the meaning clear. He says that when Jesus told the disciples in Acts 1:5 that "ye shall be baptized with the Holy Ghost not many days hence," that referred to the origin of the church and that the Holy Spirit at that time united Christians together in one body with God, and so the church was formed. And interpreting I Corinthians 12:13, our brethren teach that although now people are put into the body when they are saved, that potentially happened for all us Christians at Pentecost.

Dr. Ironside and others say, "The baptism of the Spirit is therefore collective, and, as I have remarked, dispensational. It is not something to be sought or prayed for, nor yet tarried for, since the body has already been formed." It is an over and done matter.

In effect, Dr. Scofield says the same thing when he insists "one baptism, many fillings."

But if "baptized with the Spirit" at Pentecost meant the origin of the church, what does it mean in Acts 11:15-17? Peter, explaining what happened at Cornelius' household, said,

"And as I began to speak, the Holy Ghost fell on them, as on us at the beginning. Then remembered I the word of the Lord, how that he said, John indeed baptized with water; but ye shall be baptized with the Holy Ghost. Forasmuch then as God gave them the like gift as he did unto us, who believed on the Lord Jesus Christ; what was I, that I could withstand God?"

Note the same thing happened to them as happened to the apostles at the beginning, that is, the same as Pentecost. And what did Peter remember? Not the term "filled with the Spirit" but the promise "baptized with the Holy Ghost." And then he said, "Forasmuch then as God gave them the like gift as he did unto us, who believed on the Lord Jesus Christ; what was I, that I could withstand God?" So, at Pentecost they were baptized with the Spirit, and so here Peter says that Cornelius and his household got the same baptism. That is the term he used, so I must use it.

Now if the church started at Pentecost and they were baptized with the Holy Ghost, did a church start again at Cornelius' household when he was baptized with the Spirit? No. There is only one honest way to take it, it seems to me, and that is that "baptized with the Spirit" meant endued with power from on High. That is the historic Christian teaching, the teaching of Moody, Torrey, Finney and other great soul winners, the generally held position until the Plymouth Brethren and the Scofield Reference Bible influenced the fundamental, independent Bible institutes and Dallas Theological Seminary in America and elsewhere. And baptism of the Spirit does not mean the origin of the church in Acts 1:5 unless it means the origin of another church in Acts 11:16!

CHAPTER V

The Historic Christian Position Is That Baptized With the Holy Ghost Meant the Promised Enduement of Power

It is a strange fact of history that certain doctrines rise with a cult or leader and become a fad, accepted without serious questions by those with a bias for that leadership. So the rise of the mass, the prayers to Mary, the papacy. So the cults of Christian Science, of Jehovah's Witnesses. So the modern tongues movement. So Plymouth Brethren and Dr. Scofield and his followers took up the fad doctrine that "baptized with the Holy Ghost" meant the origin of the church at Pentecost. That modern fad is wrong.

The historic Christian position for centuries has been that "baptized with the Spirit" referred to the enduement of power for soul winning.

I. SO D. L. MOODY TAUGHT

D. L. Moody plainly believed and taught that to be baptized with the Spirit meant the enduement of power promised at Pentecost and that was the same as "filled with the Spirit" or the Holy Spirit "coming upon" one. At Moody's funeral service, Dr. C. I. Scofield himself, then pastor of Mr. Moody's church at Northfield, Massachusetts, said that "Mr. Moody was baptized of the Holy Ghost and knew it." He was referring to the enduement of power. Later, under Plymouth Brethren influence, he left the historic, Moody-Torrey position.

II. DR. R. A. TORREY, FATHER OF BIBLE INSTITUTES, SO HELD

Dr. R. A. Torrey, the closest associate of Mr. Moody, preached again and again on "The Baptism of the Holy Ghost," and has a book by that title. In his memorial sermon on "Why God Used D. L. Moody," he said that Moody had a definite baptism of the Holy Ghost for power. And remember that again and again Moody insisted that everywhere Dr. Torrey should go, he should preach on this baptism of the Holy Ghost or enduement of power.

Later Dr. C. I. Scofield fell under the influence of the Plymouth Brethren. So did Dr. James M. Gray. There came a time when some of the teachers in Moody Bible Institute decided to take out of the curriculum the teaching of Moody and Torrey on the Holy Spirit and substitute the Plymouth Brethren teaching. Some years ago one of the teachers told my then associate, Dr. Robert Wells, that he himself helped in that decision. Dr. Scofield was greatly impressed, as he should have been, with the Bible scholarship of Plymouth Brethren, Darby, Kelley, and many of the others. And so in the Scofield Bible, which is so often right and which is by all odds the most useful reference Bible in the world in general, he left out the historic teaching of Moody, Torrey and others through all the years. And so the fad, and the Scofield Bible and the Bible institutes in many fundamental circles left people to disregard that clear Bible teaching that one can have a mighty enduement of power by waiting on God for soul-winning power.

Dr. H. A. Ironside, for eighteen years pastor of the Moody Memorial Church, Chicago, was a very dear friend of this author. He sent me many sermons for THE SWORD OF THE LORD. He helped me in conferences on revival and soul winning. He was a blessed Bible teacher, a warmhearted preacher, and he regularly preached on Sunday to 3500 or more people. And usually there was someone saved, sometimes two or three or five or six in the services. He had been active in the Salvation Army and as a street preacher and soul winner, but he had seen the mistakes of Holiness doctrine and had gotten into the fine Bible teaching of the Plymouth Brethren on most Scriptures and so became one of them in his convictions and practice.

Dr. Ironside wrote the book, *A Historical Sketch of the Brethren Movement*, published by Zondervan. I remember that in that book he lamented the divisions and strife among Plymouth Brethren leaders, and at one place, as I recall, he expressed sorrow and surprise that there were no outstanding evangelists among the Plymouth Brethren.

I remember that I urged him to accept some big revival opportunities and give himself more to revivals and soul winning on a large scale. He was so greatly loved and respected and his influence so widespread he would have been invited to many such united campaigns, instead of giving simply Bible conference messages week after week as he did.

But he was hesitant, saying he was afraid of taking the awesome responsibility of revival campaigns and feared he could not have the mighty power of God that would be necessary for such campaigns.

He was kind to me. He was on the platform with me in the great citywide campaign in Chicago in 1946. He invited me to speak in the Moody Church once during his Week of Prayer. But Dr. Ironside felt he did not have enough Holy Spirit power for the work of an evangelist in great congregations.

I mention these things only to show that there is a deadness in the Plymouth Brethren position about the Holy Spirit. If you simply tell people, "You already have all there is; if you just obey the Lord, that is all you can do now to be useful," then people do not wait on God nor seek nor pray for the mighty power of God for soul winning. That means there will be no great evangelists among people who hold very clearly to the teachings of Plymouth Brethren on the Holy Spirit.

Oh, people would do well when they come to study about the power of God to read and follow the men who had the power of God, men such as Spurgeon, Moody, Torrey, Chapman, Earle and L. R. Scarborough, instead of following James M. Gray and Plymouth Brethren teachers and teachers from the Bible institutes and Dallas Theological Seminary. The clear truth is that the doctrine that there is no such thing now as being baptized or overwhelmed with the power of God and that one ought not seek that, tends to make powerless Christians or those with little power.

No, the baptism of the Holy Spirit, as Jesus promised in Acts 1:5, meant the same thing as the fullness of power which Christians received at Pentecost and which all of us should seek and have for soul winning.

III. THE INTERNATIONAL STANDARD BIBLE ENCYCLOPAEDIA SAYS SO

I am saying the historic Christian position has been that "baptized with the Spirit" meant enduement of power. *The International Standard Bible Encyclopaedia* says:

> . . .In John 1:33, John the Baptist declares that the descent of the Spirit on Jesus at the baptism of the latter marked out Jesus as "he that baptizeth in the Holy Spirit." Again in John 7:37, 38 we read: "Now on the last day, the great day of the feast, Jesus stood and cried, saying, If any man thirst, let him come unto me and drink. He that believeth on me, as the scripture hath said, from within him shall flow rivers of living water." Then the evangelist adds in verse 39: "But this spake he of the Spirit, which they that believed on him were to receive: for the Spirit was not yet given; because Jesus was not yet glorified." These are the specific references in the four Gospels to the baptisms of the Holy Spirit. In Acts we find direct reference by Luke to the promised baptism in the Holy Spirit. In 1:5 Jesus, just before the ascension, contrasts John's baptism in water with the baptism in the Holy Spirit which the disciples are to receive "not many days hence," and in verse 8 power in witnessing for Jesus is predicted as the result of the baptism in the Holy Spirit.

The above article was written by E. Y. Mullins, president of the Southern Baptist Theological Seminary, president of the Southern Baptist Convention, in *The International Standard Bible Encyclopaedia*. He teaches the historic doctrine that "baptized with the Holy Ghost," meant endued with power.

IV. CLASSIC MATTHEW HENRY'S COMMENTARY UNDERSTOOD "BAPTIZED WITH THE HOLY GHOST" TO MEAN ENDUEMENT WITH POWER

Matthew Henry's Commentary says on this matter, referring to Acts 1:5:

> The blessing designed them shall come, and they shall find it worth waiting for. *"You shall be baptized with the Holy Ghost;"* that is (1.) "The Holy Ghost shall be poured out upon you more plentifully than ever." They had already been breathed upon with the Holy Ghost (John xx. 22), and they had found the benefit of it; but now they shall have larger measures of his gifts, graces, and comforts, and be baptized with them. . . .

Again he says:

> As the prediction of John Baptist; for so far back Christ here directs them to look (v. 5): "You have not only heard it from me, but you have had it from John; when he turned you over to me, he said (Matt. iii. 11), I indeed baptize you with water, but he that cometh after me shall baptize you with the Holy Ghost." It is a great honour that Christ now does to John not only to quote his words, but to make this great gift of the Spirit, now at hand, to be the accomplishment of them.

He continues by saying that this baptism of the Spirit was fulfilled in the next chapter. He said nothing about an origin of a church at Pentecost in this passage.

V. ELLICOTT SAID "BAPTIZED WITH HOLY GHOST" MEANT "PLUNGED INTO POWER"

Ellicott's Commentary on the Whole Bible, commenting on Acts 1:5, says:

> Some of them, at least, must have remembered also the teaching which had told them of the new birth of water and of the Spirit (John iii. 3-5). Now they were told that their spirits were to be as fully baptized, i.e. plunged, into

the power of the Divine Spirit, as their bodies had then been plunged in the waters of the Jordan. . . .

VI. DR. B. H. CARROLL, GREATEST THEOLOGIAN AMONG SOUTHERN BAPTISTS, SAID "BAPTIZED WITH HOLY GHOST" MEANT "TO CONFER POWER"

In his *Book of Sermons*, Dr. B. H. Carroll has a sermon on "Baptism of the Spirit." He says on page 319:

> The design of the baptism of the Holy Ghost was to confer power on Christians, whether they had once been baptized in water or not, as you will see directly.

So the historic position among Bible-believers through the centuries has been that "baptized with the Spirit" referred to enduement of power, the same as "filled with the Spirit" and "gift of the Spirit" in Acts 2.

VII. DR. W. B. RILEY SAYS "BAPTIZED WITH HOLY GHOST" MEANT "OUTPOURING OF THE SPIRIT AT PENTECOST"

In his forty-volume set of *The Bible of the Expositor*, (Vol. 6, p. 16) Dr. W. B. Riley says, commenting on Acts 1:5:

> But there was further blessing for them "not many days hence." The reference here plainly to the outpouring of the Spirit at Pentecost, which came ten days later.

VIII. DR. W. A. CRISWELL USES THE TERM AS ENDUEMENT OF POWER

Following the historic Christian position of Spurgeon, Mullins, Carroll, Scarborough, Moody and Torrey, Dr. W. A. Criswell writes me and then comments on my book, *Power of Pentecost*, "Your messages have thrilled and blessed my heart. Thank you again and again. Oh, that I might know the baptism of the Spirit and all the fullness of the meaning of the word."

IX. DR. L. R. SCARBOROUGH

It was my great privilege to be two years in the

evangelism classes of the late Dr. L. R. Scarborough, president of Southwestern Baptist Seminary and famous soul winner. My, how he held up Moody and Torrey and pleaded with us to seek and have the mighty power of God, as they had!

It is important to note the inspired usage of the term "baptized" when it is used figuratively. When Christ baptizes, He baptizes or overwhelms a Christian *"in the Holy Spirit."* When one is buried in the body of Christ, it is the Spirit who baptizes one *into the body.* The baptizer and the element are different. To make that figurative baptism in II Corinthians 12:13 to be the same as the different figure of baptism in Acts 1:5 disregards the language itself, the ones to whom it is spoken and the occasion.

The evidence of Holy Spirit baptism is soul-winning power, as we will show you in the next chapter.

CHAPTER VI

Gifts of the Spirit in I Corinthians 12

There are two passages in I Corinthians 12 that deal with the gifts of the Spirit. First are verses 4 to 11 as follows:

"Now there are diversities of gifts, but the same Spirit. And there are differences of administrations, but the same Lord. And there are diversities of operations, but it is the same God which worketh all in all. But the manifestation of the Spirit is given to every man to profit withal. For to one is given by the Spirit the word of wisdom; to another the word of knowledge by the same Spirit; To another faith by the same Spirit; to another the gifts of healing by the same Spirit; To another the working of miracles; to another prophecy; to another discerning of spirits; to another divers kinds of tongues; to another the interpretation of tongues: But all these worketh that one and the selfsame Spirit, dividing to every man severally as he will."

I. HOLY SPIRIT BRINGS DIFFERENT GIFTS TO DIFFERENT CHRISTIANS

Verse 7 says that "the manifestation of the Spirit is given to every man to profit withal." Every Christian can have some manifestation of Holy Spirit blessing. But they are all not the same. There are "diversities of operations." There are "diversities of gifts, but the same Spirit." Note the gifts that are given in verses 8 to 10: (1) the word of wisdom; (2) the word of knowledge; (3) faith; (4) gifts of healing; (5) working of miracles; (6) prophecy; (7) discerning of spirits; (8) foreign languages; (9) interpretation of languages.

II. THIS DIVISION OF GIFTS TO CHRISTIANS IS BY GOD'S CHOICE, NOT MAN'S

". . .the selfsame Spirit, dividing to every man severally as he will." This is abundantly clear that those signs which are to follow those who believe in Christ, those who believe on Him for miraculous manifestations as promised in Mark 16:17, will vary depending on the circumstances and need and in particular, as the Spirit Himself decides. Different people have different gifts. No one is taught that he could have or ought to have the same gifts.

And in verses 12 to 27 of the same chapter, God takes great pains to show that each one should be satisfied with whatever gifts God gives him, and we are all members of the body of Christ although we may have different manifestations of the Spirit's power and blessing.

This does not change the fact that every Christian is to win souls and is to have the power of the Holy Spirit for that. But these particular gifts of the Spirit named here are divided severally, as God wills.

In this same 12th chapter of I Corinthians, verses 28 to 31 tell us further:

"And God hath set some in the church, first apostles, secondarily prophets, thirdly teachers, after that miracles, then gifts of healings, helps, governments, diversities of tongues. Are all apostles? are all prophets? are all teachers? are all workers of miracles? Have all the gifts of healing? do all speak with tongues? do all interpret? But covet earnestly the best gifts: and yet shew I unto you a more excellent way."

Again it is emphasied that not all Christians are to have the same gifts. Are all apostles? Obviously not. Nor are all prophets or teachers. All do not work miracles. All do not have the gifts of healing. All do not speak with foreign languages nor interpret foreign languages.

When anyone sets out to teach that every Christian should speak in tongues or foreign languages miraculously, then he teaches what is not in the Bible and what contradicts the plain inspired Word of the Apostle Paul here.

III. GIFT OF LANGUAGES LAST AND LEAST OF THE SPIRIT'S GIFTS

Note that the gift of tongues or foreign languages and interpretation of tongues are the very last mentioned gifts here. Notice the order in verses 28 to 31. *"First"*—apostles; *"secondarily*—prophets; *"thirdly"*—teachers; *"after that"*—these other gifts that are less important, and last of all, speaking in tongues and interpreting. God gave this order—I did not. Do you think the gift of languages is as important as the gift of apostles? Certainly not. And here, verse 31 commands us that we are to "covet earnestly *the best gifts*," not the least. In I Corinthians 14:1 He commands us to "desire spiritual gifts, but rather that ye may prophesy," (or witness) in the power of God. Best of all is to have the power of God for soul winning.

Now, if God put these gifts in order and named one, two, three, and then after that, others, we should suppose He means them in order. The simple truth is that in Bible times the gift of foreign languages was necessarily counted least important. Here we have the gift of tongues mentioned at Pentecost in Acts, chapter 2. It is eight years later (in Acts, chap. 10), before there is any mention of tongues again. In this case, again, there is a crowd who speak several languages, from Rome and Jerusalem, and the servants and Jews present. The Scripture does not say that the languages there were miraculously given. We do not know. At any rate, that is the first time in eight years that the question has come up again with New Testament Christians. Why? Simply because there was no occasion for it. When everybody in my audience and everybody I meet can speak English, then why should I not be satisfied to speak to them in English?

Oh, to witness (prophesy) in the power of God is more important than tongues! This writer studied a good many languages. I had two years of Latin, two years in Hebrew, two years of German, some in Greek and some in French. I have spoken through interpreters in Japanese, Korean, Tamil, Telugu, and in sign languages. But any one or all these languages are incidental and unimportant compared to the matter of simply having the power of God to preach the Gospel and win souls in whatever language I speak to people. Prophesying, witnessing in the power of God as all did at Pentecost according to Acts 2:14-21, is the thing, whatever the language. Speaking in tongues is a lesser and unusual, not often-needed gift. Why should we be magnifying what God plainly plays down as less important?

The sad truth is that those who magnify "tongues" are often poorest soul winners. Let us say, they often do very little about soul winning.

CHAPTER VII

Is Speaking in Tongues "The Initial Evidence of Holy Spirit Baptism"?

Pentecostal people generally teach two separate doctrines about speaking in tongues. First, that when one is baptized of the Holy Ghost or filled with the Spirit there ought to be an initial evidence of the fullness of the Spirit by speaking in tongues. Second, that Christians ought to be able, at will, to speak regularly and often in tongues in private prayer and sometimes in public.

But is speaking in tongues the initial evidence of being baptized with the Spirit or the fullness of the Spirit? Or, since we are speaking about what happened at Pentecost and the use of the word "tongues" in the Bible, is speaking in *foreign languages* always the initial evidence of being filled with the Spirit? For the word "tongues" in the Bible always means "languages," foreign languages, when it does not refer to the literal, physical tongue in one's mouth.

I. PENTECOSTALISTS CLAIM THIS WITHOUT A SINGLE BIBLE STATEMENT TO VERIFY IT

It is a shock to careful and unbiased Bible students that anybody should claim that speaking in tongues is required evidence for the initial baptism or fullness of the Spirit, but that is widely held Pentecostal doctrine.

"The baptism of believers in the Holy Ghost is witnessed by the initial physical sign of speaking with other tongues as the Spirit of God gives them utterance," says the constitution of the Assemblies of God.

The Declaration of Faith of the Church of God says, "We believe in speaking with other tongues as the Spirit gives utterance, and that it is the initial evidence of the baptism in the Holy Ghost."

(Both the above quotations are from the book, *They Speak With Other Tongues*, by John L. Sherrill, a Pentecostal writer.)

He does not say which one of the three or four bodies called the "Church of God" he quotes.

From the headquarters and publishing house of the Assemblies of God in England, the pamphlet, *What Is the Good of Speaking With Tongues?* by Harold Horton, says on page 6, "(1) 'What is the good of speaking in tongues?' First of all, we reply, speaking in tongues is the scriptural evidence, the initial scriptural sign, of the baptism in the Holy Ghost." And then he insists repeatedly that that is the "scriptural sign," although he can give no Scripture that says so.

In the pamphlet, *How to Receive the Holy Spirit Baptism*, Gordon Lindsay says, "The Scriptures indicate rather strongly that the initial evidence of the baptism of the Spirit is the speaking in other tongues."

In the book, *These Are Not Drunken As Ye Suppose*, on page 105 Howard M. Ervin, says, "And whether stated, or implied, it is a fair conclusion from the biblical evidence, that tongues are the 'external and indubitable proof' of the baptism in/filling with the Holy Spirit." And he continues, "In the author's opinion, a baptism in the Spirit without the charismatic evidence is not a Biblical datum."

Note that he says, "In the author's opinion. . . ." He says it may be implied and "it is a fair conclusion." Of course he does not say, as no one can say, that the Bible states any such thing.

A little more scholarly man, Laurence Christenson, writes the book, *Speaking in Tongues*, with a Foreword by Corrie ten Boom, and he says, "The book of Acts contains not a single theological statement or precept in reference to speaking in tongues, It simply records the occurrence of the phenomenon" (p. 31). Read it again carefully: *"The book of*

Acts contains not a single theological statement or precept in reference to speaking in tongues."

I remember that a good many years ago Donald Gee, then one of the most prominent writers among Pentecostalists, frankly acknowledged the same thing.

Larry Christenson goes a little further to show how and why he inferred that speaking in tongues is the initial evidence of the baptism in the Holy Spirit. Again on pages 31 and 32 he says:

> What kinds of examples of speaking in tongues do we find in the Book of Acts? It is mentioned three times: Acts 2:4, on the Day of Pentecost; Acts 10:45, in the household of Cornelius, about 12 years after Pentecost; Acts 19:6, in Ephesus, about 24 years after Pentecost. The most striking similarity is that in each case the speaking in tongues is directly connected with an initial outpouring of the Holy Spirit upon a group of believers.

Note that he mentions three times in the book of Acts when people talked in foreign languages, when the Holy Spirit was poured out upon them. He ignores all the other times in the Bible when people were filled with the Holy Spirit: Jesus, Elisabeth, Mary, Zacharias, John the Baptist, the seven deacons in Acts 6, Stephen particularly in Acts 7, the Apostle Paul in Acts 9:17, Barnabas in Acts 11:24, and elsewhere. And he picks out these three cases when, because of local conditions, people spoke in foreign languages, and from that he infers, and Pentecostalists generally do infer, what the Bible does not say—that speaking in tongues or foreign languages goes with and is the proof of the baptism of the Holy Spirit in the initial case or first time. He ignores the fact that there is no command anywhere to talk in tongues or to seek to talk in tongues. And he ignores also the fact that Jesus gave entirely different evidence, that is, soul-winning power, as the evidence of the power of the Holy Spirit (Luke 24:46-49; Acts 1:8; and the example of Pentecost itself).

But in *I Believe in the Holy Ghost*, published by Bethany Fellowship, Minneapolis, Maynard James reminds us that many ardent Pentecostalists are not satisfied with making a doctrine without a single statement of Scripture to back it. He says:

> We are glad that certain Pentecostal leaders have had both discernment and courage to acknowledge that a person can be filled with the Holy Spirit without speaking in tongues. Among them were the late T. B. Barratt and George Jeffreys. Even more authoritative is the statement by the European Pentecostal Conference held in Stockholm in the early summer of 1939. It admitted that tongues might occur apart from the Spirit's action; and that a Christian could be filled with the Spirit without the sign of tongues.

Then Maynard reminds us that the Christian and Missionary Alliance which, because they had the same emphasis on divine healing, were often involved in the tongues question, had a rule, "Seek not, forbid not." That is, they allowed speaking in tongues, but they did not claim it was the evidence of Holy Spirit baptism or fullness.

You can nowhere prove by the Bible that speaking with tongues is the initial evidence required of the baptism of the Holy Spirit.

II. NO OTHER BIBLE DOCTRINE ACCEPTED IN HISTORIC CHRISTIANITY IS EVER BELIEVED ON SOME IMPLICATION AND WITHOUT CLEAR STATEMENT IN BIBLE

How do we know that the Bible is inspired? Well, the grandeur of the Bible, its influence on society, its revelation of Christ, its marvelous moral standards, are all good indications, but that is not why we believe in the inspiration of the Bible. We believe it because it is explicitly stated again and again!

Why do we believe in the virgin birth of Christ? Because He lived and talked as no one else ever lived and talked? No. We believe it because the Bible plainly says it again and again, in Isaiah 7:14, in Matthew 1:20-23, in Luke 1:34,35, besides being implied many times.

How do we know that Christians will rise from the dead? You may say it might be inferred from the resurrection of

Jesus. No. That is not enough. It is expressly and literally taught again and again, as in I Corinthians 15; Romans 8:11 and many other Scriptures.

How do we know about the Bible doctrine of the new birth? Well, it is implied, you may say, because we see the difference in various Christians in the New Testament. No. That is not how we know "ye must be born again." Jesus said it so plainly, in John 3, in John 1:12,13; in I Peter 1:23 and in many, many other Scriptures.

How do we know that we have a right to pray to God? Well, we might infer it because some people in the Bible did pray. Oh, no! But we are plainly invited, commanded and exhorted to pray again and again and again in the Bible and told how to pray and what to expect.

And should we simply infer that because Jesus on the cross prayed for forgiveness for those who crucified Him, we then should forgive our enemies? Well, that was a good example all right, but the Lord Jesus did not leave it to example but expressly commanded it again and again, as in Mark 11:25, in the Lord's Prayer and elsewhere.

So the warning about drink—we don't have to go by the sad example of Noah and Lot and so infer it. We learn by direct commands in the Bible.

Do we learn the great moral principles of the Ten Commandments just by inferring them from some Scriptures or incidents that happened? Oh, no! They are expressly commanded in Exodus 20 and again in Deuteronomy 5, and the moral commandments, that is, all but the Sabbath commandment, are repeated in the New Testament.

Not a single doctrinal teaching in the Bible is left to be inferred by somebody's interpretation of an obscure passage.

If we could infer from what happened at Pentecost, that one baptized of the Spirit must talk in other tongues as an evidence, then we could also infer that there must be a cyclonic wind filling the house and tongues like fire sitting upon people.

Again, if we can infer from the case at Pentecost that people must talk in tongues as the *initial* evidence of the baptism of the Spirit, then we might infer from Acts 4:31 that the *second* time people are filled with the Spirit they would have an earthquake, for, "When they had prayed, the place was shaken where they were assembled together; and they were all filled with the Holy Ghost, and they spake the word of God with boldness." No, it is wrong to infer what the Bible does not say. That would always depend on a subjective attitude of the one who reads.

If you are to infer doctrine with no further teaching, without any Bible statement, then, since John baptized people in the River Jordan, you might infer there is no valid baptism unless done in a river. In fact, some have made that silly conclusion. Inference is unreliable.

Our Catholic friends infer that Peter was the first pope; they infer that he went to Rome (although the Bible makes clear he never did and history never proves it); and they infer that from that time on the bishop at Rome is to rule the world as God's vicegerent on earth in spiritual matters. And they infer that the priest therefore has a right to forgive sins. But all that is inference, not stated in the Bible. And that is the way people go into heresies.

The Bible does not say anywhere that speaking in tongues is the initial evidence of the baptism of the Holy Spirit. To infer that and say that is heresy and shows an improper irreverence toward the Word of God and its authority.

III. BIBLE EXAMPLES SHOW TO BE FILLED WITH SPIRIT OR BAPTIZED WITH SPIRIT NEED NOT INVOLVE TALKING IN A FOREIGN LANGUAGE

1. Jesus Did Not Speak in Foreign Languages

In Luke 3:21,22 we find that when Jesus was baptized in the River Jordan, "the Holy Ghost descended in a bodily shape like a dove upon him, and a voice came from heaven, which said, Thou art my beloved Son; in thee I am well pleased." And the Scripture continues that Jesus was now thirty years old. Up to this time He had never preached a sermon, nor worked a miracle, nor won a soul. But here He began His public ministry, was tempted in the wilderness and then "returned in the power of the Spirit into Galilee," and explained that now the Scripture in Isaiah 61:1 was fulfilled this day before them. And Acts 10:38 reminds us "how God anointed Jesus of Nazareth with the Holy Ghost and with power: who went about doing good, and healing all that were oppressed of the devil; for God was with him."

So Jesus, filled with the Spirit, and for the first time, and beginning His ministry, did not talk in foreign languages. Why should He? Nobody was present who could not understand the Aramaic, the language they all spoke. But why wouldn't Christians be satisfied to have just what Jesus had, the power of the Holy Ghost to preach and witness and win souls, without some jabber you could brag about?

2. Spirit-Filled John the Baptist Never Spoke in a Miraculous Language

Luke 1:15 and 16 gives a sweet promise about John the Baptist, that "he shall be filled with the Holy Ghost, even from his mother's womb. And many of the children of Israel shall he turn to the Lord their God."

Now there is no indication that John the Baptist ever spoke in any foreign languages. In fact, we are told in John 10:41 that "John did no miracle." But the foreign languages spoken at Pentecost were miraculously given; John had nothing like that. Now, would God make a rule, then break His own rule? No. Speaking in foreign languages or tongues is not the Bible initial evidence of the baptism of the Holy Spirit, not any evidence at all.

3. Samaritan Converts, First Filled With Spirit, Had No Language Evidence

The great group of converts at Samaria had been wonderfully saved, and then Peter and John came to pray for them that they might receive the Holy Ghost. In Acts 8:14-16 we read:

"Now when the apostles which were at Jerusalem heard that Samaria had received the word of God, they sent unto them Peter and John: Who, when they were come down, prayed for them, that they might receive the Holy Ghost: (For as yet he was fallen upon none of them: only they were baptized in the name of the Lord Jesus.)"

Notice that they had been saved but had not before received the Holy Spirit. The term "fallen on them" is used also in other cases for "filled with the Spirit." Now, if the Lord had intended us to understand that always people filled with the Holy Spirit at first speak in other languages, He could have said so there, or He could have told that they did, and in all these other cases when people were filled with the Spirit. But if the Spirit-filled people at Samaria did not talk in foreign languages or tongues, then there is no need for others to expect that.

4. Paul, First Filled With Spirit, Did Not Speak in Foreign Languages

Again in Acts 9:17 we find where Paul the apostle, wonderfully saved on the way to Damascus and who had been fasting and praying for three days and nights, now received the Holy Spirit. Acts 9:17 says, "And Ananias went his way, and entered into the house; and putting his hands on him said, Brother Saul, the Lord, even Jesus, that appeared unto thee in the way as thou camest, hath sent me, that thou mightest receive thy sight, and be filled with the Holy Ghost." Now straightway the following Scripture tells us that Paul was baptized and began to witness with power about Jesus as the Son of God. But there is no hint that he talked in foreign languages or tongues.

Why ignore all these cases, then pretend that by three cases in particular circumstances where people of other languages were present, therefore one is always supposed to talk in tongues or a foreign language when filled with the Spirit? That contradicts the Bible doctrine. It is a shoddy kind of Bible exposition to infer what the Bible does not teach and what did not happen in other cases when people were filled with the Spirit.

IV. BIBLE HAS CLEAR COMMANDS, PROMISES ABOUT BEING FILLED WITH SPIRIT THAT DO NOT INVOLVE SPEAKING IN FOREIGN LANGUAGES OR TONGUES

In Luke 24:46-49 Jesus said:

"Thus it is written, and thus it behoved Christ to suffer, and to rise from the dead the third day: And that repentance and remission of sins should be preached in his name among all nations, beginning at Jerusalem. And ye are witnesses of these things. And, behold, I send the promise of my Father upon you: but tarry ye in the city of Jerusalem, until ye be endued with power from on high."

Note that what He is talking about is enduement of power to win souls. It is connected with carrying out the Great Commission. Now one has a right here to connect what Jesus connected, that is, Holy Spirit power with preaching the Gospel and winning souls. But one has no right to connect something else with it that Jesus didn't mention.

Again in Acts 1:4 and 5 Jesus told the disciples:

"And, being assembled together with them, commanded them that they should not depart from Jerusalem, but wait for the promise of the Father, which, saith he, ye have heard of me. For John truly baptized with water; but ye shall be baptized with the Holy Ghost not many days hence."

They were to wait for a promise of the Father. How often in the Old Testament had God promised that Christians could have the power of the Holy Spirit! It was so in Joel 2:28-32 which Peter said was the beginning of the fulfillment on the day of Pentecost. That promise did not mention talking in foreign languages.

In Isaiah 44:3 the Lord had promised, "For I will pour water upon him that is thirsty, and floods upon the dry ground: I will pour my spirit upon thy seed, and my blessing upon thine offspring." This is the promise of the

Father about the Holy Spirit to be poured out upon people. And no mention is made of tongues or foreign languages.

To Ezekiel the Lord again and again promised that He would put a new Spirit of the Lord in Jews when He comes back to the earth to reign (Ezek. 11:19; Ezek. 18:31; Ezek. 36:26,27; Ezek. 39:29). Now, why should all these promises about the pouring out of the Holy Spirit be given without any mention or even inference that it would involve talking in a foreign language or other tongues?

The disciples thought Jesus perhaps referred to the coming restoration of Israel at His second coming. No, He was referring to the enduement of power for getting out the Gospel. So in Acts 1:8 He said, "But ye shall receive power, after that the Holy Ghost is come upon you: and ye shall be witnesses unto me both in Jerusalem, and in all Judaea, and in Samaria, and unto the uttermost part of the earth."

And Peter promised those Jews who wanted to be saved and wanted the power of the Holy Spirit, ". . . and ye shall receive the gift of the Holy Ghost. For the promise is unto you, and to your children, and to all that are afar off, even as many as the Lord our God shall call" (Acts 2:38,39). He made no reference, did not even imply that along with this gift of the Holy Ghost would be talking in foreign languages or tongues. Why read into a few passages a doctrine never clearly stated and that doesn't fit all the other Scriptures involved?

No, speaking in tongues or foreign languages is not the initial evidence of the baptism of the Holy Ghost.

V. THROUGH THE CENTURIES, GREATEST CHRISTIANS, GREATEST SOUL WINNERS, FILLED WITH SPIRIT, HAVE NOT TALKED IN TONGUES OR FOREIGN LANGUAGES

Here you may begin to see why godly Christians everywhere are impatient at the rather arrogant claims of Pentecostal people. They say that only those who talk in tongues have the fullness of the Spirit. Thus they claim to be better Christians than all the great soul winners of the ages who did not talk in tongues.

When I spoke in Toronto at the Avenue Road Church to a great congregation, I think some fifteen people came weeping to trust in Christ and claim Him as Saviour. Immediately after I stepped out of the pulpit, a man approached me and asked if I had been baptized with the Holy Ghost. He had, he said. But when I inquired, he told me frankly that he had never won a soul to Christ. Yet he thought himself superior to me and other Christians who win souls! That kind of arrogance, that "holier-than-thou" attitude, is not the attitude of good Christian humility, and it is unfitting and is indication that they are deceived in a false doctrine.

1. Would You Deny Spurgeon Had God's Mighty Power?

I do not now deal so much with Savonarola, John Huss, Martin Luther, John Knox—none of these claimed to talk in tongues. But what about Charles Spurgeon who preached in London to the greatest crowds assembled, up to 5,000 people regularly, and sometimes up to 12,000 or 20,000 when he got a great Exposition Building to preach in? Multiplied thousands were saved under his ministry. Now, because he did not talk in tongues, do you tell me that he was not filled with the Spirit? Oh, how wonderfully he preached about the power of the Holy Spirit! And how he believed in that power! And how he manifested it! It is shameful and shortsighted and, I think, not very intelligent for someone to claim he has the power of God because he talks in tongues and Spurgeon, who won many thousands, did not.

2. John Wesley

What about blessed John Wesley? Oh, what a preacher! How lovingly and with holy dedication and sacrifice he worked, wrote, preached and won souls! What a blessing it is to read John Wesley's *Journal*. But since John Wesley didn't talk in tongues, you think he was never filled with the Spirit of God. I do not believe you.

3. John Knox, George Whitefield

And what about John Knox in Scotland? What about Whitefield, that flaming preacher in England who then came to the American colonies and won so many thousands? Do you think he was not filled with the Spirit? He did not talk in tongues.

4. Charles G. Finney Won Hundreds of Thousands

In America, Charles G. Finney was wonderfully baptized with the Holy Spirit and said so, but he did not talk in tongues. Because he plainly said he was baptized with the Spirit, ignorant and loose thinking people have sometimes accused him of talking in tongues.

Rev. Jerry Jensen, Managing Editor of the Full Gospel Men's Voice, in his pamphlet, *Baptists and the Baptism of the Holy Spirit*, says:

> From the vivid accounts of the mighty moving of the Holy Spirit in the Book of Acts, through the great revivals of yester-year when Dwight L. Moody, Charles Finney and others testified of speaking in other tongues as they received the Baptism with the Holy Spirit, we are brought today, to another mighty outpouring of the Spirit of God on people of all denominations.

That is an inexcusable, false statement.

Now, with the most casual reading of Charles G. Finney's autobiography and his accounts of how he was filled with the Spirit or baptized with the Spirit and had mighty power to win souls and how he returned again and again to pray for "new baptism of the Spirit," any honest man will see that Finney never claimed to talk in tongues. And the history of his work, written by more than one, gives no such intimation. The poor man, Jensen, without much background, jumped to the conclusion that Finney talked in tongues since he said he was "baptized with the Holy Spirit."

5. D. L. Moody, "Baptized With Holy Ghost," Did Not Talk in Tongues

Again D. L. Moody is charged that he "testified of speaking in other tongues" as he "received the Baptism with the Holy Spirit." He testified to nothing of the kind. We have republished *The Life of D. L. Moody by His Son*, a book of 590 pages. I have perhaps a dozen books before me on the life of Mr. Moody. I have his sermons on the Holy Spirit. I have probably published more sermons by D. L. Moody than any man in America. Mr. Moody tells how he was filled with the Holy Spirit after he had pleaded for God's power for some time and how many were saved thereafter. But he does not even hint that he talked in tongues.

That kind of talk is dishonest and comes from ignorance and presuppositions. Intelligent Christians ought not listen to that kind of dishonest and misleading teaching.

Ah, but now consider someone who talks in tongues and perhaps never wins a soul or wins very few; is he therefore a better Christian than Mr. Moody? Is he on the inside with a New Testament experience which Moody never had? There is something strangely wrong with the mentality of people who think so.

6. Other Mighty Soul Winners Did Not Talk in Tongues

What about the greatest evangelists: A. B. Earle, R. A. Torrey, J. Wilbur Chapman, Gipsy Smith, William Biederwolf, Sam Jones, Billy Sunday, Mordecai Ham, Abe Mulkey, and a multitude of others? At one time there were a thousand evangelists holding citywide campaigns in America and uniting in the association meeting held once a year in Winona Lake with Dr. Bob Jones, Sr., as president. They did not claim that they talked in tongues. Many, many of them are on record that they did have a special enduement of power from on High, a fullness of the Spirit, in answer to prayer, as they sought to have power to win souls and received it.

It is a common practice among Pentecostal people to pick out soul winners and report that they have talked in tongues. A woman wrote me recently that Dr. J. Frank Norris sought long for the "baptism" and to "speak in tongues" but could not "pay the price." I probably knew him better than any outside his family and office staff. I know he did not. So one wrote to me that Dr. Hyman Appelman had talked in tongues, a man I have known for many years. I have his book of sermons on the Holy Spirit before me just now. I know better than that, of course.

Someone wrote me the other day asking, "Is it true, as they say, that Dr. Jack Hyles talks in tongues?" Of course he does not. I have had very intimate association with him for twenty years.

No, I am saying that those who have been most mightily used of God, with obvious enduement of power of the Holy Spirit down through the ages, usually have not talked in tongues. And that disproves the claim that in the initial fullness of the Spirit one must talk in tongues. It is simply not taught in the Bible; and human experience, of course, proves the claim is unfounded.

CHAPTER VIII

Real Purpose and Evidence of Holy Spirit Baptism or Fullness

Our Pentecostal friends infer that speaking in tongues, foreign languages, is the necessary initial evidence of the baptism of the Holy Spirit. I say they infer that, though there is not a single Scripture in the Bible which says so.

As the scholarly Pentecostal writer Larry Christenson says in his book, *Speaking in Tongues*, "The Book of Acts contains not a single theological statement or precept in reference to speaking in tongues. It simply records the occurrence of the phenomenon."

I. MANY SCRIPTURES DECLARE THAT FULLNESS OR BAPTISM OF SPIRIT IS FOR SOUL-WINNING POWER

So, then, why must we infer what is the purpose and the evidence of the gift of foreign languages as at Pentecost? The truth is, we have explicit statements and teaching in the Word of God. Christenson could say that "the Book of Acts contains not a single theological statement or precept in reference to speaking in tongues," but he could not say that about Holy Spirit power for soul winning.

There is an abundance of statements and precepts about seeking and having the Holy Spirit as at Pentecost. Whether you call it baptism of the Spirit, or the gift of the Spirit, or the fullness of the Spirit, or the Holy Spirit coming upon Christians, the purpose of the pouring out of the Holy Spirit at Pentecost is simply to carry out the Great Commission, to win souls.

1. Prophecy of Joel in Acts 2:14-21 Shows Meaning of Pentecost Beyond Doubt

Acts 2:14-21 says:

"But Peter, standing up with the eleven, lifted up his voice, and said unto them, Ye men of Judaea, and all ye that dwell at Jerusalem, be this known unto you, and hearken to my words: For these are not drunken, as ye suppose, seeing it is but the third hour of the day. But this is that which was spoken by the prophet Joel; And it shall come to pass in the last days, saith God, I will pour out of my Spirit upon all flesh: and your sons and your daughters shall prophesy, and your young men shall see visions, and your old men shall dream dreams: And on my servants and on my handmaidens I will pour out in those days of my Spirit; and they shall prophesy: And I will shew wonders in heaven above, and signs in the earth beneath; blood, and fire, and vapour of smoke: The sun shall be turned into darkness, and the moon into blood, before that great and notable day of the Lord come: And it shall come to pass, that whosoever shall call on the name of the Lord shall be saved."

Peter said, "This is that," so what Joel prophesied for a period of time is called "the last days," including not only Pentecost but going right on down to the "great and notable day of the Lord." That pouring out of the Spirit was to enable people to prophesy or witness for the Lord Jesus in the power of the Spirit and the result would be that "whosoever shall call upon the name of the Lord shall be saved."

Some say that only Peter prophesied or witnessed or preached publicly at Pentecost. But that is not true. His message was addressed to "Ye men of Judaea, and all ye that dwell at Jerusalem," those native Jews who spoke the Aramaic language. But the others who were filled with the Spirit spoke, prophesied, in the languages of "Jews, devout men, out of every nation under heaven" who were there that day. Whether it was Peter speaking in the Aramaic language to the dwellers in Jerusalem, or to the rest of them speaking to all these other Jews from other nations speaking foreign languages, remember that it was all called "prophesying," which means speaking in the mighty power of God and witnessing. As Joel had said, the result was 3,000 people saved.

Do you want some evidence, some indication of what the meaning at Pentecost was? Then listen to the prophecy of Joel which Peter said was fulfilled then. It is so people might prophesy in the power of God, witness in the power of God; and as a result, 3,000 people were saved. Is not the soul-winning power itself, which was promised, evidenced when the power was displayed and souls were saved?

2. Luke 24:46-49 Teaches They Were Waiting for Power to Win Souls

We come again to the Great Commission in Luke 24:46-49:

"And said unto them, Thus it is written, and thus it behoved Christ to suffer, and to rise from the dead the third day: And that repentance and remission of sins should be preached in his name among all nations, beginning at Jerusalem. And ye are witnesses of these things. And, behold, I send the promise of my Father upon you: but tarry ye in the city of Jerusalem, until ye be endued with power from on high."

Now, since they were tarrying to be endued with power, what kind of sign would they want? The power, and the fruits of that power! So when the power of God came and the multitude were saved, sensible people who were waiting on God for His power would surely rejoice that the power came. What evidence would you need besides those thousands of people saved and the joy of having part in their salvation?

So the soul-winning power is itself the evidence of the fullness of the Spirit.

3. In Acts 1:8 Jesus Told Them the Results They Should Seek and Expect

In Acts 1:8 Jesus said:

"But ye shall receive power, after that the Holy Ghost is come upon you: and ye shall be witnesses unto me both in Jerusalem, and in all Judaea, and in Samaria, and unto the uttermost part of the earth."

Here is the express statement that Bible believers ought to take to heart. Why look for some other strange kind of evidence that you might infer or hope for, when the Lord clearly tells us they were to receive power when the Holy Ghost came on them and they were to be witnesses, soul-winning witnesses, for Him?

And it was done. Even if God had to work some incidental miracles and help them with foreign languages they did not know, the power of God was there to win souls; and soul-winning power itself was what they sought and what they had and was its own authentication. Soul-winning power is the evidence of the fullness of the Spirit.

II. BIBLE EXAMPLES ALSO SHOW WHAT IS BIBLE EVIDENCE OF FULLNESS OF SPIRIT

We have not only the promises about Pentecost but the blessed results: 3,000 souls saved and baptized are good enough evidence for anyone who wants what Bible Christians had. The fullness of the Spirit at Pentecost meant saving souls.

1. John the Baptist Saw Multitudes Saved

John the Baptist was a blessed soul winner. And remember, the angel said about him:

"For he shall be great in the sight of the Lord, and shall drink neither wine nor strong drink; and he shall be filled with the Holy Ghost, even from his mother's womb. And many of the children of Israel shall he turn to the Lord their God."—Luke 1:15, 16.

John the Baptist was filled with the Holy Spirit, just like they were at Pentecost, only in his case it was from the time of his birth. There must have been some time when he came to see himself a sinner. So, conscious of sin, he turned to the Lord and was saved and so continued in the power of God. The Lord gave him the spirit and power of Elijah. We need not dodge the simple, exact language used. He was "filled with the Spirit," and the result was, "And many of the children of Israel shall he turn to the Lord their God."

We do not know of any incidental miracles in the

ministry of John the Baptist. There were no tongues like as of fire sitting upon him, no sound of a rushing, mighty wind, no need for and no giving of understanding some modern language. But the evidence is plainly given: "And many of the children of Israel shall he turn to the Lord their God." So he did, the Scripture tells us.

Matthew 3 tells us how John the Baptist came preaching in the wilderness of Judaea and saying, "Repent ye: for the kingdom of heaven is at hand." And verses 5 and 6 tell us, "Then went out to him Jerusalem, and all Judaea, and all the region round about Jordan, And were baptized of him in Jordan, confessing their sins." The people saved were the evidence of the power of God.

2. Disciples, Again Filled With Holy Spirit After Pentecost, Saw Many Saved

In Acts 4:31 the disciples needed power again and they prayed again and God's soul-winning power came. That verse says, "And when they had prayed, the place was shaken where they were assembled together; and they were all filled with the Holy Ghost, and they spake the word of God with boldness."

Oh, the boldness of these Spirit-filled preachers! Verse 33 says, "And with great power gave the apostles witness of the resurrection of the Lord Jesus: and great grace was upon them all." There follows the story in the next chapter of how "believers were the more added to the Lord, multitudes both of men and women" (5:14).

Do you suppose Peter and John and the other apostles needed some other special evidence of the fullness of the Spirit when multitudes came to be saved?

Oh, but one may say that was not an *initial* fullness of the Spirit. No, but that idea of an *initial* evidence is not mentioned in the Bible. The fullness of the Spirit in Acts 4:31 was given for the same reason as Acts 2:4. Exactly the same nine words are used to describe it—"And they were all filled with the Holy Ghost." It is given for the same reason promised in Luke 24:49 and in Acts 1:8; they had the evidence—souls saved.

3. Spirit-Filled Stephen Won Paul

Stephen, one of the seven deacons, was arraigned before the high priest and Jewish leaders. And how his words burned!

"Ye stiffnecked and uncircumcised in heart and ears, ye do always resist the Holy Ghost: as your fathers did, so do ye. Which of the prophets have not your fathers persecuted? and they have slain them which shewed before of the coming of the Just One; of whom ye have been now the betrayers and murderers: Who have received the law by the disposition of angels, and have not kept it. When they heard these things, they were cut to the heart, and they gnashed on him with their teeth. But he, being full of the Holy Ghost, looked up stedfastly into heaven, and saw the glory of God, and Jesus standing on the right hand of God, And said, Behold, I see the heavens opened, and the Son of man standing on the right hand of God."—Acts 7:51-56.

So they ran on Stephen and gnashed on him with their teeth and beat him to death with stones. You do not at once see the results of souls saved here. Ah, but wait. A little later in the story you will see Saul of Tarsus who held the garments for those who stoned Stephen. He is on his road to Damascus breathing out threatenings and slaughter. Oh, but one thing keeps pricking him like an oxgoad. It is the glorified face of Stephen, like the face of an angel. It is his Spirit-filled testimony and his prayer. Ah, Paul told the story later when he stood before Agrippa. He saw a vision of Jesus, and Acts 26:13-15 tells us of the conviction of his heart:

"At midday, O king, I saw in the way a light from heaven, above the brightness of the sun, shining round about me and them which journeyed with me. And when we were all fallen to the earth, I heard a voice speaking unto me, and saying in the Hebrew tongue, Saul, Saul, why persecutest thou me? it is hard for thee to kick against the pricks. And I said, Who art thou, Lord? And he said, I am Jesus whom thou persecutest."

Stephen, here is your fruit—that blaspheming Pharisee

who hated Christians could not get away from the pricking oxgoad of Spirit-filled Stephen's testimony.

4. Samaritan Converts Spirit-Filled, Did Not Speak in Foreign Languages

In Samaria, the converts under the preaching of Spirit-filled Philip were not immediately filled with the Spirit until the apostles Peter and John came from Jerusalem and laid hands upon them. Acts 8:14-17 tells us:

"Now when the apostles which were at Jerusalem heard that Samaria had received the word of God, they sent unto them Peter and John: Who, when they were come down, prayed for them, that they might receive the Holy Ghost: (For as yet he was fallen upon none of them: only they were baptized in the name of the Lord Jesus.) Then laid they their hands on them, and they received the Holy Ghost."

The term "receive the Holy Ghost" here obviously refers to the special witnessing power, the enduement of power which came on some at Pentecost. They had already believed, and the Holy Spirit had already worked a miracle of regeneration in them and had come in to dwell. So we think the receiving of the Holy Ghost here is the enduement of power.

In John 20:22 Jesus breathed on the disciples and told them, "Receive ye the Holy Ghost." We take it that that was the fulfillment of the promise of the Holy Spirit that "he dwelleth with you, and shall be in you," from John 14:17. But it is important to notice that there is NO indication here that they talked in foreign languages. And why should they? There is no evidence that people of foreign languages were present who needed to hear the Gospel in their own tongue.

5. Paul, Filled With Spirit, "Straightway" Won Souls

Paul the apostle was filled with the Holy Spirit also. After he was converted on the road to Damascus and had fasted and prayed for three days, God sent Ananias to him who said, "Brother Saul, the Lord, even Jesus, that appeared unto thee in the way as thou camest, hath sent me, that thou mightest receive thy sight, and be filled with the Holy Ghost" (Acts 9:17).

What evidence was there of the power of God? Verse 20 says, "And straightway he preached Christ in the synagogues, that he is the Son of God."

The people were amazed. Some set out to kill him, so he had to run for his life. And henceforth everywhere Paul went blessed fruitage of souls saved followed his ministry.

Was not that enough evidence for Paul? There is never any indication that he talked in some jabber as an evidence, but there was the evidence of souls saved, and that was enough for him, as it ought to be for us.

But someone will be quick to say, "Oh, but Paul talked in tongues." In I Corinthians 14:18 he said, "I thank my God, I speak with tongues more than ye all." Let us make it a little clearer. "Tongues" in the New Testament refers to foreign languages, as it does here. So Paul said, "I speak in foreign languages more than all of you." You see, Paul spoke the Aramaic language which was the common language throughout Judaea in his time. But Acts 21:40 tells us that Paul stood and talked to the people "in the Hebrew tongue." So he spoke Hebrew also. Then Paul spoke in Koine Greek, for all his letters in the New Testament were written in the Greek language.

Paul also boasted that he was a Roman citizen. It may well be that he spoke Latin also. That we do not know, but he was a highly educated, cultured man, and he spoke in a number of foreign languages. He did not say, in I Corinthians 14:18, that he spoke in some unknown tongue, and he was explaining to them very carefully that although he knew more languages than they did, he did not use them where they could not be understood. He was rebuking them for using foreign languages in public services when others could not understand them.

Paul's evidence of the fullness of the Spirit was souls saved, of course.

III. GREATEST SOUL WINNERS WHO CLAIMED TO HAVE BEEN FILLED OR BAPTIZED WITH HOLY SPIRIT, WON THOUSANDS, DID NOT TALK IN TONGUES

1. Charles G. Finney

In his autobiography, Finney tells of his conversion. He had a great deal of a struggle getting assurance that he was saved. And after he had trusted the Lord the best he knew, he kept waiting on God and praying. Then he tells us on pages 20 and 21:

> . . .But as I turned and was about to take a seat by the fire, I received a mighty baptism of the Holy Ghost. Without any expectation of it, without ever having the thought in my mind that there was any such thing for me, without any recollection that I had ever heard the thing mentioned by any person in the world, the Holy Spirit descended upon me in a manner that seemed to go through me, body and soul. I could feel the impression, like a wave of electricity, going through and through me. Indeed it seemed to come in waves and waves of liquid love; for I could not express it in any other way. It seemed like the very breath of God. I can recollect distinctly that it seemed to fan me, like immense wings.
>
> No words can express the wonderful love that was shed abroad in my heart. I wept aloud with joy and love; and I do not know but I should say, I literally bellowed out the unutterable gushings of my heart. These waves came over me, and over me, one after the other, until I recollect I cried out, "I shall die if these waves continue to pass over me." I said, "Lord, I cannot bear any more;" yet I had no fear of death.

Immediately there was an amazing series of conversions. He talked to a young man about his soul, who was very careless and worldly. And the young man fell upon his knees and begged Finney to pray. And he was saved.

Then on pages 22 and 23 he tells us further:

> When I awoke in the morning the sun had risen, and was pouring a clear light into my room. Words cannot express the impression that this sunlight made upon me. Instantly the baptism that I had received the night before returned upon me in the same manner. I arose upon my

knees in the bed and wept aloud with joy, and remained
for some time too much overwhelmed with the baptism of
the Spirit to do anything but pour out my soul to God. It
seemed as if this morning's baptism was accompanied
with a gentle reproof, and the Spirit seemed to say to me,
"Will you doubt?" I cried, "No! I will not doubt; I cannot
doubt." He then cleared the subject up so much to my
mind that it was in fact impossible for me to doubt that
the Spirit of God had taken possession of my soul.

Now, Finney knew he must preach; he wanted to preach.
He must begin immediately. He sallied forth. A shoemaker
was talking with a Universalist. That young man was cut
to the heart, went into the woods, and there gave his heart
to God.

Finney said,

I spoke with many persons that day, and I believe the
Spirit of God made lasting impressions upon every one of
them. I cannot remember one whom I spoke with, who
was not soon after converted.

He visited a home. A young woman was converted. A
young man, a relative and a Universalist, was immediately
converted. He fled to his room, locked himself in, and did
not come down until the next morning when he came and
claimed the Saviour.

His marvelous soul winning continued and he said,

The Word of God had wonderful power; and I was every
day surprised to find that a few words, spoken to an
individual, would stick in his heart like an arrow.

He visited his own home and his father and mother,
both soon in tears, were saved.

Soon Finney was preaching in the mighty power of God
and hundreds of thousands of souls were saved in his
marvelous campaigns.

Mr. Finney never talked in tongues. Why should he? The
people who heard him could understand the English
language. But he did have what God promised, that is, he
received power when the Holy Ghost came upon him and
many were saved.

Soul-winning power is the Bible evidence of the fullness
of the Spirit.

2. Evangelist A. B. Earle Won 150,000 With No Tongues

A. B. Earle was a Spirit-filled evangelist, author of the books, *Bringing in the Sheaves* and *The Rest of Faith.* James Gilchrist Lawson says,

> In fifty years he traveled 325,000 miles in the United States and Canada, preached 19,780 times, and 150,000 persons professed conversion in his meetings.

He began preaching in 1830 and he said,

> I have observed for nearly forty years past, that the secret of success in promoting revivals of religion is in having our own hearts filled with the Holy Spirit.

And again he says,

> Nothing can be a substitute for real power from on high. No amount of study, or talent, or effort, however untiring, can take the place of the fulness of Christ's love; "Not by might, nor by [human] power, but by my Spirit, saith the Lord."—Quoting from *Deeper Experiences of Famous Christians* by James Gilchrist Lawson.

3. Billy Sunday Used to Win Perhaps a Million Souls; No Tongues!

Billy Sunday was a Spirit-filled evangelist and it is supposed that a million people came to Christ in his great campaigns. And whence came his power? He was only a high school graduate, baseball player, colloquial and sometimes uncouth in his language, yet God saved multitudes under his ministry. Why? He knew why. Every time he went to the pulpit he opened his Bible to one passage of Scripture, Isaiah 61:1, 2,

> *"The Spirit of the Lord God is upon me; because the Lord hath anointed me to preach good tidings unto the meek; he hath sent me to bind up the brokenhearted, to proclaim liberty to the captives, and the opening of the prison to them that are bound; To proclaim the acceptable year of the Lord, and the day of the vengeance of our God; to comfort all that mourn."*

Then he laid his sermon notes on top of the Bible, whatever his text, but always as a testimony to God and to his own heart he remembered that his power lay in the fact that he was anointed to preach, that the Spirit of God was upon him! Billy Sunday never talked in tongues. Why should he? He had the Bible evidences of the power of God when the Spirit of God was on him.

Dr. Bob Jones, Sr., told me of a time when he went to an altar and waited on God and he said, "I do not know what to call it, and I don't care what you say. I know that from that time forward a great increase of power and blessing was on my ministry."

The Bible evidence of the fullness of the Spirit is soul-winning power.

IV. THOSE WHO PUT MOST EMPHASIS ON "SPEAKING IN TONGUES" PUT LESS EMPHASIS ON SOUL-WINNING POWER

I have before me some thirty books and pamphlets by Pentecostal writers on the tongues business. They make a great deal to do about experiences, feelings, what they saw and felt.

A good example of this is *They Speak With Other Tongues* by John L. Sherrill, the story of a reporter, editor of *Guideposts* magazine, who went to study all about the matter of tongues and became a tongues speaker himself. Beginning on page 12 he tells about Harald Bredesen, a Reformed Church pastor, who had a wonderful experience. He spoke in tongues and one man said it was Polish. A woman said he spoke in Arabic. No mention of soul winning.

Then he tells about visiting a Pentecostal church where they spoke in tongues, and he went into a room where a number spoke in tongues, and swayed and sang and clapped hands and had interpretation. Then there was a sermon. The services lasted three hours. No invitation, nobody saved!

Then he tells how the modernist Dr. Henry Van Dusen approved the tongues meeting of Pentecostalists.

Then there is a chapter about Parham, a Methodist preacher who learned to speak in tongues—page after page.

If there were any saved, Sherrill doesn't mention that or doesn't care about it. That is not usually what the tongues people are interested in.

Then Sherrill goes on for nearly fifty pages telling of the history of the Pentecostal movement and churches but nothing about people being saved.

Then on page 52 begins a chapter on David du Plessis, a principal leader in the Pentecostal movement. There is a great deal about the Pentecostal movement, about speaking in tongues, about conferences with liberals, but nothing about soul winning.

Then Sherrill tells how he went to the Full Gospel Business Men's Fellowship International meeting. He tells how a number of Episcopalians and Catholic priests were "baptized with the Holy Ghost" so that they talked in tongues. He tells how Methodist pastors and Lutherans and theological professors talked in tongues. But he never mentions whether any of them won any souls. That is not the principal burden of those who promote Pentecostalism, it seems.

I read through the book very carefully and reviewed it carefully. Lydia Maxam, an Episcopalian, talked in tongues into Sherrill's tape recorder. He enjoyed that, and his wife got a story finished she was writing. Then on pages 83 and 84 Sherrill names ten different cases in history of people speaking in tongues. Nothing is said about whether souls were saved. That had no special part in the motive of the book.

At last, Sherrill tells how he himself got the blessing he sought, that is, he spoke in tongues. He did not seek, evidently, and says nothing about desiring, soul-winning power. In chapter 12 he tells of his experience with the Holy Spirit and talking in tongues. If he ever won a soul he does not say so.

Is it not strange that a man of education, setting out to examine the whole matter of tongues, talking to principal leaders, checking on the testimony of thousands, taking down the talking in tongues on a recorder, and then beginning to talk in tongues himself, has not a word to say about ever winning a soul to Christ or expecting to? Is not that a strange case? Is that like at Pentecost?

I have gone through the famous book, *With Signs Following,* by Stanley H. Frodsham. I have gone through book after book here before me, pamphlet after pamphlet, written by Pentecostalists on the tongues issue. It is obvious, and I speak in kindness and with a genuine love for people whom I know are often very sincere and devoted to Christ, that they generally are not talking about soul-winning power when they speak of the fullness of the Spirit. They are talking about tongues experiences.

Oh, they tell about falling in a faint, or seeing a great light. They tell how you can practice to learn to talk in tongues. There is a great deal about feeling, emotion and joy, but they miss the point of what happened at Pentecost. Where is their Pentecost with thousands saved?

A Pentecostal brother wrote to me in great detail, and I answered that I know the best soul-winning churches in America. I keep careful account. I preach in many of them. I have published from time to time the record of the churches that win the most souls to make public profession and who baptize the converts, and of these churches, not one have I found was a Pentecostal church.

This brother protested, however, that there was such a church in Sweden and one in Korea with thousands of members and many people saved. I do not doubt it and I am glad there are. But why not in America? I am sure that many other Pentecostal churches have some people saved. But that is not the main thing with them. They do not have multitudes saved. They do not go out and get them in great crowds and bring them in with earnest prayer and weeping and testimony win them to Christ. I am saying soul winning is not the main thing with the people who put tongues first. They are more concerned to get Baptists, Lutherans, and Catholics to talk in tongues than to have lost people saved.

The Bible evidence of the fullness of the Spirit is the power of God to win souls.

CHAPTER IX

Foreign Languages in I Corinthians 13 and 14

What a wonderful thing it is that we can go to the Bible and take it by simple childlike faith, examine every sentence of it involved, and find what God wants us to know on this or other questions.

Since I Corinthians 13 has only two mentions of languages, and since that is closely connected with the 14th chapter, we deal with both passages together. You see, there was no dividing chapter heading in the original manuscript, as Paul wrote it.

I. TONGUES IN I CORINTHIANS 13

You will notice that here Paul discusses the matter of the gifts of the Spirit and blessings of God. Prophecy, understanding mysteries and knowledge and faith and talking in foreign languages—all these are nothing if you do not have brotherly love.

1. Tongues of Angels

Verse 1 says, "Though I speak with the tongues of men and of angels, and have not charity, I am become as sounding brass, or a tinkling cymbal."

Angels have no special tongue of their own. They talk in all the languages of earth when they come to talk to men. We suppose no man in the world knows all the languages, all the dialects in the world, but angels do. Yet, if one had mastered every language in the universe, as the angels do, then he still would be nothing if he did not have brotherly love. In other words, Paul is playing down the matter of languages. The language in which you speak is not as important as what you speak. And what you say with your mouth is important only as the heart is right with love and obedience.

The people at Corinth should not make so much of languages. They should make more of love.

2. When Will "Tongues" Pass Away?

Verse 8 says, "Charity never faileth: but whether there be prophecies, they shall fail; whether there be tongues, they shall cease; whether there be knowledge, it shall vanish away."

And verses 9 and 10 continue, "For we know in part, and we prophesy in part. But when that which is perfect is come, then that which is in part shall be done away."

Some good men have argued that therefore when the Scriptures were all written, then the gift of tongues would cease, as well as these other gifts. I do not believe that is a proper interpretation of this Scripture. "That which is perfect" has not come to us, will not until the resurrection.

Verse 12 says, "For now we see through a glass, darkly; but then face to face: now I know in part; but then shall I know even as also I am known." That could not refer to the time the Scriptures were completed. When the Scriptures were finished, that did not mean that anybody knew everything even as God knows one. No, that refers to resurrection time, no doubt.

I think that when the rapture comes and all the saved are caught up to meet Christ in the air, all of us then will know as we are known. All of us then will see face to face. All of us then will be of one language. The divisions that separate people now will be gone then, including the language barrier.

Ellicott's Commentary, Barnes, Thayer, The Expositors Greek New Testament, all say "when that which is perfect is come" (I Cor. 13:10) and tongues shall cease, must be in Heaven after Christ comes.

In the first place, I do not believe that God intended a period of great blessings in Bible times that we cannot have now. I do not believe God had the mighty power of the Holy

Spirit available then and does not have it available now. I do not believe God would work miracles then when He gave faith for miracles and He would not work miracles now when they are necessary and He gives faith for them. I do not believe any gifts of the Spirit were available then that would not be available now as needed and as the Spirit of God Himself is "dividing to every man severally as he will" to fit the occasion.

No, good men, jumping to a foolish conclusion that speaking in tongues was some ecstatic and heavenly language in Bible times, think that now there is no such language. No, there never was! The modern tongues business of a jabber nobody understands for the personal enjoyment of those who like to be carried away with such a fantasy—they are not what they had in Bible times. The gift of tongues as in the Bible has not passed away and will not pass away until the time comes "when that which is perfect is come, then that which is in part shall be done away."

But Paul is inspired here to remind the people of Corinth that language and these other things about which they are quarreling and divided are passing things and in the heavens and in the millennial reign of Christ we will still have love and they should cultivate that instead of the divisions and strife that prove they are carnal, as he said.

II. PAUL WRITES TO CORINTHIAN CHRISTIANS AS CARNAL BABES IN CHRIST

First Corinthians is remarkable in that more than any other of the epistles in the New Testament, yes, more than all of them together, he rebukes particular sins of Christians.

Will you note the emphasis Paul has in rebuking of these carnal Corinthians on languages? You see, Corinth was a great city of a quarter of a million people. It was one of the great trade centers in the Roman world, and had many races and many languages in it. We need not be surprised, then, that there had risen a great deal of pride among them of their languages and they needed a very serious rebuke about their use of foreign languages in the church services.

Consider how carnal, worldly, and immature were these Corinthian Christians. Paul starts in the first chapter of I Corinthians and rejoices that they were enriched "in all utterance, and in all knowledge," and God had richly blessed them.

1. Division and Strife Prove Them Carnal

But after only nine verses, Paul began to remind them of their carnal ways, their divisions and strife. Some of them had lined up to be followers of Paul, others of Apollos, others of Peter or Cephas. They had grown away from the leadership of Paul who won them to Christ. They were just recently come out of heathendom, and they were easily divided and led astray. So Paul must defend his ministry through the first and second chapters, as he will do again and again through I and II Corinthians. He must particularly warn them of thinking they are wise. He tells them plainly that they are carnal. He warns them in chapter 3 of the judgment seat of Christ where the works of wood, hay and stubble will be burned and those whose works are burned will suffer loss. So therefore they should set out to glorify God in their bodies.

Through chapter 4 he must still defend his apostleship to these baby Christians who now think they have gotten beyond Paul who won them: "Now some are puffed up, as though I would not come to you," he says in I Corinthians 4:18, and he warns them solemnly, must he come with a rod to punish or with love and meekness?

2. Fornication Accepted, Defended by These Worldly Christians

Fornication was common among them evidently, and chapter 5 tells us of that kind of fornication not even mentioned among heathen people—a man living in adultery with his stepmother!

Offended by these carnal Christians, Paul demands, "Purge out therefore the old leaven," withdraw from that man you have been defending. In chapter 6 he tells how they go to law, one with another, and disgrace the cause before heathen judges.

And then he mentions more disgraceful sins. There is a great tendency there still to fornication, the very common sin in Corinth where they had prostitutes in heathen worship in heathen temples. And so fornication is to be hateful. They had defended it, now they must beware of it. Fornication is a greater sin, and should a member of the body of Christ be joined to a harlot? "What? know ye not that he which is joined to an harlot is one body? for two, saith he, shall be one flesh" (I Cor. 6:16). And he reminds them again that the body of a Christian belongs to Christ and is the temple of the Holy Spirit (vs. 19).

3. Led Astray About Meats Offered Idols

In chapter 8 he deals with a quarrel they have there about meats offered to idols. An idol is nothing, but why lead to guilt and sin by carelessness here and so destroy some of these weak brethren by eating meats offered to idols? Part of their division and strife and self-righteousness is involved here.

Now in chapter 9 we find they had not supported Paul as others had. People from Thessalonica and Philippi had sent money to him, but these people where he preached for eighteen months had not. And he says in verse 14, "Even so hath the Lord ordained that they which preach the gospel should live of the gospel." He had not demanded that and does not now demand it, but he reminds them of their fault in this matter.

4. Like Israel's Rebellion and Sin in Wilderness

In chapter 10 he goes back to liken their sins and divisions to that which Israel had in the wilderness and so were punished for them—the sins of idolatry, fornication and murmuring. And Paul reminds them that the way God dealt with Israel is reported for our admonition.

Then in that chapter Paul takes up the matter of the

Lord's Table. It demands separation. One cannot drink the cup of the Lord and the cup of devils.

5. Drunkenness at the Lord's Table; Many Die Because of This

Chapter 11 takes in detail the matter of women's wearing long hair as a type of their submission to husbands and fathers, and it is a shame for a man to have long hair, he says. Again he takes up the matter of the Lord's Table. Some have great feasts at the table and shame poor people who cannot bring a big dinner; others get drunk at the Lord's Table. That is the way of carnal Christians and gives us some insight into the need they had for further instruction.

And then come the chapters 12, 13 and 14, dealing particularly with this matter of languages in the church.

In II Corinthians Paul finds some improvement. They had repented about the man's living in adultery. But they still questioned Paul's authority. So in II Corinthians 13:3 he said, "Since ye seek proof of Christ speaking in me. . . ," and in verse 10 he is trying to get the thing settled by his letter, ". . .lest being present I should use sharpness" when he comes to them.

So now we approach Paul's rebuke and instruction to the carnal, baby Christians of Corinth on the question of languages in the church.

III. ALL DISCUSSION IN CHAPTER 14 ABOUT FOREIGN LANGUAGES

Sometimes speaking in tongues is called "glossolalia." That high-sounding word is simply from the word *glossa,* the Greek word for tongue or language. And the Greek word *glossa,* in the Greek New Testament, all the way through the 14th chapter of I Corinthians, is simply translated "tongues." Since it is in the plural, it would be proper to translate it "foreign languages." And always the term means regularly used national languages, known and used by some people. So Paul said in I Corinthians 14:10,

"There are, it may be, so many kinds of voices in the world, and none of them is without signification." Every language has some regular meaning to some groups of people.

And remember the word *unknown* before the word "tongues" in I Corinthians 14 is simply put in by translators; it was not in the original manuscript at all. The word "tongues" means regular foreign languages.

Note also that nowhere in this chapter is it stated that the people at Corinth had the *gift* of tongues and so were miraculously talking in tongues, in foreign languages. No, they were not. And they were putting on a show in their pride of their many languages in this great cosmopolitan city, and Paul rebukes them. God would not have rebuked it if it had been miraculous. God never does wrong when He works a miracle, and neither God nor anybody else has a right to rebuke a miracle. Their use of languages is not miraculous. They are using foreign languages in services and thus simply "mimicking" what the gift of tongues had been at Pentecost. It was not the miraculous gift of tongues. The Bible does not say so and, of course, no one else has a right to say so.

The "tongues" in I Corinthians 14 were regular foreign languages.

So when Paul said, "I would that ye all spake with tongues, but rather that ye prophesied," he simply meant, "I would like for all of you to be able to speak foreign languages, but far more important it is that you witness for Christ in Holy Spirit power." He did not say he wished they all had a gift of tongues. And, of course, we cannot say so. In chapter 12 He plainly said all are not to speak in tongues with the miraculous gift.

When Paul said in verse 18, "I thank my God, I speak with tongues more than ye all," he was simply saying, "I speak more foreign languages than all of you: Aramaic, Greek, Hebrew," and perhaps Latin. And in the next verse he plays that down and said he would rather speak five words that could be understood and teach others than to speak ten thousand words in a language not known to those present.

So when Paul says, ". . .forbid not to speak with tongues," in verse 39, he simply meant, "Don't forbid people to speak their regular foreign languages," just so some people present can interpret.

Remember, if you read in a lot of tradition and opinions in I Corinthians 14, you will go wrong. If you simply take the Scripture at face value, then you will get what God means by it. The tongues in I Corinthians 14 are simply foreign languages, natural languages.

IV. WHOLE CHAPTER ABOUT PUBLIC SERVICES NOT PRIVATE PRAYER

Pentecostal people would generally try to find instruction here for some private worship and that every Christian should privately talk in tongues as a matter of praise and for private enjoyment and perhaps as evidence of spirituality. They think that in verse 5 when Paul says, "I would that ye all spake with tongues," that he means he wants everybody privately to speak in tongues again and again. Actually what he is saying is that he would be glad if everybody knew as many foreign languages as he does.

1. Paul Insists He Must Use His Mind, His Understanding When He Speaks

In verses 14 and 15, Paul was inspired to say, "For if I pray in an unknown tongue, my spirit prayeth, but my understanding is unfruitful. What is it then? I will pray with the spirit, and I will pray with the understanding also." They think that means that Paul would sometimes pray knowing what he said and other times he would pray in an unknown tongue and have no idea what he said. That is not what it means, of course. There Paul is saying that he will always pray in a language that is known to himself so that his mind will be fruitful as well as his tongue saying words. The word for "with the understanding" is simply the Greek word *nous,* which is translated fifteen times in the New Testament as "mind." So Paul would speak in the

Holy Spirit but speak with words he could understand, too, and so could people who heard him.

And they quote verse 18 to say that Paul spoke in unknown tongues: "I thank my God, I speak with tongues more than ye all." But remember, the word "tongues" in the Bible is "languages" and the plural means foreign languages, so Paul means he spoke regularly the Aramaic language current in all Judaea; he spoke in the Koine Greek and wrote all his epistles in Greek. Also, Acts 21:40 told us that he addressed the people at Jerusalem in the Hebrew tongue, which Jewish leaders understood but many others did not. And since Paul was a Roman citizen, he may also have known Latin. He was an educated man and that is possible. Yes, he spoke more foreign languages than any of them. And he did not forbid them to speak in foreign languages, but he is speaking about natural foreign languages, of course, and that is all the word means unless the other words are used like in Acts where they spoke in "other tongues, as the Spirit gave them utterance." Nothing like that is said here in I Corinthians 14.

2. All This Chapter Discusses Public Services, Not Private Worship

Now back to the subject. All the instructions in I Corinthians 14 are about the matter of languages IN THE PUBLIC SERVICES. That you can see by checking carefully.

Verse 1 says they should desire "that ye may prophesy." But *prophesying* is always witnessing to others; it is not private devotions.

Verses 2 and 3 say that they are speaking to men unless they speak in a foreign language that no one understands.

And how much better, verse 4 says, when they prophesy and *edify the church.*

Verse 5 says his desire is "that *the church may receive edifying.*"

Verse 6 says, "If I come unto you speaking with tongues, *what shall I profit you,* except I shall speak to you either by revelation, or by knowledge, or by prophesying, or by doctrine?" He is speaking about public services of the church.

One plays a musical instrument so people *may know* "*what is piped or harped.*" They blow a trumpet for men to prepare themselves to the battle. That is for people to hear. This is not talking about private devotions.

So people should speak, verse 9 says, "*words easy to be understood,*" so people will know what is spoken.

Verse 11 says if you are talking in a language that people do not understand, those who hear in an unknown foreign language will be like a barbarian to the speaker and the one who is speaking will be like a barbarian to the hearer and God is talking about speaking in the hearing of others here.

3. All This Is "to the Edifying of the Church," Not Private Enjoyment

Verse 12 reminds them that whatever spiritual gifts they get they should "seek that ye may *excel to the edifying of the church,*" and so they must always have an interpreter if they speak in a language that is not known. Any praying in a language not known to others is not fruitful to others who hear and how else, verse 16 says, "shall he that *occupieth the room of the unlearned* say Amen at thy giving of thanks, seeing he understandeth not what thou sayest?" So then, in the church people should use language people can understand and even when you pray or sing, so they can say Amen to it.

In verse 19 Paul says, "Yet *in the church* I had rather speak five words with my understanding, that by my voice I might *teach others also*, than ten thousand words in an unknown tongue."

Verse 23 says, "If therefore the *whole church be come together* into one place. . . ." Verse 24 says, "But if all prophesy." And verse 26 says, "*When ye come together,* every one of you hath a psalm, hath a doctrine. . . ."

In a service those who talk in a foreign language, let it be only with not more than two or three consecutively and somebody to interpret. He is talking about services in the crowd. Verse 28 says, otherwise, *"let him keep silence in the church."* In verse 33 God warns against confusion. Not in private worship, he is talking about the services. In verse 34, he says, "Let your women keep silence *in the churches."* In verse 40 Paul says that in the churches, "Let all things be done decently and in order." You will understand, then, that in this whole chapter there is not any license for any use of foreign languages as such in private praise or worship.

V. WHOLE DISCUSSION ABOUT FOREIGN LANGUAGES NOT MIRACULOUSLY GIVEN

If you go through this 14th chapter of I Corinthians carefully, you will see that God is talking about natural languages not miraculously given.

1. "Unknown" Tongue Is Not Inspired, Is Added

Three or four times in the chapter in verse 4, verse 13, verse 14, verse 19, verse 27—this chapter uses the term "unknown tongue." But look at it carefully and you will see that in every case the term "unknown" is spelled in italics which means that it was not in the original Greek manuscripts at all, but was inserted by the translators trying to make it clearer. The languages mentioned here are foreign languages unknown to some people but not heavenly languages, rather languages regularly spoken by certain nationalities.

2. Whole Chapter Never Speaks of Their Tongues Being Given of God

Again, you must notice that the Scripture never indicates that these languages discussed here are miraculously given languages. The promise in Mark 16:17 was that those who were given faith for it and, of course, where God was willing to give the faith and work the miracle, some should "speak with other tongues" or languages. That is clearly intended as a miracle. In Acts

2:4 they spoke "with other tongues, as the Spirit gave them utterance." That is clearly miraculous, a gift of tongues. But nothing like that is said anywhere in I Corinthians 14, and nobody has a right to put in the chapter what God left out.

3. This Chapter Speaks of Foreign Languages That May Be "Learned"

Another evidence that the languages used were natural languages is given in verse 14. If they talk in such a foreign language in the church then "how shall he that occupieth the room of the *unlearned* say Amen at thy giving of thanks, seeing he understandeth not what thou sayest?" You might be testifying and mean it and the Spirit might be on your testimony, but the *unlearned* man who hadn't learned the language you learned, could not understand it.

Again in verse 23, "If. . .all speak with tongues [foreign languages], and there come in those that are *unlearned*, or unbelievers, will they not say that ye are mad?" Here the subject is regular foreign languages which *unlearned* people would not have. In that great city of Corinth many, many people spoke a number of languages, unlearned people did not. They ought to consider them in the services.

In the next verse also, verse 24 says, "But if all prophesy [that is, if they witness in the power of God], and there come in one that believeth not, or one unlearned, he is convinced of all, he is judged of all. . ." because he can understand the words that are given. But the term "unlearned," speaking of people who hear, means that they were using regular languages but foreign languages which some present could not understand. And that is not praised but condemned.

VI. MIRACLES NEVER MISUSED, NEVER PUT UNDER RULES, NEVER REPROVED BY THE LORD

The tongues, that is, the foreign languages that are discussed in the 14th chapter of I Corinthians, were not miraculous languages. They were not the miraculous gift of the Spirit, could not have been, since they are openly rebuked for misuse.

Remember that what was promised in Mark 16:17, "other tongues," or languages, is listed along with miracles as healing and such matters and referred to the miraculous gift of tongues at Pentecost and perhaps some other times. That means, of course, there were no restrictions on it. God gave it, "dividing to every man severally as he will." They spoke always "as the Spirit gave them utterance" and not according to their own will or choice. The real gift of tongues is miraculous.

1. Old Testament Miracles Never Rebuked

Now go back and consider all the miracles in the Bible, if you will. You never find that God gave somebody a right and power to work miracles indiscriminately, and that they must follow certain rules and sometimes be controlled or reproved. No, a miracle, every particular miracle, is a direct act of God. Consider the miracles of Moses when he held out his rod over the Red Sea and it opened and the children of Israel could walk through, or when he pronounced the special plagues one by one on Pharaoh. Every one was a separate miracle, every one given directly by the Lord. When Moses asked God that the ground should open and swallow certain of his enemies and detractors and it was done, or when God gave the manna from Heaven, or when Moses smote the rock and the water gushed forth, you will notice in every single case it was a separate miracle and the one who worked the miracle was in touch with God, acted by faith for that particular miracle. Now Moses might do wrong by smiting the rock on the second occasion, instead of speaking to it, but God did the miracle and did nothing wrong about it.

Consider the miracles of Elijah. He called down fire from Heaven at Mount Carmel. He raised the widow's son from death. I counted that Elijah was given to perform eight separate major miracles. Elisha, the following prophet, was given to perform sixteen major miracles. In every single case it was a direct act of God. Did Elisha do wrong when he had Naaman dip into the River Jordan seven times and was healed of the leprosy? Did Elisha do anything wrong, did he need any restraint or control or rebuke from God when he made good that tainted spring in Jericho which still runs today? Was Elisha wrong when he worked a miracle by retrieving the lost axhead from the waters of Jordan? I am just saying—go through the miracles and you will never find a single case where God put any restrictions, where God put any bounds on it, or rebuked it or criticised it, or of anyone who worked a miracle that was not directly in the will of God.

2. Miracles by Peter, Paul Never Rebuked: Could Not Be

When Peter pronounced the death of Ananias and then of Sapphira, that was a great miracle. Was it a mistake? Or was he in the perfect will of God? When Peter prayed and Dorcas was raised from the dead, was that a mistake? When Paul struck Elymas the sorcerer blind, was that right or wrong? Search through the Bible and you will never find a miracle but what it was immediately given in the will of God as a particular act and it was never done wrong, never criticised by the Lord and there was no restraint about it.

So the gift of miracles is actually a gift at one particular time for a particular miracle or series, in the will of God. It was never given to anybody just to work miracles whenever they wanted to, to heal people who ought not to be healed, or to condemn to death people who ought not die, or even to speak in a foreign language which was not the will of God. The miracles of the Bible in every case were particularly given just as at Pentecost every man spoke "as the Spirit gave utterance." It was a particular miracle.

3. Tongues, Foreign Languages, at Corinth Not Miraculous Because Wrong, Rebuked

But here in I Corinthians 14 Paul tells them they are

misusing languages. Then the languages were not divinely given. It was not a miraculous gift. First Corinthians 14 speaks only of natural languages. And Paul sets up rules about it. They should not speak in a language people did not understand but "words easy to be understood." He would rather speak five words that could be understood than ten thousand words not understood. They were never to have more than two or three speaking in a foreign language in any one service and that was to be consecutively and somebody must explain it. And the women were to keep silent in the churches. You see, God is *not* talking here about miracles which have gone wrong, He is talking about a human practice of carnal Christians that was wrong, carnal, worldly. That is the use of natural languages in a way that was wrong but not a miraculous gift of tongues.

Just as the people at Corinth had been carnal and baby Christians about putting up with fornication, about division and strife, about meats offered to idols, about going to law one with another, about making the Lord's Supper a great feast and some of them getting drunk, just as these carnal Christians at Corinth had been wrong on those things and needed restraint, so they need restraint and instructions and warnings about the way they use foreign languages in the church. The languages were not supernatural languages miraculously given, they were natural languages where these carnal and proud young Christians wanted to show off the many languages. And I think they were mocking and copying what they thought was the gift of tongues, but they were wrong.

4. Pentecostal People Admit Their "Tongues," Like Natural Languages at Corinth, Need Regulation

Surprisingly, Pentecostal people and teachers indicate that the kind of "tongues" they speak are not really miraculously given separate miracles given separately, but are something else besides miracle languages. For example, Dr. Howard M. Ervin, in his book, *These Are Not*

Drunken as Ye Suppose, (He is a teacher in Oral Roberts University.) says on page 125,

> Certainly Paul's counsels to regulate the Spirit's gifts of tongues and prophecy at Corinth indicate that he did not regard them as spurious.

But that is a thoughtless kind of conclusion. Paul's counsel to *regulate* the tongues at Corinth indicates that they were not miraculously given so they needed reproof or correction or regulation. God never has to regulate miracles, they are never wrong. If God did it, it doesn't need correction or regulation.

John L. Sherrill, editor of Dr. Norman Vincent Peale's *Guideposts* magazine, in his book, *They Speak With Other Tongues,* says on page 80, that as he read the Bible,

> I noticed first of all Paul's attitude toward the happenings in Corinth. There was no suggestion of surprise, no overtone of What's-going-on-over-there! He was obviously quite familiar with the various phenomena being reported. He accepts them without discussion as a genuine part of the Christian experience, and is concerned only that they be put into proper perspective.

Now Sherrill is a careless student of the Scriptures and if he thinks that Paul had no rebuke for what was going on and if he thinks Paul accepted all that was going on in Corinth as "a genuine part of the Christian experience," he did not read very carefully. But he did say, "Paul is concerned only that they be put into proper perspective." Ah, so then, the kind of tongues they had at Corinth needed to be controlled and guided and sometimes suppressed and "put into proper perspective"! But that talk doesn't fit a miracle. Nobody ever set out to put a miracle in proper perspective or to control it or set rules for it, or to rebuke it.

5. Sherrill Admits His "Tongues" Need to Be Corrected Too!

After this Pentecostal editor got to talking in tongues, then he did that frequently whenever he liked. On page 143 he says,

> I used my new tongue, too, during this period. There were two kinds of occasions when it seemed to come naturally. Once was in response to beauty. . . .Something moving would happen, something which once might have sent a shiver up my spine, but now brought out the response of tongues instead.

Then he said,

> The other times when I used them were in intercessions. I remember praying in tongues one evening for a man in our parish whose wife had confided to us that her husband wasn't sleeping nights.

A friend's teenage daughter had tried to commit suicide and was close to death. So Sherrill prayed in tongues, as he says on page 145.

He admits that he himself sometimes "did mouth nonsense syllables in an effort to start the flow of prayer-in-tongues."

On page 146 he says,

> I had a sudden, violent reaction. It centered chiefly on tongues: I became suspicious that I was generating the whole thing. Indeed I often did mouth nonsense syllables in an effort to start the flow of prayer-in-tongues. But sometimes the easy, effortless flow never came. I'd be left listening to the sound of my own foolishness. It was obvious to me that the Holy Spirit was no part of these noises: the ridiculousness of it would sweep over me, and from there it was not far to wondering if the Holy Spirit had ever been a part of tongues.

So sometimes when he tried to talk in tongues it was foolishness. But he worked at it! But, consider, is it a miracle when you start talking syllables hoping you can talk in tongues when that needs to be controlled and regulated? That is not the way God does about miracles. A miracle is of God. It needs never to be controlled or rebuked or regulated. And the real gift of tongues like at Pentecost was "as the Spirit gave utterance." That is not what happened in I Corinthians, chapter 14, and that is not what happens in most of the Pentecostal meetings.

"Nonsense syllables" are not a way to God's miracle. But Pentecostal people do not really regard usual cases of "speaking in tongues" as a miraculous gift. They feel they can control it, talk in these nonmiraculous "tongues" at will.

Then the tongues in I Corinthians 14, the tongues as a usual thing in Pentecostal assemblies are not the same as the gift of tongues in the Bible.

6. Oral Roberts Admits Pentecostal "Interpretation of Tongues" Not Miraculous, Needs Careful Wisdom

Dr. Oral Roberts, famous preacher, in his book, *The Baptism of the Holy Spirit and the Value of Speaking in Tongues Today*, on page 84, says,

> I am pointing this out because of the fact that no matter how the gift of the Spirit may be manifested through a believer, he is still a human being and needs improvement. It is a beautiful and powerful thing when one is exercising the gift of interpretation of tongues and gives a prophecy or exhortation, especially when he leaves the results with God. On the other hand, one's zeal can run beyond his knowledge and he can go beyond what the Spirit seeks to do through him. If he does not use wisdom, he can follow his exhortation with a spirit of attempting to correct and rebuke which normally came through the Word of God and the anointed preaching of God's Word. Even when Paul was distressed over the abuses in the Corinthian Church concerning Holy Communion, tongues and interpretation, prophecy, lack of love, and other things, he used words of helpfulness and encouragement.

Note carefully, Dr. Oral Roberts plainly says that "Paul was distressed over *the abuses in the Corinthian Church concerning* Holy Communion, *tongues and interpretations*, prophecy, lack of love, and other things." In other words, when the carnal Christians in Corinth were wrong about the Lord's Supper, wrong about taking up for fornication and wrong about going to law and wrong about the use of the Lord's Supper, they were wrong also in the same fleshly, carnal way about tongues. Dr. Oral Roberts does not note the fact, probably, but when the people of Corinth did wrong about the Lord's Supper and about the prophecy and about the lack of love and such matters, those things were not under the control of God, just as the tongues they were using (foreign languages) were not under the control of God. They were not the gift of tongues, they were not miraculously given. It is not proper to compare them with the gift of tongues as at Pentecost for example, and with other miraculous gifts.

No, there was a tongues heresy at Corinth. They were using natural languages to put on a show, it was carnal and worldly and wrong and was rebuked by Paul. And God does not ever rebuke a miracle. So they were not miraculously given.

7. Tongues Speaker Says "Tongues Were Greatly Abused"

Rev. Laurence Christenson, Lutheran tongues speaker, in his book, *Speaking in Tongues,* pages 18 and 19, says:

> St. Paul warns that the tongue can have a false note—like a noisy gong or a clanging cymbal—if the speaker does not manifest the gift *in love* (I Cor. 13:1); it may be used out of turn (I Cor. 14:27), or at the wrong time (I Cor. 14:28). But not even in Corinth, where tongues were great abused. . . ."

So the use of foreign languages at Corinth was not miraculous, and the "tongues" as used among Pentecostal people today are certainly not, as a usual thing, a miraculous gift. As at Corinth, Pentecostal people today confuse human manifestation, among good people (sometimes with God's blessing, sometimes without), with the Bible miraculous gift of tongues.

8. Gordon Lindsay Tries to Explain but Cannot

Gordon Lindsay, well-known Pentecostal author, in his pamphlet, *All About the Gifts of the Spirit*, page 13, acknowledges this human control and error and variation in modern use of tongues. He says:

> Gifts can be misused. Careful consideration of the subject shows that the individual is a full partner in the manifestations of the gifts. As such, he has a certain responsibility in their operation. Otherwise, if it is wholly the initiative of the Spirit, it would be impossible for a gift to be misused.
>
> For whatever the Holy Spirit does by Himself, He does perfectly and well. Yet, the evidence of the Scriptures is overwhelming that it is possible that gifts can be misused.
>
> When Moses smote the Rock twice in the wilderness, he erred in not sanctifying the Lord before the children of Israel. (Num. 20:11-12) Notwithstanding, the water flowed out of the Rock anyway. Moses' faith caused the miracle to take place, even though he had misused his gift by not sanctifying the Lord in the eyes of Israel when performing the miracle.
>
> In another instance, the disciples of the Lord would have brought fire down out of heaven upon the heads of the people in a village of Samaria, if Christ had not restrained them. (Luke 9:51-55).
>
> Paul makes it very clear that the speaking in other tongues can be misused by being exercised at the wrong time. (I Cor. 14:23) Prophets are to manifest their gift in the Assembly in proper order, and under certain circumstances to restrain it. (I Cor. 14:29-32)
>
> We all know that it is possible to misuse the gifts of God. This being true, it is evident that there is a joint responsibility of both God and man in their manifestation.

However, his explaining the miracle of Moses is not adequate. It is true that Moses did not have the right attitude, but the miracle was the bringing the water out of the rock and God did that. And it was God's plan. Moses did not change it or could not change it or control it. I do not say that Moses was himself perfect. I say the miracle was wholly of God, and not controlled by Moses.

In the case where Peter and John suggested that they call down fire from Heaven on the village in Samaria, he suggests that "the disciples of the Lord would have brought fire down out of heaven upon the heads of the people. . .if Christ had not restrained them." No, they suggested it, but they had no power to do it unless Jesus gave the miracle. Again let me insist, a miracle is of God and miracles cannot be misused. If men control it at will, it is not a miracle of God. It is true as I Corinthians 14:32 says, "And the spirits of the prophets are subject to the prophets." Yet in testifying or prophesying in any language, that is a different thing from controlling a miracle. In testifying, one can control himself, but cannot control a miracle or do wrong with a miracle. Men do not use God. God may use men.

9. W. Herbert Brown Thinks Tongues at Corinth Used Carnally and Childishly

In his book, *Pentecostal Fire Radiance and Love, Evidence of Baptism in the Spirit,* by W. Herbert Brown, he clearly takes the Pentecostal position. He thinks that what the people at Corinth had were gifts of the Spirit but not very important, not very good nor very inportant gifts! He said about the gift of tongues there,

> This was the most showy gift, and it gratified only the individual himself. Neither was the church edified by it when there was no interpreter (14:28). It was associated, moreover, particularly with emotions. Its overemphasis led to the neglect of those gifts associated with the intellect and the will. The carnal use of the gift was childish (14:20); and brought disunity, indecency, and disorder (14:10). When Paul wrote to more normal Christians, those in Rome, he didn't even mention tongues.—Pages 149,150.

Then on page 151 Brown says,

> A comparison at this point of the supernaturalism of Corinthians with that of Romans proves very helpful: the miracles prominent in Corinthians are abnormal and on a lower spiritual plane than the miracle-life pictured in Romans 8. There's no doubt about that. In fact, the supernaturalism of Corinthians *without* that of Romans is unfruitful (I Cor. 13). Romans, it's easy to see, is basic and reveals the main thrust of Biblical Christianity.

Now isn't that a strange way to talk about the tongues at Pentecost if they were really a supernatural gift, a miraculous gift? No, supernaturalism, that is, miracles, are never childish, are never carnal, are never unfruitful. What they had at Corinth was not the miraculous gift of tongues. Why do not those who realize the faults at Corinth simply admit that what they had was rebuked because it was not right?

10. Miracles Cannot Be Wrong, Are Never Reproved

Again, speaking of the gifts of the Spirit, nobody ever misused the gift of healing and healed somebody who ought not to have been healed. Concerning the gift of the Spirit working miracles, nobody ever worked a miracle when God did not want him to work a miracle.

It is important to note that the gift of tongues at Pentecost was a one-time miraculous gift. There is no indication that those one hundred and twenty people who witnessed in the power of the Spirit and prophesied to those Jews from every nation and had three thousand people saved—there is no indication that any of these after that talked in foreign languages. It was a one-time gift. The truth is that so with all the gifts, if they are miraculous, the occasion of their use is determined by the Lord and God distributes them "severally as he will," and when He will, too, and when He has a purpose in it.

God never gave anybody power to go out and work miracles before breakfast, raise the dead or make a show or do whatever he wanted or to make a million dollars at a man's own discretion. God never gave anybody power to go around and miraculously decree the death of every enemy he had. No, the gift of miracles and the other miraculous gifts were separate occasions and always the decision of God, not simply the decision of men.

The idea that anybody can get a gift of tongues and use it at will anywhere, that idea is utterly foreign to the miraculous gifts of the Spirit as used in the New Testament times.

CHAPTER X

Foreign Languages in Acts 10 and Acts 19

There are only three cases in the New Testament where we are explicitly told that certain people were filled with the Holy Spirit and talked in foreign languages. The first of these is in Acts 2:4, where we are plainly told that the gift was miraculous and that each one spoke in a foreign language "as the Spirit gave them utterance." We learn that although they were Galileans, they spoke to these people in the different languages in which they were born. The context tells us plainly, so we know that was a supernatural gift of tongues or languages.

I. HOUSEHOLD OF CORNELIUS IN ACTS 10

The other two cases are not as clear as that. In Acts 10:43-47 we have the story of the conversion of Cornelius and his household:

"To him give all the prophets witness, that through his name whosoever believeth in him shall have remission of sins. While Peter yet spake these words, the Holy Ghost fell on all them which heard the word. And they of the circumcision which believed were astonished, as many as came with Peter, because that on the Gentiles also was poured out the gift of the Holy Ghost. For they heard them speak with tongues, and magnify God. Then answered Peter, Can any man forbid water, that these should not be baptized, which have received the Holy Ghost as well as we?"

1. Saved Witnessed, Praised God in Foreign Languages

The new converts gave witness to God in power. They did it in foreign languages, that is, in more than one language. Did they use the natural languages they already knew, or was this a miraculous gift of tongues? The Scripture does not say.

We know Cornelius was a centurion of the Italian band. He was from Rome and so spoke Latin. We take for granted that his relatives and close friends also spoke Latin, if they were of his family or connected with the Italian band of soldiers. But Jewish servants of the family would speak the Aramaic language. It is also true that these from Rome and the Jews also probably spoke Koine Greek, the common language throughout the empire.

Now, when these new converts were filled with the Spirit, did they praise God in these various languages, each of which some of them knew? That may be so. In that case, what impressed Peter and the others was that they heard them magnify God, they heard them witnessing in the power of the Spirit.

Some people think that these people were given the power miraculously to speak in other languages to which they were not accustomed. In that case, we would suppose that people who knew Latin now would suddenly be given the power to speak in Aramaic or Hebrew so Peter and the other Christian Jews with him could understand them. We do not know.

At any rate, if it followed the pattern of Pentecost they would have been genuine, natural languages, and the speaking would have been in the language of those who heard and understood. There was no jabber in some unknown tongue that nobody could understand.

I personally think it was probably just natural languages and that each one, when filled with the Spirit, praised God in his Latin or Aramaic or Greek. If in this particular case Peter and the other Christian Jews who had never seen a Gentile saved and who doubted that Gentiles could be saved—if in this case some think God allowed them to see and hear a miraculous sign to convince them that they must carry the Gospel to Gentiles as well as Jews, that would be proper. The Scripture does not say that that was the case. If it were, it still would not indicate that always the talking in tongues is the initial evidence of the fullness of the Spirit. The Bible nowhere claims that and many, many cases prove it was not true.

2. They, Too, Were "Baptized With the Holy Ghost"

Later when Peter reported this matter to the other Christians at Jerusalem who were shocked that he went in to preach to Gentiles, he said:

"And as I began to speak, the Holy Ghost fell on them, as on us at the beginning. Then remembered I the word of the Lord, how that he said, John indeed baptized with water; but ye shall be baptized with the Holy Ghost. Forasmuch then as God gave them the like gift as he did unto us, who believed on the Lord Jesus Christ; what was I, that I could withstand God? When they heard these things, they held their peace, and glorified God, saying, Then hath God also to the Gentiles granted repentance unto life."—Acts 11:15-18.

Notice the one great thing is the Jews were thus assured that Gentiles could be saved. And Peter did not mention the matter of different languages if that was an important part of the story. He mentioned that they did receive the Holy Ghost and they are on the same basis as Jews in the matter of salvation.

The conclusion of the saints at Jerusalem was that God has now granted repentance to the Gentiles.

II. ONLY OTHER SPECIFIC INSTANCE WHERE FOREIGN LANGUAGES ARE MENTIONED IN CONNECTION WITH THE HOLY SPIRIT IN BOOK OF ACTS IS ACTS 19:1-7

That Scripture says:

"And it came to pass, that, while Apollos was at Corinth, Paul having passed through the upper coasts came to Ephesus: and finding certain disciples, He said unto them, Have ye received the Holy Ghost since ye believed? And they said unto him, We have not so much as heard whether there be any Holy Ghost. And he said unto them, Unto what then were ye baptized? And they said, Unto John's baptism. Then said Paul, John verily baptized with the baptism of repentance, saying unto the people, that they should believe on him which should come after him, that is, on Christ

Jesus. When they heard this, they were baptized in the name of the Lord Jesus. And when Paul had laid his hands upon them, the Holy Ghost came on them; and they spake with tongues, and prophesied. And all the men were about twelve."

These twelve men were "disciples." They had "believed." So there is every reason to take it that they were saved but they did not have the enduement of power which Christians everywhere could have. Apollos, from Alexandria, Egypt, who had not been present at Pentecost and may not have known what to teach about the power of the Holy Spirit, had been at Ephesus, and these, we suppose, had been saved under his ministry. Now Paul came and inquired. No, they said they did not know about the Holy Spirit. Paul explained that when they were baptized in water that ought to have meant they counted the old man dead and gave themselves over to the power of God and they ought to have expected the power of God upon them. So now they were baptized and Paul laid his hands upon them: ". . .the Holy Ghost came on them; and they spake with tongues, and prophesied."

They spoke with foreign languages. Was it miraculous? The Scripture does not say. Again, Ephesus, like Corinth, was a great cosmopolitan city and the trade routes from Asia to Europe passed through this area. And here was a great center of learning with many languages and many races. Did each of these men speak in his own native language praising God? We do not know. The Bible does not say in this case that they spoke "as the Spirit gave them utterance," as it was at Pentecost, and there is no indication it was miraculous. The Scripture does not say that the languages were "the initial evidence of the fullness of the Spirit," and it would be presumption for us to say so. The Bible nowhere says that that was the evidence, and many other examples disprove that.

1. Note How Rare Was Any Occurrence of Foreign Languages as an Issue, Whether Miraculous or Natural, in New Testament Churches

It is important to notice that the matter of foreign

languages in the church, or tongues, is not nearly so prominent in New Testament churches as Pentecostal people would make their speaking in tongues now.

The events at Pentecost were in the year 33 A.D. Ussher's chronology tells us that it was eight years later, in 41 A.D., when Cornelius heard the Gospel. Eight years went by without a mention of any repetition of this matter of foreign languages. You see, unless there were some particular need for it, and occasion, God would not have people speaking in a foreign language.

The years go by. When Paul comes to Ephesus, according to Ussher's chronology, it was either in the year A.D. 54 or 56, twelve or fourteen years later, that the matter of languages in connection with the Holy Spirit is mentioned. It is obvious that it was not a principal issue in New Testament churches. The gift of languages at Pentecost was for a particular, needed purpose. That occasion did not often occur or there would be a need for people to learn to speak in other languages they did not know.

2. No Teaching on "Tongues" in Any Other New Testament Epistle

After one verse in Mark 16:17, no epistle in the New Testament even mentions tongues except I Corinthians.

Paul wrote, we think, fourteen epistles in the New Testament. Only at Corinth, where the carnality was so great and foreign languages wrongly used in services, was there need for any mention of the "gift of tongues" or the use of foreign languages.

In Paul's journeys and in his founding of new churches, the record never mentions this unimportant, rarely needed gift except in Acts 19:1-7. In his letters to others besides the Corinthians it is never mentioned!

So we can understand why an interpretation of tongues is the very last of the list of gifts of the Spirit. It is the least important. And when Paul said, "Covet earnestly the best gifts" (I Cor. 12:31), he obviously meant to leave out tongues. There might be many occasions, day after day, week after week, when one would long to have the power of healing given in particular cases, and so with wisdom, and so with discernment, and so with other gifts of the Spirit. But it was rare when there was any occasion for the gift of languages. It did not occur often in the New Testament and has very little prominence there. And there is no indication that Christians should ever seek to talk in tongues. No, they should covet rather to prophesy, that is, to witness in the power of God.

CHAPTER XI

Second Pentecostal Doctrine of Tongues

1. Are "tongues" given for private prayer and praise, self-edification?

2. Are they for every Christian and to be eagerly sought?

3. Does "praying in the Spirit" mean without any understanding of your prayer, or any conscious, intelligent request?

4. Are "unknown tongues" to be on tap every day, to use rightly or wrongly at one's own pleasure?

I. PENTECOSTALISTS HAVE TWO KINDS OF TONGUES

The first distinctive teaching of Pentecostal people was that "speaking in tongues" (unknown tongues), as at Pentecost, was the "initial evidence" or "personal witness" that one is "baptized with the Holy Ghost." Most Pentecostal people even yet insist that those of us who never talked in tongues have never been filled with the Spirit or baptized with the Spirit. That meant that they lost sight of the meaning of the Spirit's fullness. They generally lost sight of the fact that the fullness of the Spirit at Pentecost, as in the case of John the Baptist (Luke 1:15), Barnabas (Acts 11:24), and as plainly promised by the Saviour in Luke 24:46-49 and in Acts 1:8, was simply to be "endued with power from on high" and to be soul-winning "witnesses."

Their teaching that only those who talked in tongues had the baptism meant that what Moody, Torrey, Finney, Billy Sunday, Sam Jones, Spurgeon and other countless numbers of great soul winners had was something else. So their doctrine led them away from seeking and from having soul-winning power. I do not mean no Pentecostal people had soul-winning power, but it is obviously not the one intent of the tongues doctrine. Many Pentecostal people are far more concerned about getting some Baptist or Methodist or Lutheran to talk in tongues than to get a drunkard saved.

But it turned out that the "unknown tongues" they so proudly claimed did not, except in rare cases, pretend to approach people with the Gospel in their own tongues in which they were born, as happened at Pentecost. So the unknown tongues of Pentecostal people were not like at Pentecost. Besides, it was so distinctive it set them off as spiritual with special gifts, they thought, so why not demand that everybody speak in tongues? And why not have everybody do it often, perhaps daily? And they figured it could be called prayer, or their elation in the matter could be called "edifying self." So these dear people developed the other doctrine about speaking in tongues. It is not simply the doctrine that speaking in tongues is the initial evidence of the baptism of the Holy Spirit, but the doctrine that every Christian in the world ought to seek and ought to have a gift of tongues and be able to talk in tongues at any time he wishes, for his own edification and in private worship and prayer and sometimes in the public assembly, if there are interpreters.

II. EVANGELIST ORAL ROBERTS SPEAKS ABOUT THIS DOCTRINE

In *The Baptism With the Holy Spirit and the Value of Speaking in Tongues Today* by Oral Roberts, chapter 2 is entitled, "Your New Tongue of Prayer and Giving Thanks to God."

1. He Thought Mark 16:17 Taught Continual Miracles for All Christians

In the first two paragraphs Brother Roberts says:

In Mark 16:15-20, we are given several evidences of

vital Christian experience. They were given by Jesus possibly near the time that He gave us Acts 1:8. The statement starts with the Great Commission to go into all the world and to preach the Gospel to every creature and to win souls; that is, to be a witness for Jesus Christ wherever one is in the world. Then Jesus said, "These signs shall follow them that believe. . . ." These signs are five in number: (1) Casting out devils. (2) Speaking with new tongues. (3) Taking up serpents (enemies). (4) Drinking some deadly thing without being hurt by it (accidental). (5) Laying hands upon the sick that they may recover. The chapter ends with these words, "And they went forth, and preached every where, the Lord working with them, and confirming the words with signs following."

All five evidences or signs followed the believing members of the Early Church. They cast out demons. The records of Acts and of the Early Church fathers indicate that they continued to speak with new tongues. They took up serpents.

The next to the last sentence above is inaccurate: "The records of Acts and of the Early Church fathers indicate that they continued to speak with new tongues." No, they did not. They only occasionally had a reason for this miracle. It was not a regular practice. There were eight years between the occasion in Acts 2:4 and the occasion of Cornelius and his people, which may not have been miraculous at all. It was twelve or fourteen years later before the mention in Ephesus of the men for whom Paul prayed and they "spake with tongues," that is, with foreign languages. And even if that were miraculous, that is not very often, and there is no mention in any other church to whom Paul wrote letters or to whom John or Peter or James wrote letters, of any that ever had talked in tongues.

2. Evangelist Roberts Supposed Jesus Had Promised "Tongues" for Everyone

At the bottom of page 17 Mr. Roberts says:

Tongues
"They shall speak with new tongues," is one of the evidences which Jesus promised of vital Christian experience. Jesus had carefully prepared His disciples to

be ready to receive the Holy Spirit. To the very last minutes before His ascension, He was sharing with them what they would receive and how they would be witnesses unto their world. He talked about a new kind of power coming upon them after they received. Doubtless He spoke of the new tongue that was to be given them. It is evident that He mentioned this tongue prior to their receiving the Holy Ghost, because of their ready acceptance of it. "And they were all filled with the Holy Ghost, and began to speak with other tongues, as the Spirit gave them utterance" (Acts 2:4).

Tongues were not to be some freakish experience that would be present one moment and gone the next. It was actually a *point of power release* in those early disciples. Much later Paul said, "I thank my God, I speak with tongues more than ye all" and, "I would that ye all spake with tongues" (I Corinthians 14:5,18). Today we are finding that it is a source of power release in us, too.

Of course the Scriptures are very explicit and tell us what God wanted us to know. There is not even a hint that Jesus told the disciples He would have them speaking in new tongues regularly, nor for everybody. The Bible never mentions at all that "it was actually a point of power release in those early disciples."

And then Oral Roberts quotes Paul in I Corinthians 14:5,18 as if Paul were saying that he spoke in *unknown* tongues. No, his regular preaching was in the Koine Greek, Aramaic and Hebrew languages. We will deal with that careless use of Scripture later.

Notice what Evangelist Oral Roberts is saying in another paragraph later:

The Book of Acts clearly points out that speaking in tongues was a practice of those who received the fullness of the Holy Spirit. It was a meaningful part of Paul's experience.

But on that he speaks purely from guesswork. There is no hint in the Bible that Paul ever spoke in an unknown tongue or that he taught anybody else to do so. He said:

We are not told when Paul began to speak in new tongues, although it is implied that he began when he received the gift of the Holy Ghost by the laying on of hands by Ananias in Damascus.

Implied how? It is not even hinted at nor mentioned in all the passage telling of Paul's conversion or of the two or three times that Paul referred to it later telling others about it. Some would like to have Paul speaking in unknown tongues as evidence of the fullness of the Spirit, but he did not. And no one has a right to make a doctrine which the Bible doesn't even mention.

". . . speaking in tongues was a practice. . ."—by that, evidently Brother Roberts intends us to believe that it was a regular, frequent, perhaps daily custom for all Christians to talk in tongues. That is never mentioned nor implied in the Bible. Only he must lay some kind of a foundation for the teaching that Christians ought to have "Your New Tongue of Prayer and Giving Thanks to God."

Now consider again the fourfold function Oral Roberts says that tongues has. On page 19 he says:

> It is indicated both in the Book of Acts and in Paul's teaching, speaking in tongues has a fourfold function in the believer's life and witness. First, he speaks in tongues as a part of his private devotions to God.

Not a word like that in the Bible. That is wholly made up to speak from people's experience and not from the Word. Continue the quotation:

> "Second, for his personal edification and release."

Again the Bible says nothing of the kind. Paul did say that when those carnal and worldly Corinthians spoke in foreign languages in the church, they themselves enjoyed it when they testified, but nobody else was blessed. It did not edify the church. But nothing there in I Corinthians 14 is said about the gift of tongues or any miraculous tongues as his personal edification and release.

Then continuing, Mr. Roberts says tongues are:

> "Third, to edify the Body of Christ."

No, that is the exact opposite of the meaning throughout the 14th chapter of I Corinthians. Everywhere they were told that they must say words "easily to be understood." They must not speak in a foreign language unless somebody explained it. Paul would rather speak five words with people understanding than ten thousand words in an "unknown tongue."

I was in a revival campaign once in Oklahoma City. An Indian was there who had been converted, I think of the Kaw tribe. He asked the friend by him to inquire if he could give a testimony? He did not speak English well, but he wanted to tell why he loved the Lord and that he had been saved. I had his friend tell him that if he would testify and his friend could tell us what he said, it would be all right. Otherwise, it would do no one any good.

The Bible never intimates that talking in some foreign language that people would not understand will edify them, or anyone else. Oh, they may, with a sense of pride, think, "Our denomination has got it; all the other folks are wrong." But that carnal enthusiasm is not edification in the Bible sense. They may enjoy it but it does not edify the church.

3. Perverts the Reference in I Corinthians 14

At the bottom of page 18 and the top of page 19 Mr. Roberts says:

> Speaking in tongues was such a normal experience in Paul's life that he made many definite statements concerning speaking in tongues. These in I Corinthians 14 include: "I would that ye all spake with tongues" (verse 5). "He that speaketh in an unknown tongue speaketh not unto men, but unto God" (2). "If I pray in an unknown tongue, my spirit prayeth" (14). "I thank my God, I speak with tongues more than ye all" (18). "Forbid not to speak with tongues" (39).

Now, so you will not be misled, you must remember several truths and you will see how Brother Roberts is far afield from the scriptural teaching here.

1. The "other tongues" in the Bible were always natural languages, like at Pentecost when people heard the Gospel "in our own tongue, wherein we were born." There is nothing in the Bible about some especially holy, heavenly language which nobody understands but God. All the teaching about languages on I Corinthians 14 was of

certain foreign languages and the unlearned people did not know those languages and so they ought to speak in words people could understand and should not use a foreign language unless somebody there could explain what was meant. He said in verse 2, "For he that speaketh in an unknown tongue speaketh not unto men, but unto God."

Note here that if a man speaks in the Latin language and nobody present can understand Latin, then only God would hear him and understand. He is not speaking to the men there in any language they can understand. Why make that a spiritual miracle? In fact, that is the very thing Paul is rebuking.

2. Oral Roberts quotes, "If I pray in an unknown tongue, my spirit prayeth." That is, a man may be with his own mind saying things but it is not fruitful, it does not mean anything to anybody else. It is not spiritual prayer led by the Spirit. The word "spirit" there refers to man's own spirit, of course. The man Paul rebukes means well and enjoys it but in his spirit he prays, but his words are not fruitful, do not edify the church.

3. In verse 18 (Mr. Roberts quotes), "I thank my God, I speak with tongues more than ye all." Of course Paul did. He spoke more foreign languages. And remember, tongues always mean foreign languages in the Bible. He spoke in Koine Greek and all his New Testament epistles were written in Greek. He spoke in the Aramaic tongue that all Palestine knew regularly. He also spoke in Hebrew, as Acts 21:40 tells us. Yes, he spoke more foreign languages than any of them. But he was not talking about some unknown tongue that didn't have meaning to people who heard him. He was not speaking of the miraculous gift of tongues. That he is plainly rebuking all the way through—any talking to people that they cannot understand.

And then Paul said in verse 39, "Forbid not to speak with tongues." That is, in that great cosmopolitan city of many races and many languages, of course, you would not shut people out of a service who had a different language from you. Don't forbid people to speak in whatever language they knew; only if it is going to be in public, let somebody interpret for him.

4. Pentecostal People Do Not Notice That All 120 at Pentecost Prophesied, Witnessed, Preached

He thinks that the tongues at Pentecost were not witnessing to get people saved but were simply making a show of personal enjoyment and worship. Like other Pentecostalists, Mr. Roberts would like to insist that Peter did all the preaching and soul winning and that speaking to people in their own language in which they were born had nothing to do with the three thousand people saved. He says on the value of tongues, page 19:

> As we study the second chapter of Acts, we sense that the 120 men and women who received the baptism with the Holy Ghost on the Day of Pentecost found release while speaking in tongues. Those that heard them and understood said, "We do hear them speak the wonderful works of God." It is evident that something which was pent-up in them was released while they were speaking with tongues. There has been conjecture that the 120 were attempting to preach the Gospel to the foreign Jews gathered there that day. We now know that is not according to the facts. When it came time to preach, Peter did that in his own normal tongue (Acts 2:14).

Note Mr. Robert's statement,

> "There has been conjecture that the 120 were attempting to preach the Gospel to the foreign Jews gathered there that day. We now know that is not according to the facts."

He knows nothing of the kind. There are no facts that show only Peter preached. Will you note two or three evidences that people heard the Gospel in their own language and thus that all the 120 were winning souls that day.

First, that was a promise. They were to tarry to be "endued with power from on high" to carry out the Great Commission that "repentance and remission of sins should be preached in his name among all nations, beginning at Jerusalem" (Luke 24:46-49). That was for all the 120, of course. The purpose was not to talk in tongues and to show an example of worship and praise and some sign for them to think how wonderful Christians these were. No, they heard the Gospel every one "in our own tongue, wherein we were born."

In the second place, the meaning is very clear, and neither Mr. Roberts nor anybody else ought to dodge it. Peter said plainly that what happened at Pentecost was a fulfillment of Joel's prophecy in Joel 2:28-32. He said, "But this is that which was spoken by the prophet Joel; And it shall come to pass in the last days, saith God, I will pour out of my Spirit upon all flesh: and your sons and your daughters shall prophesy." And the word "prophesy" is the word for speaking the Gospel and speaking in the power of the Holy Spirit whatever the language. And that is what Paul said people should seek to do, instead of simply talking in foreign languages.

So what happened to Peter and to all the rest of the 120 is that they were "endued with power from on high," as was promised. They received power to be witnesses of Jesus as He had promised in Acts 1:8. And what happened was that all of them alike "prophesied" or witnessed in the power of God and got people saved.

And Peter quoted in that passage from Joel, the closing part, "That whosoever shall call on the name of the Lord shall be saved." What are these old men, young men, sons and daughters, servants and handmaids whom Joel said would be filled with the Holy Spirit—what were they to do? They were all to witness in power. They were to get people saved. And that is what did happen.

If you want to make a distinction between talking in tongues as a kind of personal enjoyment and showing what a wonderful Christian you are, etc., instead of doing what God had told them to do to get out the Gospel, you will have to make it without any scriptural background. There is not a particle of evidence except that at Pentecost they preached the Gospel to people in their own language in which they were born, who otherwise would not have heard the Gospel and so three thousand people were saved.

5. Peter Addressed Jerusalem Jews, Others Addressed Jews "Out of Every Nation Under Heaven"

It is clear also that the preaching of Peter was addressed particularly to Jerusalem Jews. In Acts 2:14 he said, "Ye men of Judaea, and all ye that dwell at Jerusalem, be this known unto you, and hearken to my words." So his address was not to these fifteen or sixteen different nationalities of Jews, but all of these also heard in their own tongue the wonderful works of God and not from Peter.

Again Mr. Roberts says, "Fourth, as a sign to unbelievers." Yes, at Pentecost, when people heard the Gospel in their own tongue in which they were born, it was obvious to them that God was speaking to them through His servants and many were saved. That is the way the miracle of tongues at Pentecost was a sign to unbelievers. But the kind of jabber that nobody understands and that has no special message to the unsaved, people putting on a show of talking in some language they think is from God although it doesn't say anything and doesn't mean anything to anybody who hears it, was never a sign to unbelievers. In fact, as you see when you read I Corinthians 14, unbelievers coming in where people talk in foreign languages you don't understand, they will think you are crazy or that you are a barbarian (I Cor. 14:23,24). Speaking in tongues (natural languages), miraculously given, as at Pentecost when it was necessary, is a sign to unbelievers. The kind of tongues that Pentecostal people use today does not get people saved. Neither did the kind they were using at Corinth! In fact, now the more people talk in tongues the less there is of soul winning in the churches.

6. Bible Never Hints That Praying Should Be in an "Unknown Tongue"

The Bible is full of illustrations on prayer. Why does it never suggest prayer in tongues?

On page 22 Mr. Roberts says:

> "Paul continues, 'What is it then? I will pray with the spirit [in tongues] and I will pray with the understanding [my intellect] also: I will sing with the spirit [in tongues], and I will sing with the understanding [by my intellect] also' (I Corinthians 14:15)."

Does Paul mean that he will sometimes pray and not know anything about it and that therefore he is praying in the Spirit? Actually, he is saying the exact opposite, as a careful reading of I Corinthians 14 shows. Paul was rebuking them for using natural languages in the service which some could not understand. He said he would rather speak five words that could be understood than to speak ten thousand words that could not. He never inferred that he ever talked in an unknown tongue, whether in prayer or anything else. That is paying little attention to the context and the teaching throughout the passage. And it is not quite honest to insert in the Scripture "in tongues" when Paul said, "I will pray with the spirit," or when he says, "I will sing with the spirit." That is wresting the Scriptures and is unjustified.

Again on page 23, Mr. Roberts says:

> When one is praying "in the Spirit," he is praying or speaking in tongues. Paul uses this term again in Ephesians 6:18 and refers to it as a part of the whole armor of God which the believer is to put on to help him stand successfully against all the wiles of the devil. "Praying always with all prayer and supplication IN THE SPIRIT." Here again Paul links speaking in tongues with prayer and supplication, pointing out that our new tongue is devotional, a tongue of prayer and praise TO GOD.

But "in the Spirit" never refers to speaking in tongues. Man may pray in his own spirit in a foreign language nobody knows but not in the Holy Spirit. And to say that Paul was pointing out in Ephesians 6:18 "that our new tongue is devotional, a tongue of prayer and praise to God" is a careless treatment of the Word of God.

I have quoted Mr. Roberts because he is well known and

is representative. I could quote like statements from Rev. Laurence Christenson from his book, *Speaking in Tongues and Its Significance for the Church*, and so with other Pentecostal writers, declaring this second doctrine on tongues by Pentecostal people, that Christians all ought to speak in tongues regularly, in their own prayer and praise and devotion.

On page 37 Mr. Roberts says:

> "Ephesians 6:18 inspired me to believe that as often as I prayed, which has always been very frequently, I should and could use my new tongue devotionally toward God. I too thank God for the richness and depth and dimension of this experience which is daily in my life."

Daily speaking in tongues!

Again on page 40 Mr. Roberts tells of his dealing with a man he got to talking in tongues:

> "He said, 'What am I to do now?' I said, 'Use your new tongue every day to pray in the Holy Spirit and to give thanks with your spirit. Gradually you will become more fluent in the Spirit.' "

And again at the bottom of page 41 he says:

> "It is by our desire and by the desire of the Holy Spirit, by the exercise of our will and the exercise of the will of the Holy Spirit, through an act of faith, that we may speak at any moment."

So here is the teaching that every Christian ought to seek to talk in tongues, ought to seek to talk in tongues every day, ought to use these tongues in prayer and praise. But there is no such teaching in the Bible.

III. FOLLY OF THIS PENTECOSTAL TEACHING

This idea that every Christian should talk in tongues and should seek to talk in tongues, should seek to talk in tongues again and again, that talking in tongues is a favorite way of prayer and praise, is wholly unscriptural. I think that any honest heart should prayerfully consider these facts.

1. Gift of Tongues Never Given to Many

The Scripture says in I Corinthians 12:8-11:

"For to one is given by the Spirit the word of wisdom; to another the word of knowledge by the same Spirit; To another faith by the same Spirit; to another the gifts of healing by the same Spirit; To another the working of miracles; to another prophecy; to another discerning of spirits; to another divers kinds of tongues; to another the interpretation of tongues: But all these worketh that one and the selfsame Spirit, dividing to every man severally as he will."

Note carefully, ". . . to another divers kinds of tongues." Not to all. God Himself decides, "dividing to every man severally as he will." And in I Corinthians 12:30, "Have all the gifts of healing? do all speak with tongues? do all interpret?" The honest and obvious answer is that all are not supposed to.

Tongues very rarely appeared in Bible times, in a miraculous sense. They appeared at Pentecost; they may have appeared in the 10th chapter of Acts eight years later, though we cannot be sure and it may have been simply foreign languages without a miracle. They may have appeared twelve or fourteen years further still at Ephesus, though again the Scripture says foreign languages and we do not know whether they were miraculous. But to suppose that every Christian is expected to speak regularly in tongues and do it for their own prayer and praise is unheard of in the Bible.

2. None of the Other Miraculous Gifts or Works of Holy Spirit Left to Choice of Every Christian

Note that the promises about tongues are right along with other promises. In Mark 16:17, "And these signs shall follow them that believe; In my name shall they cast out devils; they shall speak with new tongues. . . ." Does that mean that everyone who trusts in Christ shall drink poison and be delivered? Does it mean that every person who trusts Christ for salvation will be snake-bitten without harm? If every Christian should go through that, then those illiterate snake handlers in the backwoods mountains are right to set out to have Christians bitten by snakes and have faith enough to be healed. Obviously that is not the meaning of the Scripture.

But if the Bible doesn't mean that about snake handling, it doesn't mean it about tongues either. In every case a gift of tongues was given, if at all, only to honor God in getting the Gospel to people who ought to hear it; and in every case of healing, as of Paul delivered from a snake bite on the island of Malta, when it was necessary. It would be foolish to suppose that everyone of the things promised there would happen to every Christian or happen every day.

Do you really believe that every Christian who was saved went about healing people every day?

3. Gifts of Spirit Were Each Single, Separate Gifts

Again, it is obvious that even the gift of miracles was always a particular gift, at a given time. It was a separate gift on every occasion it was given. For example, in Acts 16 Paul was confronted with the devil-possessed girl. She followed Paul and Silas for days and in deepest concern of heart Paul was exercised about it. At last he had faith to claim the blessing and he demanded the demon to come out of the girl, and it did.

You will note, then, that it was not just a miraculous dispensation that Paul had the right to cast out every demon any time at any whim, right or wrong. Well, if that is not the way God gives a miraculous gift, it is not the way He gave the gift of tongues either.

In the matter of healing of the sick, the plain statement of James 5:15 is, "And the prayer of *faith* shall save the sick, and the Lord shall raise him up; and if he have committed sins, they shall be forgiven him." Note carefully that healing is one of the gifts. But in every particular case the healing is given only in answer to faith for that particular healing. The Lord never gave anybody in the Bible the power to go about healing everybody he wanted to heal. It was only when God gave the faith. Every healing is in answer to a new act of faith. Paul left Trophimus sick at

Miletum (II Tim. 4:20). Paul could not heal him. Though Timothy had a weak stomach and often infirmities and needed fruit juice for the vitamins, yet Paul could not heal him (I Tim. 5:23). Paul himself had a thorn in the flesh and besought the Lord again and again and again, yet God did not take away that thorn in his flesh. He did not give faith for that particular healing.

There is no way for anybody to boss God around and get a miraculous gift of tongues or a gift of miracles or a gift of healing that he can use permanently, just any time he wants it. Each one of those was a particular gift of God and God "divideth them severally as he will," and no one person is to get all the gifts and no person is to get any gift indiscriminately without limitation or control and claim it as a permanent, abiding gift of God.

4. Is "Praying in the Spirit" Talking in Tongues? So Mr. Roberts and So Other Pentecostal Teachers Say

But the simple truth is that prayer is many times discussed in the Bible. Oh, thank God for the multitude of promises about answers to prayer and how to pray! We are to pray for daily bread. We are to pray for cleansing and forgiveness of our daily trespasses. We are to pray for Holy Spirit power. We are to pray for our enemies and those who despitefully use us and persecute us. We are to pray for wisdom, James 1:5 tells us. We are to pray, "What things soever ye desire, when ye pray, believe that ye receive them, and ye shall have them" (Mark 11:24). We are to ask in Jesus' name, when we can honestly know that it is the will of Jesus we want satisfied.

I am saying there are many, many instructions about prayer. Then how is it that the Bible never even mentions or never hints that prayer ought to be, much of the time, or any of the time, in an unknown tongue? You see, that is a man-made doctrine, made without the Bible.

There is no Scripture that says one must talk in tongues as the initial evidence of the fullness of the Spirit. There is not a single Scripture in the Bible that instructs Christians to pray or worship in an unknown tongue. The whole matter, I am sorry to say, is not good Bible teaching, nor good Christianity. There are some good Christians who go wrong on this, but they don't get it from the Bible.

It is sad that good people who mean well and who want, they say, to restore New Testament Christianity with its joy and power, lose the point that God has that all of us are to have Holy Spirit power to win souls. And it is especially sad that they make up other things that appeal to the carnal mind like talking in tongues and such matters and put the emphasis on that which is not taught in the Scriptures at all.

There was a tongues heresy at Corinth which Paul rebuked in I Corinthians 14. There they were using natural languages but using them in pride and in carnal, childish ways in the services and in kind of an imitation of the Bible gift of tongues but not miraculous there and not blessed of God there. Paul plainly rebuked it. Now, why should anybody take that which God is clearly rebuking and set out to follow the same pattern of heresy that they had, a carnal, worldly teaching not taught in the Bible?

No wonder there is division and strife wherever it goes and good Christians are deceived and led away in broken fellowship, and often lost people around them are left to go to Hell while people talk in tongues or enjoy their private devotions in tongues.

CHAPTER XII

What Really Happens When People Talk in Tongues?

It is very hard to convince people to leave a position who have come to that position through their feelings, their emotions, their experiences, even their happiness. In their consideration of the problem, they are subjective, not objective. But the matter is so serious that honest Christians ought to consider what the Bible itself says on this matter of tongues.

We do not deny that many have been happy and many have claimed to be greatly blessed and became better Christians after talking in tongues. And the speaking in tongues phenomena is so widespread that it deserves the honest consideration of Christian people.

We know there is a great mixture of sincere devotion to Christ, some earnestly seeking after the best from God, along with a lot of naive lack of discernment, some evident fraud, some things that seem to be clearly of God, and some things that surely must be from evil spirits. It is fair to honestly search out this matter. What really happens when people talk in tongues?

I. HAPPINESS, DEVOTION, SINCERITY DO NOT NECESSARILY PROVE PEOPLE RIGHT IN RELIGION

A Christian Science woman told me what great peace of heart she had had, how her troubled mind had settled down, when she learned through Christian Science that there is no such thing as sin, that it is only an error of mortal mind, etc. She insisted that she had the peace she had long sought.

A Catholic woman wrote me the other day of what great joy and peace she had in the Catholic faith, how precious Mary was to her, and how she enjoyed praying to Mary! And what a great comfort the priest had been when he came to their home in a time of sickness. And how sad she felt that I did not have the joy and privilege of being in the Roman Church. She was sincere. But the simple truth is that praying to Mary, confessing to a priest, having masses said for people's souls, etc., are not scriptural nor right. And she did not know the joy of salvation by personal faith in Christ.

How arrogant and sure of themselves are Jehovah's Witnesses missionaries! Some of them spend years in house-to-house visitation trying to propagate the Jehovah's Witness doctrines. Yet most of them do not know that they are saved or have not the assurance of salvation. Again and again when I pressed the matter, "Ye must be born again," Jehovah's Witnesses at my door had no idea what it meant. Satisfaction with their religion does not prove that they are right. I remember the astonishment and conviction of such a man at Hastings, Minnesota. He then came to trust Christ and be saved.

In Rome, which I visited about fourteen times, I always go when I can to the Church of the Holy Stairs. There we see people climbing those twenty-eight steps on their knees, steps that tradition says Queen Helena, the mother of Emperor Constantine, brought from Jerusalem from Pilate's Judgment Hall. Always those stairs have been crowded. Often people are weeping as they climb the stairs and stop to kiss each step. My heart bleeds when I see them. I have no doubt of their sincerity, their deep seeking after God, their constant faith that they will gain credit in Heaven. Oh, but there is an easier, surer way to peace with God! These people are sincere, though they are wrong. And it is said that Martin Luther, climbing these "holy stairs" long ago, suddenly remembered the Scripture, "The just shall live [or have life] by faith." And he immediately gave up seeking after favor by his good works, trusted Christ and walked down those steps to start the Reformation.

Among many good Christian people, strange doctrines are held sincerely. My father was sprinkled as a baby by his Methodist parents. And until he was about thirty-five years old, a wild, rough, drinking lost man, his only hope of Heaven was that he had been sprinkled and surely his father and mother knew what they were doing. Any confidence he had in that religion was a false confidence. Then he got saved.

Can honest people, even scholarly, devoted ministers of the Gospel, hold to sprinkling for baptism and sprinkling babies instead of converts? Oh, yes, many of them do! They didn't get that from the Bible, but they inherited the doctrine and now try to find proof texts to satisfy their hearts. To convince one against his will, leaves him of the same opinion still.

Good people can be misled on doctrine. Because four thousand people at Catholic Notre Dame University talked in tongues is no sign that speaking in tongues is from God. Because people enjoy it and think it brings great blessing does not mean it is scriptural. We still need to check carefully the Scriptures.

II. SPEAKING IN TONGUES NOT NECESSARILY CHRISTIAN; WIDESPREAD IN HEATHEN RELIGIONS

Some Christians talk in tongues. So do some Mormons, some devil-possessed spiritists, heathen witch doctors in Africa and Asia. Ages ago many heathen religions talked in tongues. It is not of itself necessarily of God.

In his book, *New Testament Teaching on Tongues*, Dr. Merrill Unger calls attention to this fact, on pages 163-165:

> That tongues can be and are counterfeited by demon spirits is evidenced by the fact that spiritistic mediums, Muslim dervishes, and Indian fakirs speak in tongues. It must be remembered by those who try to make tongues a badge of spirituality or a status symbol of saints who have

attained the height of spiritual experience, that speaking in tongues and their interpretation are not peculiar to the Christian church but are common in ancient pagan religions and in spiritism both ancient and modern.

The very phrase "to speak with tongues" (Greek *glossais lalein*, Acts 2:4; 10:46; 19:6; I Cor. 12-14; cf. Mark 16:17) was not invented by New Testament writers, but borrowed from the ordinary speech of pagans. Plato's attitude toward the enthusiastic ecstasies of the ancient soothsayer (*mantis*, diviner,) recalls the Apostle Paul's attitude toward glossolalia among the Corinthian believers.

Virgil graphically describes the ancient pagan prophetess "speaking with tongues." He depicts her disheveled hair, her panting breast, her change of color, and her apparent increase in stature as the god (demon) came upon her and filled her with his supernatural afflatus. Then her voice loses its mortal ring as the god (demon) speaks through her, as in ancient and modern necromancy (spiritism).

Phenomena of this type are common among savages and pagan peoples of lower culture. Ecstatic utterances interpreted by a person in a sane state of mind have been verified. In the Sandwich Islands, for example, the god Oro gave his oracles through a priest who "ceased to act or speak as a voluntary agent, but with his limbs convulsed, his features distorted and terrific, his eyes wild and strained, would roll on the ground foaming at the mouth, and reveal the will of the god in shrill cries and sounds violent and indistinct, which the attending priests duly interpreted to the people."

So, intelligent and concerned people will want to find out what is of God and what is of evil spirits.

The matter is so important, let me call to the witness stand again the assistant professor in Grace Theological Seminary, Dr. Charles R. Smith. He says on pages 20-22 of his book, *Tongues in Biblical Perspective*:

IN NON-CHRISTIAN RELIGIONS.—Tongues occupied a significant place in ancient Greek religion. The seeress at Delphi, not far from Corinth, spoke in tongues. According to Plutarch (A.D. 44-117), interpreters were kept in attendance to explain her incoherent utterances. Many scholars have stated that tongues were experienced in the mystery religions (Osiris, Mithra, Eleusinian, Dionysian, and Orphic cults). Some have concluded that the unintelligible lists of "words" in the "magical papyri" and in certain Gnostic "prayers" are records of ecstatic utterances. About A.D. 180 Celsus reported ecstatic utterances among the Gnostics. Lucian of Samosata (A.D. 120-198) described tongues speaking as it was practiced by the devotees of the Syrian goddess, Juno.

Today shamans (witch doctors, priests, or medicine men) in Haiti, Greenland, Micronesia, and countries of Africa, Australia, Asia, and North and South America speak in tongues. Several groups use drugs to aid in inducing the ecstatic state and utterances. Voodoo practitioners speak in tongues. Buddhist and Shinto priests have been heard speaking in tongues. Moslems have spoken in tongues, and an ancient tradition even reports that Mohammed himself spoke in tongues. According to his own account, after his ecstatic experiences he found it difficult to return to "logical and intelligible speech" (Kelsey, p. 143).

IN MENTAL ILLNESS.—The fact that nonreligious tongues speaking often occurs in association with certain mental illnesses is well documented. Psychiatrists have reported it in association with schizophrenia, neurosis, and psychosis. Probably all psychiatrists and psychologists are aware of the possibility of psychic damage resulting from tongues speaking (Kelsey, p. 227). It was reported that following the extended tongues meeting held by Aimee Semple McPherson, founder of the Church of the Foursquare Gospel, mental institutions in the area of her meetings were overburdened. The Episcopalian church financed a study commission which concluded that tongues are "not *per se* a religious phenomenon" and may appear among those "who are suffering from mental disorders as schizophrenia and hysteria" (Jennings, p. 11).

IN SPIRITISM.—Tongues speaking occurs among anti-Christian spiritistic mediums. Contrary to *popular* belief among tongues speakers, a few years ago the European Pentecostal Conference admitted that "tongues might occur apart from the Spirit's action" (Brown, p. 151).

IN THE DEMON POSSESSED.—Even Pentecostal authors grant that there are cases where demonic influence is apparently responsible for tongues utterances. Some feel that this is why "the gift of discernment of spirits" is necessary.

Again on page 38 Dr. Smith says:

In extrabiblical literature this word was used to

describe the "inspired" utterances of diviners. Moulton and Milligan cite three occurrences of the word in Vettius Valens where it designates irrational or unintelligible speech. It is stated that the speakers' minds had "fallen away," they were overcome with "madness," and they spoke in "ecstasy" (p. 72). *Apoptheggomai* was almost a technical term for describing the speech of oracle-givers, diviners, prophets, exorcists, ecstatics, and other "inspired" persons (Kittel, I, 447; Arndt and Gingrich, p. 101). The basic idea is "an unusual utterance by virtue of inspiration." Though the word obviously cannot be limited to unintelligible speech, it is certainly appropriate for such. Its usage in Greek literature, in fact, definitely suggests a connection with ecstatic, often unintelligible, utterances.

If a Mormon talks in tongues with his false religion, is that speaking with tongues the Bible gift of tongues? I think not. If an unconverted Catholic who prays to Mary, confesses to a priest, hopes to get out of purgatory if enough people pay for masses and if he hasn't sinned too badly, talks in tongues, is that the Bible gift of tongues? I think not.

Evidently Satan can have people talk in tongues also, and we need to carefully consider that when we talk about the gift of tongues.

III. FALSE PROPHETS, EVIL SPIRITS CONTINUALLY TRY TO MISLEAD GOD'S PEOPLE

Jesus said, "Beware of false prophets, which come to you in sheep's clothing, but inwardly they are ravening wolves" (Matt. 7:15). And He says that after death

. . . *many will say to me in that day, Lord, Lord, have we not prophesied in thy name? and in thy name have cast out devils? and in thy name done many wonderful works? And then will I profess unto them, I never knew you: depart from me, ye that work iniquity."*—Matt. 7:22,23.

So evidently there are preachers and leaders in religion who themselves are unsaved and have never known Christ and we are to beware of them.

Paul was troubled because in the churches which he had founded there came in false prophets with evil doctrines.

And he said:

"For such are false apostles, deceitful workers, transforming themselves into the apostles of Christ. And no marvel; for Satan himself is transformed into an angel of light. Therefore it is no great thing if his ministers also be transformed as the ministers of righteousness; whose end shall be according to their works."—II Cor. 11:13-15.

We would be foolish if we did not take to heart such solemn warnings. Not everyone who claims to be for God and the Bible can be trusted. And not everybody with a smiling face and a testimony for Christ is really right in doctrine.

We are warned in I Timothy 4:1:

"Now the Spirit speaketh expressly, that in the latter times some shall depart from the faith, giving heed to seducing spirits, and doctrines of devils."

So some do depart from the faith, and all of us need to be watching.

Second Peter 2:1,2 says:

"But there were false prophets also among the people, even as there shall be false teachers among you, who privily shall bring in damnable heresies, even denying the Lord that bought them and bring upon themselves swift destruction. And many shall follow their pernicious ways; by reason of whom the way of truth shall be evil spoken of."

Ah, here we have it again. There are false workers, false prophets, and many will follow their pernicious ways. We do not believe that everyone who is led astray by false teachers is intentionally wicked. Sometimes they are simply naive, not well-founded in the Scriptures, and so easily led astray.

In I John 4:1 we are commanded to be on our guard:

"Beloved, believe not every spirit, but try the spirits whether they are of God: because many false prophets are gone out into the world."

Do these lessons apply to the charismatic movement? I am sure the warnings are needed in this movement, because if the unconverted and false cults and heathen religions, unconverted modernists and Catholics and immoral people sometimes talk in tongues, we would be advised to search carefully to see that we be not misled and do not go along with other false cults in this matter.

IV. HOW EXPLAIN TONGUES?

Consider what really happens. How can you explain it when people talk in tongues? Is it miraculous? Is it the miraculous gift of tongues like they had at Pentecost and elsewhere?

Is it self-hypnotism induced by earnest seeking and going through a prescribed rigmarole and practicing until it is fluent? Is it demon-possession like with heathen witch doctors? Is it intentional fraud, a fake, deceit? How can you explain people's talking in tongues?

1. When Miraculously Useful in Winning Souls Like at Pentecost, It May Be Counted of God

At Pentecost people talked in natural languages, miraculously given, languages they had not previously learned. They spoke to people in their own tongue in which they were born. People who heard it understood. And in those tongues they "prophesied," as Peter himself explained it in quoting from Joel in Acts 2:14-21. And the result was that people were saved as Joel had "prophesied" in Acts 2:21. That was clearly of God. People spake as the Spirit gave them utterance. There was a sensible reason in it. They prophesied to people in their own languages and they helped to have 3,000 people saved.

Any time you have that kind of talking in tongues, I think you have a right to say it is the Bible kind, supernaturally given from God. Any so-called "speaking in tongues" that doesn't fit that pattern is suspect.

You will understand that very rarely, even in Bible times, did anybody need or use this miraculous gift of tongues. It happened at Pentecost about the year 33. If the speaking in foreign languages by Cornelius and his group was a miraculous gift, then that was eight years later, according to Ussher's chronology, and there is not a hint that anybody in that interval anywhere used this gift of tongues.

Then, if the foreign languages spoken in Acts 19:6 were miraculous, (the Bible does not say, and we doubt it), then that was about thirteen years later, maybe fourteen, according to Ussher's chronology. And I remind you there was not a hint in all the travels of Paul and Barnabas and Silas, in the missionary journeys, nor in the work at Jerusalem or Samaria and elsewhere as reported in the book of Acts, that anybody else except in those three instances, talked in tongues in all that time of more than twenty years. If they did, it was unimportant and not recorded.

We remember, of course, that tongues are mentioned last and evidently least in importance of all the gifts of the Spirit. And the reason is simple: there would rarely be a time when one had no chance to witness to a man of another language except with a miraculously given language.

If it was like Pentecost—a miraculously given use of a foreign language which one did not know in order to speak to people in their own language and get people saved—then you may rightly think that is the Bible gift of tongues.

2. If It Is Like the Carnal, Worldly Group at Corinth, Who Used Foreign Languages Unknown to the Unlearned Present, and to Make a Show, Then That Is Probably Wrong, Worldly

There is only one honest way to read I Corinthians, chapter 14, and that is as a plain rebuke of carnal, ignorant, worldly people who were doing wrong. We have no right to say that they had a continual gift of tongues, miraculously given, and yet were free to commit all kinds of sins with that gift. I don't believe it, and I don't think you do. God never leaves miracles as human playthings for worldly or immature people.

In the case at Corinth, they used regular foreign languages, unknown to some of the unlearned present.

Paul rebuked them saying that five words that could be understood were better than ten thousand words that could not be understood. Instead of tongues, he urged them to seek the best gifts, especially prophesying.

Any time more or less immature and emotional people try to make a big splash, try to win converts to their faith, insist that they have a New Testament religion better than anybody who doesn't talk in tongues, it means they probably do not have the Bible gift of tongues, and it is more of the flesh than of God.

3. If It Is Carefully Worked Up, With Explicit Instructions How to Empty the Mind, Say Syllable After Syllable and Continue Until You Fall Into Some Pattern and Practice, Until You Become Fluent in Tongues—Then That Is Probably Some Kind of Self-Hypnotism

If Mormons can find themselves talking in tongues after similar rigmaroles, then it is probably no more from God for a Pentecostal to learn the same thing. If an unsaved Catholic, or a modernist professor in a university, or heathen American Indians, or original heathen Hawaiian leaders, or if priestesses of the Delphian Oracle in Ancient Greece can bring themselves to talk in tongues, then it is not necessarily true that tongues are from God. And people find it easy to convince themselves and to reach the state which they think is proper if they work hard enough at it and begin to jabber in what they think is a heavenly language.

In the Kathryn Kuhlman healing meetings it was the universal custom that when people came to her on the platform and she put her hands upon them, they fell immediately to the floor out of control. Was that a universal fraud? No, they thought that is what would happen, and they surrendered to it. They hypnotized themselves to it, and so they fell.

That happened, says *Blu-Print,* just the same the other day, when Oral Roberts, Rex Humbard and other

Pentecostal leaders came in Kathryn Kuhlman's meetings and had her put her hands upon their heads. Each of them crumpled to the floor.

In Kathryn Kuhlman's book, *God Can Do It Again*, pages 17 and 18, we are told of three Naval airmen from the aircraft carrier *Enterprise* who came to the meeting, and she called them to the platform.

> She walked toward the three men and placed her hands on their heads to pray for them. Immediately, two of her ushers broke from the wings and rushed to where they were standing. They knew from past experience that when Miss Kuhlman prays for people in circumstances such as this, the power of God falls in such a mysterious way that those being prayed for simply crumple to the floor. Sure enough, as she began to pray for them the young men crumpled backward. Caught by the diligent ushers, they were laid gently on the floor.

Then a footnote says,

> "The phenomenon of persons crumpling when Miss Kuhlman lays hands on them or prays for them has characterized her ministry since its inception."

Miss Kuhlman couldn't explain that; she thought it was the power of the Holy Ghost. But that is not what happened when Jesus touched people and healed them. That did not happen when James and John saw the lame man healed at the Gate of the Temple in Acts, chapter 3. That is not what happened when Ananias put his hands on the head of Saul and prayed for him in Acts 9:17-19. That is not what happened at the healing of Aeneas in Acts 9:33, 34. That did not happen when the brethren prayed for Paul and Barnabas and put their hands on them and so sent them forth by the Holy Ghost for their missionary journey. In fact, there is not a hint in the Bible that that happened anywhere as a miraculous gift accompanied with healing.

I mention this in detail to show you that people fall over in a faint because they expect to. They have come wholly committed to the idea that that is what is supposed to happen and it does happen. They are self-hypnotized and brainwashed. The mind is a strange thing, but people can convince themselves of nearly anything they want to believe.

That shows clearly that if a man wanted to talk in tongues and emptied his mind and set out making syllables and insisting and waiting and praying, then he might find himself saying over some syllables and as he practiced more and became more "fluent" (the term Pentecostal writers use), then he would be fooling himself, perhaps. One who wants to be brainwashed can be.

In his book, *They Speak With Other Tongues*, John Sherrill, editor of Norman Vincent Peale's *Guideposts* magazine, tells how he talked in tongues, then on page 146 he says:

> I have described the first flush of joy and wholeness following the Baptism as lasting three months. I'm not sure of the exact period, but after about that length of time, I had a sudden, violent reaction. It centered chiefly on tongues: I became suspicious that I was generating the whole thing. Indeed I often did mouth nonsense syllables in an effort to start the flow of prayer-in-tongues. But sometimes the easy, effortless flow never came. I'd be left listening to the sound of my own foolishness. It was obvious to me that the Holy Spirit was no part of these noises: the ridiculousness of it would sweep over me, and from there it was not far to wondering if the Holy Spirit had ever been a part of tongues."

And then he found that other Pentecostal people nearly always go through such a time also. In certain sane, reasonable moments they know that they have worked hard to get to the place of talking in tongues. They feel that sometimes it is ridiculous. In other words, although they still have been more or less hypnotized and they want to talk in tongues, they have periods of doubt as to whether it is rational and real. They worked so hard to get it and practiced on it so much, that it does not seem a clear-cut case of a miracle from God in such cases.

Self-hypnotism? Yes. Here was a woman convinced that she was healed of cancer. But she died in two months. Here is one who needs braces on his legs and crutches to walk, and at a healing meeting he throws away his crutches, convinced that he is absolutely healed. Then when he is let down he finds his body is still weak, he still needs the braces and the crutches. So people who talk in tongues sometimes more or less honestly are self-hypnotized.

Years ago there was a cult called the "Shakers." When people got converted or were under, as they thought, the power of God, they began to shake. They sometimes cultivated it, shaking hands and fingers until the whole body took up the shaking. They said it was supernatural. I think they honestly thought so. Actually, they just got themselves into a state to believe it was of God and so it came on them.

In some communities and with some sects of people it is understood that when one is converted he must shout aloud the praises of God and so sometimes people did who would never give a public testimony, would never try to win a soul. But if they felt it was proper and right, they got themselves to shout aloud and walk up and down the aisles clapping their hands saying, "Glory to God!" I am saying, one could obviously see that they were outside themselves—a woman's hair would come down and she wouldn't know it; clothes would become loosened and immodestly, maybe, and she not be conscious of it.

I am saying that one may cultivate a certain attitude of mind toward religious phenomenon like talking in tongues and, no doubt, many do.

4. Talking in Tongues Is Often Deliberate Fraud

I think that sometimes the phenomenon of tongues, even if one is self-hypnotized, is not an intentional fraud, though fraudulent. Good people think they have a gift from God when they work themselves up to believe they must talk in tongues and they get themselves to jabbering.

But many times we can be sure that the talking in tongues becomes a deliberate fraud. One by practice grows "fluent," as Pentecostalists themselves say.

I knew a godly, soul-winning preacher, a good man. He told me that he had been active in the Pentecostal churches and had talked in tongues. He said, "I will show you how," and he cut loose in a jabber and smiled at me. In other words, he was saying that he could imitate and put on the kind of show that people expected in the Pentecostal service and he had done it himself as a Pentecostalist.

I am sure that John Sherrill was right in his doubts about it and there was something that offended his own sense of honesty in putting on that kind of show. But he reconvinced himself and goes on with his tongues business.

Do not feel unkind when I say this, because in the thirty or more books I have by Pentecostal writers, they frequently say that beyond any doubt there is often fraud among the Pentecostal people on the tongues matter.

5. Sometimes Certainly Evil Spirits Get Into People Who Open Their Minds to Any Impression and Who Talk in Tongues

Who can doubt that in the heathen races, in the ancient Grecian oracles, in the heathen religion of the American Indians, Asians and Africans, sometimes evil spirits have gotten into people and had part in their speaking in tongues. Sometimes there may be miraculous revelations.

Would an evil spirit make people happier? Sometimes. Would he let them believe that now they have grown to love God better, they are more interested in the Bible and spiritual matters and prayer? Yes. Satan might do that very thing, and probably does. If he can get people to talk in tongues instead of win souls, he would rather they talked in tongues. If he can get them to talk in tongues so that they think they are better than the best soul winners in the world and have an arrogant, "holier-than-thou" attitude toward better Christians, more mature Christians, more sacrificial Christians, then Satan would certainly be glad to do that. Satan worked miracles before Pharaoh down in Egypt, before the children of Israel were brought out of Egypt. And he can do so today.

No doubt Satan has sometimes healed people in body, temporarily at least, in order to keep them from serving

God and trusting Him. There is no doubt that sometimes fortunetellers reveal things that are only supernaturally known.

My cousin near Gainesville, Texas, had some horses stolen. He went to a spiritist medium in Gainesville, Texas. They had sought for the horses all through the country and could not even find a lead. This woman fortuneteller told him that a certain man had stolen the horses and had taken them over into Ardmore, Oklahoma. My cousin went there and found the horses and brought them back. He was not a good Christian. After that, he thought more of fortunetellers than preachers.

My stepmother's mother, that is, my stepgrandmother, as I recall the story, had lost some jewelry which was very precious to her. She went to a spiritist medium who told her where the jewelry was, and she found it in the fruit cellar. This greatly impressed her. But as she was down in the fruit cellar and started to leave, God seemed to speak to her and say, "That is of Satan. Do not follow it." And she knew that the fortuneteller had been allowed to help her in a small matter to keep her mind from Christ and God and the Bible.

I am saying, evil spirits do take part in religious matters. They do deceive Christian people.

I am certain in my own mind that sometimes evil spirits lead people away from soul-winning, New Testament Christianity into a hard hyper-Calvinism, critical, unloving, unfruitful. I am sure that sometimes evil spirits take over in church and revival services and cause a big uproar religiously by people who think they are serving God but who hinder the work of God.

So note how sometimes evil spirits enter into people in connection with this tongues business.

In his book, *New Testament Teaching on Tongues*, on pages 163 and 164, Dr. Unger says:

> That tongues can be and are counterfeited by demon spirits is evidenced by the fact that spiritistic mediums, Muslim dervishes, and Indian fakirs speak in tongues. It must be remembered by those who try to make tongues a

badge of spirituality or a status symbol of saints who have
attained the height of spiritual experience, that speaking
in tongues and their interpretation are not peculiar to the
Christian church but are common in ancient pagan
religions and in spiritism both ancient and modern.

Again he says on pages 165 and 166:

Citations could be extended indefinitely to
demonstrate that speaking in tongues may be by demon
power, as is certainly the case in pagan religions,
spiritistic circles, and among Indian fakirs and Muslim
dervishes. Christians who seek a manifestation not
sanctioned by the Word of God for our day and age
likewise run a grave risk of coming under demon
influence, if not under direct demon power.

In such cases the results are physical, mental, and
spiritual breakdown. Marital infidelity, divorce, and
gross immorality often result. Christians so deceived
often resort to dishonesty, commercialism of the Lord's
work, trickery, sensational publicity, lying, and
misrepresentation with a conscience "seared with a hot
iron." Unarrested careers in this direction often lead to
the "sin unto [physical] death" (I Cor. 5:1-5; 11:30-32; I
John 5:16). God prematurely terminates the earthly life
of the believer so despoiled by Satan in order that his
"spirit may be saved in the day of the Lord Jesus" (I Cor.
5:5).

I recently had a very earnest letter from a young man
who had been in the Pentecostal movement and had sought
tongues. His wife had talked in tongues. Then he came to
feel satanic influences taking hold of him in these services
as he sought to speak in tongues. He escaped; now he writes
earnestly urging me to warn people that evil spirits may
take part when your mind turns blank and you give
yourself over to whatever may happen to you. Leave a door
into the psychic personality open and evil spirits may well
enter.

Again I remind you of quotations from pages 21-23 of
that valuable book, *Tongues in Biblical Perspective*, by
Charles R. Smith:

In mental illness.—The fact that nonreligious tongues
speaking often occurs in association with certain mental
illnesses is well documented. Psychiatrists have reported

it in association with schizophrenia, neurosis, and psychosis. Probably all psychiatrists and psychologists are aware of the possibility of psychic damage resulting from tongues speaking (Kelsey, p. 227).

He told us: "In spiritism.—Tongues speaking occurs among anti-Christian spiritistic mediums." He reminded us: "In the demon possessed.—Even Pentecostal authors grant that there are cases where demonic influence is apparently responsible for tongues utterances."

Dr. Smith also speaks of tongues groups who deny the Trinity, deny the inspiration of the Scriptures, the Virgin Birth, the substitutionary atonement, the doctrine of creation, and other vital doctrines.

Dr. Smith laments:

Roman Catholics who teach that salvation comes through the sacraments, thereby denying that it comes through faith alone, are receiving this experience. Tongues are often associated with visions and prophecies that are contradictory to the revealed Word of God.

Blasphemous utterances.—Dr. A. C. Gaebelien reported a tongues speech which included words in a Chinese dialect which were too "vile and obscene" to be repeated, according to a missionary who was present (Bauman, p. 42). A speaker on another occasion was described as "blaspheming the Lord Jesus Christ in a most awful manner" (McCrossan, p. 33). Similar reports have been given by others. V. Raymond Edman, a former president of Wheaton College, reported that during their ritual dances Tibetan monks have spoken in English, including profanity typical of drunken sailors (Jennings, p. 13). Many have felt that such instances prove demonic influence. This possibility cannot be ignored, but another explanation will be offered in a later chapter.

Immorality.—This is a distasteful subject to bring up—especially since so many people who speak in tongues are sincere Christians seeking a closer relationship with God and attempting to live unreproachably. Nevertheless, immorality *has* often followed closely on the trail of tongues utterances. This was the case even among the Corinthians—a most carnal church. The Cevenols were charged with promiscuity, as were tongues speakers at London, the French Prophets in London, and a few of the Irvingites.

The doctrines of free love and "spiritual marriages" have too often appeared in association with tongues. Perversion of the Biblical teaching relating to sex and marriage can be seen in the Mormons and the Shakers. Aimee Semple McPherson was not the only tongues leader to receive a "revelation" that her marriage was "not in the Lord" and that she should enter another union. One of the serious problems of the Pentecostal movement has been the fact that many of its leaders have fallen into immorality. One well-known Pentecostal preacher, a woman widowed for three years, professed to be "with child of the Holy Ghost." Parham, "father of the modern Pentecostal movement," was arrested for the grossest of immoralities (Bauman, p. 34). Bauman quotes one young man as saying, "To my surprise, I found that these blessed emotions in my soul seemed to be accompanied with sexual passion in my body" (p. 37).

I have a sad clipping in my Bible telling of how a famous Pentecostal evangelist was found dead in a San Francisco hotel. An autopsy proved he was an alcoholic and was killed by an excess of liquor.

V. SOME SERIOUS AND SHOCKING THINGS THAT MAKE US GREATLY CONCERNED AND WARY OF PENTECOSTAL PEOPLE

1. So-Called Interpretations of Tongues Often a Fraud

In Pentecostal services, often someone speaks in tongues and then another gives what is pretended to be a divinely given "interpretation." But a few words may result in a long interpretation. Or a long speech in tongues may be interpreted in few words. Prophesies are made that are never fulfilled.

In my experience in Pentecostal meetings and those reported to me it is nearly always said that the one who interprets somebody's speaking in tongues says that it included "Jesus is coming soon." Now the truth is, Jesus may come soon or He may not. The Bible makes it quite clear that no one can know. So that statement which contradicts the plain statement of the Bible is obviously wrong and was not from God.

2. Careless, Naive, Unreliable Reports and Lack of Discernment Belie Pentecostal Claims

Second, there is among Pentecostal people a carelessness that grows from lack of spiritual discernment. They do not tell things straight. They regularly say that D. L. Moody talked in tongues, that Torrey talked in tongues, that Charles G. Finney talked in tongues. The same has been said about the principal Christian leaders that I know today, and it is utterly untrue.

One of the most scholarly of the writers advocating speaking in tongues quotes the word of D. L. Moody about some Christian brethren, saying they need to be baptized with the Holy Ghost and he leaves the impression that Moody is talking about the same thing he is advocating—talking in tongues. And since he quoted from *The Life of D. L. Moody,* it is nearly certain that he knew that was a dishonest use of the term.

I have letter after letter from people saying I have committed the unpardonable sin since I do not believe in talking in tongues. They accuse me of resisting the Holy Ghost. It is the customary thing for them to run down fundamental Christian leaders who win many, many souls and build great churches and accuse them of not being good Christians and not wanting to know the truth, of being second-rate and certainly of not having the Spirit of God upon them. I say, that undiscerning and sometimes ignorant, dishonest practice so widespread among Pentecostal people, would make good Christians wary of tongues.

3. Company With Heretics and Unconverted

Another sad fact which makes serious Christians troubled about Pentecostalism is their tendency to run with Bible believers or infidels—no matter who, just so they talk in tongues. They are proud that 4,000 Catholics talked in tongues at Notre Dame University. Oral Roberts leaves the Assemblies of God and joins the Methodist Church which is the hotbed of modernism. He was not offended to have fellowship with the late Bishop Oxnam, or others equally as unbelieving and opposed to fundamental Christianity.

What is wrong with a man who does not have discernment about infidels and false doctrine? What is wrong with a man who doesn't mind if people depend on prayers to Mary and confession to a priest and masses in the church, repeating, they claim, the sacrifice of Christ? These people are so absorbed in the tongues business that they do not mind about every kind of false doctrine that dishonors Christ and often sends people to Hell.

Let us say that there is much evidence that Pentecostal people do not have good judgment, do not usually have spiritual discernment, are proud, haughty, and think that one who talks in tongues but never wins a soul to Christ has something that the best soul winners do not have. That surely is a poor recommendation for the doctrine of talking in tongues.

PART II:

HEALING: Does Jesus Heal Today?

CHAPTER VIII—AN HONEST APPRAISAL OF DIVINE HEALERS' HEALING MEETINGS AND THEIR FALSE TEACHING

Was Healed, Threw Away Braces Still Needed
2. Two Elderly Women Told to Throw Away Crutches: Both Fell and Broke Hips
3. Dr. Price's Healing Campaign in Vancouver

VI. REPUTABLE, SCHOLARLY SURGEON STUDIES KATHRYN KUHLMAN'S HEALINGS
    1. A Scholarly, Kindly, Thorough Study of Kathryn Kuhlman
    2. Serious Follow-Up of Those "Healed" in Kuhlman Meetings
    3. A Doctor's Diagnosis

VII. THE DISILLUSIONMENT, HURT AND HEART-BREAK OF DECEIVED PEOPLE IS TRAGIC
    1. Because Her Mother Died, She Said God Failed Her
    2. Dr. Torrey Tells of Man Who Claimed Healing Died a Few Days Later Insane
    3. Disillusionment and Heartbreak of Two Famous Men

VIII. GREAT TEMPTATIONS COME TO DIVINE HEALERS
    1. The Money Temptation
    2. Immorality Is Too Often Observed Among Pentecostal Leaders
    3. Association With Heretics and Unsaved People in Pentecostal Movement
    4. But Failure of Some Men Does Not Change Heart of God Who So Often Heals the Sick

Introduction

It is an unspeakable tragedy, we believe, for Christians to miss the power, the joy, the answers to prayer, the manifest presence and intervention of God, that many New Testament Christians had. Where are the thousands saved like at Pentecost and following? Where are the missionary results such as Paul, Barnabas and Silas had with great new churches springing up and thousands of converts among heathen people? Where are the new men delivered from prison or from death as Peter in Acts, chapter 12, or as Paul and Silas in Acts 16 and elsewhere? Where are the miraculous healings that went with the personal ministry of the Lord Jesus and of Peter and of Paul? Yes, we believe we should sometimes see miraculous healings in answer to prayer.

We know, thank God, that New Testament power, answered prayer, seeing multitudes saved, are the blessed experience of some, but we believe they ought to be evident wherever there are born-again, Bible-believing Christians.

CHAPTER I

Where Is the God of Miracles?

God called Gideon to deliver Israel and said:

"The Lord is with thee, thou mighty man of valour. And Gideon said unto him, Oh my Lord, if the Lord be with us, why then is all this befallen us? and WHERE BE ALL HIS MIRACLES WHICH OUR FATHERS TOLD US OF, SAYING, DID NOT THE LORD BRING US UP FROM EGYPT? . . ."—Judges 6:12,13.

When Elijah went to Heaven in a whirlwind and a chariot and horses of fire, with him was the younger Elisha who had determined to be a prophet, who had insisted to Elijah that he wanted ". . . a double portion of thy spirit . . . upon me." So Elisha cried out and the mantle of Elijah fell from him, and smote the waters, and said, Where is the Lord God of Elijah? and when he also had smitten the waters, they parted hither and thither: and Elisha went over."

Let me ask every reader, "Where is the Lord God of Elijah?" Has God quit blessing men who insist on His power? Must we never expect any of the mighty power that God gave to Elijah and Elisha?

In Psalm 44 is the plaintive cry, "We have heard with our ears, O God, our fathers have told us, what work thou didst in their days, in the times of old." But is it all in vain, all that God tells us about His miracles in bringing Israel out of Egypt, the crossing of the Red Sea, the manna from Heaven, the garments that waxed not old for forty years, the water out of the rock, the Jordan opening wide for the nation to pass through, God's casting out the heathen from the land of Canaan? Does that mean nothing to us?

Or let us put it this way: Did God put all that in the Bible in vain and not mean us to ever depend upon that kind of a God?

I think we have a right to ask like Gideon, "Where be all his miracles which our fathers told us of?"

There are too many people who never saw a divine intervention, so clearly supernatural that they could know God still exercises His mighty power in the affairs of men.

Psalm 81:10 says, "I am the Lord thy God which brought thee out of the land of Egypt: open thy mouth wide, and I will fill it." But does God not mean that for Christians today? Must we throw away all the Bible as out of date, if it tells about miracles of the past, since God has now quit doing that kind of business and quit answering the prayers of people in that kind of trouble? I do not believe it.

God told Abraham that ninety-year-old Sarah would bear a child. When Abraham doubted and Sarah laughed in unbelief, God answered back, "Is any thing too hard for the Lord? At the time appointed I will return unto thee, according to the time of life, and Sarah shall have a son" (Gen. 18:14). Oh, are things changed now so some things are too hard for God? Did not God intend that kind of promise to lift our hearts to faith again?

God had told Jeremiah that the nation Israel was going into captivity, that Jerusalem would be destroyed. So the Chaldeans surrounded the city and it was about to fall; but God told Jeremiah to go buy a field for money and take witnesses and that one day that land would be inhabited again by Israel. Oh, Jeremiah must have trembled at the thought: Could God undo the awful ruin that was coming on Israel? "Then came the word of the Lord unto Jeremiah, saying, Behold, I am the Lord, the God of all flesh: is there any thing too hard for me?" (Jer. 32:26,27).

Did God mean that kind of a question and that kind of an answer for us today? Surely He did. Are you going to throw away all the great promises of the Bible and all the great examples of the Bible to have a God with no power, Christianity with no miracle?

I. CHRISTIAN RELIGION A MIRACLE RELIGION

You had better let that soak in. If this Bible is the miraculous Word of God, not written with men's wisdom but "every word . . . proceedeth out of the mouth of God," then that is a miracle. The words that are forever settled in Heaven are now put in the Bible for us, the miraculous promises and miraculous revelations of the dealings of God.

Creation was a miracle. God made everything that is, out of nothing. The creation of man was not the evolution of an animal but God made the form of Adam out of the ground and breathed into him the breath of life and Adam became a living soul. The flood was a miraculous destruction of all the world that then was—the people, the nations, the cities, all except Noah and his sons. And down through the years God's deliverance of Israel from Egypt with mighty miracles proved that He was the living God. God proved with miracles at the hand of Moses and Elijah and Elisha and many another.

Then the birth of the Saviour was a miraculous virgin birth. God's Spirit moved upon the womb of a virgin and God became Man. Then Jesus not only worked many miracles but He arose bodily from the grave.

Not only that, but regeneration, the saving of a soul, is a miracle so that one who is a child of Hell becomes a child of God. One who is dead in trespasses and sin becomes alive to God.

If someone says, "Oh, that is a spiritual miracle, not physical," then I remind you that every time God makes a lost sinner into a new creature, it foretells and guarantees a physical miracle in the resurrection of that body from the dead or changing of that body in a moment from an earthly body to a spiritual body, to live forever.

Let's go further. Every time God answers a prayer and brings about something that would not have occurred had we not appealed to God—that means a divine intervention, a controlling of the forces of nature so that is not ordinary but extraordinary, not natural but supernatural. It is a miracle for God to intervene in the affairs of men even to answer prayer. The Christian religion is a miracle religion. Oh, how sad is the state of those who leave out a miracle-working God from Christianity today!

II. MANY, MANY PROMISES IN NEW TESTAMENT GUARANTEE MIRACLES TO CONTINUE THROUGH THIS AGE

Following the Great Commission in Mark 16:15,16, Jesus said, "And these signs shall follow them that believe; In my name shall they cast out devils; they shall speak with new tongues; They shall take up serpents; and if they drink any deadly thing, it shall not hurt them; they shall lay hands on the sick, and they shall recover." Some doubt whether the last part in the King James Version is a proper ending to the book of Mark. I think it is in the inspired ending. But, like it or not, these things actually happened to New Testament Christians. It is a promise of miracles, and God fulfilled the miracles.

In John 14:13,14, Jesus said, "And whatsoever ye shall ask in my name, that will I do, that the Father may be glorified in the Son. If ye shall ask any thing in my name, I will do it." That is an unlimited promise, limited only that one should ask in the name of Jesus. And the promise is of no avail and is no promise at all, or it is good for today. Isn't that a promise of miracles if a miracle be asked in Jesus' name?

In Mark 11:24 Jesus said, "Therefore I say unto you, What things soever ye desire, when ye pray, believe that ye receive them, and ye shall have them."

Note that this is a promise to "whosoever." If John 3:16 is good for today, then Mark 11:24 is addressed to the same group and is for today also. And it is certainly a promise of miraculous intervention to anyone to whom God gives faith for such an answer.

And so it is with John 15:7, "If ye abide in me, and my words abide in you, ye shall ask what ye will, and it shall be done unto you." That is a promise that involves miracles.

In Mark 9:23 Jesus said, ". . . all things are possible to

him that believeth." And isn't that a definite promise to an indefinite audience: "him that believeth"?

In John 14:12 Jesus said, "Verily, verily, I say unto you, He that believeth on me, the works that I do shall he do also; and greater works than these shall he do; because I go unto my Father." Again this is a promise to "he that believeth on me." Doesn't that mean Christians in this day who put their trust in Christ? Then that means that the very works of Christ, a miraculous ministry, should be done by men today who please God and walk in the steps of Jesus.

One who would say that God has no miracles for today, no wondrous answers to prayer, no signs and wonders to back up the Gospel, is really taking away from us all the heart of New Testament Christianity and all the sweet promises of God. No, we must believe that the Christian religion is still a miracle religion and that God wants to answer prayer miraculously, by divine intervention in the affairs of men.

You will understand working miracles was never just a plaything in the hands of some show-off. No man went out regularly to do a miracle before breakfast! No man in Bible times went around just to make a show of miracles. Even Jesus at one time "could . . . do no mighty work, save that he laid his hands upon a few sick folk, and healed them. And he marvelled because of their unbelief" (Mark 6:5,6). No one had the gift of miracles in the sense that without any reference to divine leading or without any special waiting on God he could just work a miracle at pleasure to the astonishment of the people. No, miracles were never playthings, were never of vain display. But surely God who intervenes in the affairs of men still can work miracles when it pleases Him to do so. So are all the promises.

III. IT IS OBVIOUS THAT IN BIBLE MIRACLES OFTEN TURNED PEOPLE TO GOD AND LED TO MANY BEING SAVED

God has a purpose in showing His power. How many

times that is made clear in the Bible.

In the time of the greatest apostasy and worldliness that Israel had ever seen, when wicked Ahab had caused Israel to sin, had married Jezebel, the Baal worshiper, and when 450 prophets of Baal were eating at the queen's table and when the preachers and prophets were hid out in caves and fed on bread and water, those who had not been slain, then Elijah on Mount Carmel prayed down the fire of God, I Kings 18 tells us. And it was made a dramatic scene that none would ever forget. He had mocked the prophets of Baal and then prayed and God sent the fire and burned up the sacrifice and burned up the wood and licked up the water out of the trench. Then the people fell on their faces and said, "The Lord, he is the God" (I Kings 18:39). Then Elijah beheaded the prophets of Baal and God gave Israel another chance.

It is obvious that God miraculously encouraged Gideon to set out to deliver Israel. In Judges, chapters 6 and 7, we read how God made dew upon the fleece and dry about it, then made it dry on the fleece and dew all about to convince and encourage Gideon. We remember that God caused a Midianite to tell another of his dream, that Gideon would be empowered of God to destroy them all. That was a miracle, and God strengthened the hand of Gideon and his 300 until they miraculously delivered Israel and the nation was blessed and restored to favor.

In the New Testament, in the 3rd chapter of Acts, Peter and John came to the Temple and there at that Beautiful Gate found a beggar, a man lame who had never walked, forty years old and more. Peter got faith to call on the man—"Look on us," and taking him by the right hand he said, "Silver and gold have I none; but such as I have give I thee: In the name of Jesus Christ of Nazareth rise up and walk." Immediately his feet and ankle bones received strength so that he leaped and walked and praised God and held Peter and John. The great multitude came together at this miracle and Peter preached to them and many were saved.

Do you mean to say that a miraculous show of God's power could not be used today to convince the gainsayer and the sinner?

After Pentecost God gave wonderful blessings whereby multitudes were saved. But there arose great threatenings against the Christians. They needed a new enduement of power, a new surge of God's miraculous manifestation. Peter and John had been arrested. The Sanhedrin had straightly threatened them to preach no more. So the whole multitude with one accord lifted up their voice in prayer:

"And now, Lord, behold their threatenings: and grant unto thy servants, that with all boldness they may speak thy word, By stretching forth thine hand to heal; and that signs and wonders may be done by the name of thy holy child Jesus. And when they had prayed, the place was shaken where they were assembled together; and they were all filled with the Holy Ghost, and they spake the word of God with boldness."—Acts 4:29-31.

Ah, they pleaded with God to stretch forth His hand to heal and that signs and wonders might be done so they would have boldness to preach the Word. And that prayer was answered. Verse 33 tells us, "And with great power gave the apostles witness of the resurrection of the Lord Jesus: and great grace was upon them all." And then there follows story after story of miracles. Ananias and Sapphira died for lying to God.

"And believers were the more added to the Lord, multitudes both of men and women.) Insomuch that they brought forth the sick into the streets, and laid them on beds and couches, that at the least the shadow of Peter passing by might overshadow some of them. There came also a multitude out of the cities round about unto Jerusalem, bringing sick folks, and them which were vexed with unclean spirits: and they were healed every one."—Acts 5:14-16.

In my early ministry, I had a deep conviction that God wanted me to go in the power of God and have wonderful results. I felt certain that God wanted drunkards made sober, harlots made pure, infidels made into saints of God. He wanted New Testament Christianity again in power.

But people told me that you couldn't have the mighty power of God as they had in Bible times and that God did not work miracles now.

I went to God in prayer, and with some holy indignation I said, "Lord, if You are going to expect me to have the kind of results Peter had, then I must have the power Peter had. If You expect me to have the results the Apostle Paul had, then I must have the kind of power he had."

I was right. No one can expect to have Bible kind of results without Bible power, miraculous power, not just personality, not just culture, not just argument, but the mighty power of God!

Note that request of those Christians at Jerusalem in Acts 4:29,30, ". . . and grant unto thy servants, that with all boldness they may speak thy word, By stretching forth thine hand to heal; and that signs and wonders may be done by the name of thy holy child Jesus." Oh, surely my heart cries out, and I think yours surely does, for the same kind of results.

Nearly two years ago Dr. Lee Roberson at Chattanooga had throat trouble. Doctors found a growth on the vocal chords. There was an operation. Then he needed another operation and there came a time when Dr. Roberson could only talk for a little bit and a little above a whisper, I think. And the doctor, sadly, after the second operation said to him, "Dr. Roberson, you will never preach again!"

I talked to Dr. Roberson on the telephone and he said, "I would rather die than not preach again."

But God put on my heart this matter so urgently, and I wrote to Dr. Roberson: "Dr. Roberson, I am asking God, like the Christians at Jerusalem, 'grant . . . that with all boldness they may speak thy word, By stretching forth thine hand to heal; and that signs and wonders may be done by the name of thy holy child Jesus.' " I said, "Dr. Roberson, I need some signs and wonders!" I can't go on preaching unless I have some evidence that God, the God of Abraham and Isaac and Jacob, the God of Peter and Paul, the God of New Testament Christianity is the same today and that He wants to manifest Himself today to His people. So many, many joined, of course, and not my prayers alone but the prayers of many were answered and in August a year ago or two Dr. Roberson announced sermons in his church and since then has been preaching regularly with great power and blessing. And when Dr. Roberson preached he said, "If I never preach again, this is a miracle." But he does preach again and again.

Oh, Christians, in Jesus' name, let us plead with God to stretch forth His hand to heal and "that signs and wonders may be done by the name of thy holy child Jesus."

CHAPTER II

Jesus Personally Healed Multitudes. Does Not That Mean Something to Us?

The emphasis on the healing of the bodies, with lepers cleansed, blind eyes opened, the dead raised, the paralyzed made normal—all these in the personal ministry of Jesus must impress everybody who sets out to read the Gospels with an open mind and to take to heart all that God tells us there.

I. TWENTY-FOUR CASES IN GOSPEL OF MATTHEW WHERE JESUS MIRACU-LOUSLY HEALED

1. *"And Jesus went about all Galilee, teaching in their synagogues, and preaching the gospel of the kingdom, and healing all manner of sickness and all manner of disease among the people."*—Matt. 4:23.

2. *"And his fame went throughout all Syria: and they brought unto him all sick people that were taken with divers diseases and torments, and those which were possessed with devils, and those which were lunatick, and those that had the palsy; and he healed them."*—Matt. 4:24.

3. *"When he was come down from the mountain, great multitudes followed him. And, behold, there came a leper and worshipped him, saying, Lord, if thou wilt, thou canst make me clean. And Jesus put forth his hand and touched him, saying, I will; be thou clean. And immediately his leprosy was cleansed."*—Matt. 8:1-3.

4. *"And when Jesus was entered into Capernaum, there came unto him a centurion, beseeching him, And saying, Lord, my servant lieth at home sick of the palsy, grievously tormented. And Jesus saith unto him, I will come and heal him. . . .And Jesus said unto the centurion, Go thy way; and as thou hast believed, so be it done unto thee. And his servant was*

healed in the selfsame hour."—Matt. 8:5-7,13.

5. *"And when Jesus was come into Peter's house, he saw his wife's mother laid, and sick of a fever. And he touched her hand, and the fever left her: and she arose, and ministered unto them."*—Matt. 8:14,15.

6. *"When the even was come, they brought unto him many that were possessed with devils: and he cast out the spirits with his word, and healed all that were sick."*—Matt. 8:16.

7. *"And when he was come to the other side into the country of the Gergesenes, there met him two possessed with devils, coming out of the tombs, exceeding fierce, so that no man might pass by that way. . . .So the devils besought him, saying, If thou cast us out, suffer us to go away into the herd of swine. And he said unto them, Go. And when they were come out, they went into the herd of swine: and, behold, the whole herd of swine ran violently down a steep place into the sea, and perished in the waters."*—Matt. 8:28,31,32.

8. *"And, behold, they brought to him a man sick of the palsy, lying on a bed: and Jesus seeing their faith said unto the sick of the palsy; Son, be of good cheer; thy sins be forgiven thee. . . .But that ye may know that the Son of man hath power on earth to forgive sins, (then saith he to the sick of the palsy,) Arise, take up thy bed, and go unto thine house. And he arose, and departed to his house."*—Matt. 9:2,6,7.

9. *"And, behold, a woman, which was diseased with an issue of blood twelve years, came behind him, and touched the hem of his garment: For she said within herself, If I may but touch his garment, I shall be whole. But Jesus turned him about, and when he saw her, he said, Daughter, be of good comfort; thy faith hath made thee whole. And the woman was made whole from that hour."*—Matt. 9:20-22.

10. *"And when Jesus came into the ruler's house, and saw the minstrels and the people making a noise, He said unto them, Give place: for the maid is not dead, but sleepeth. And they laughed him to scorn. But when the people were put forth, he went in, and took her by the hand, and the maid arose."*—Matt. 9:23-25.

11. *"And when he was come into the house, the blind men came to him: and Jesus saith unto them, Believe ye that I am able to do this? They said unto him, Yea, Lord. Then touched he their eyes, saying, According to your faith be it unto you. And their eyes were opened; and Jesus straitly charged them, saying, See that no man know it."*—Matt. 9:28-30.

12. *"As they went out, behold, they brought to him a dumb man possessed with a devil. And when the devil was cast out, the dumb spake:*

and the multitudes marvelled, saying, It was never so seen in Israel."—Matt. 9:32,33.

13. "And Jesus went about all the cities and villages, teaching in their synagogues, and preaching the gospel of the kingdom, and healing every sickness and every disease among the people."—Matt. 9:35.

14. "And, behold, there was a man which had his hand withered. And they asked him, saying, Is it lawful to heal on the sabbath days? that they might accuse him. . . .Then saith he to the man, Stretch forth thine hand. And he stretched it forth: and it was restored whole, like as the other."—Matt. 12:10,13.

15. "But when Jesus knew it, he withdrew himself from thence: and great multitudes followed him, and he healed them all."—Matt. 12:15.

16. "Then was brought unto him one possessed with a devil, blind, and dumb: and he healed him, insomuch that the blind and dumb both spake and saw."—Matt. 12:22.

17. "And Jesus went forth, and saw a great multitude, and was moved with compassion toward them, and he healed their sick."—Matt. 14:14.

18. "And when the men of that place had knowledge of him, they sent out into all that country round about, and brought unto him all that were diseased; And besought him that they might only touch the hem of his garment: and as many as touched were made perfectly whole."—Matt. 14:35,36.

19. "And, behold, a woman of Canaan came out of the same coasts, and cried unto him, saying, Have mercy on me, O Lord, thou son of David; my daughter is grievously vexed with a devil. . . .Then Jesus answered and said unto her, O woman, great is thy faith: be it unto thee even as thou wilt. And her daughter was made whole from that very hour."—Matt. 15:22,28.

20. "And great multitudes came unto him, having with them those that were lame, blind, dumb, maimed, and many others, and cast them down at Jesus' feet; and he healed them: Insomuch that the multitude wondered, when they saw the dumb to speak, the maimed to be whole, the lame to walk, and the blind to see: and they glorified the God of Israel."—Matt. 15:30,31.

21. "And when they were come to the multitude, there came to him a certain man, kneeling down to him, and saying, Lord, have mercy on my son: for he is lunatick, and sore vexed: for ofttimes he falleth into the fire, and oft into the water. And I brought him to thy disciples, and they could not cure him. Then Jesus answered and said, O faithless and perverse

generation, how long shall I be with you? how long shall I suffer you? bring him hither to me. And Jesus rebuked the devil; and he departed out of him: and the child was cured from that very hour."—Matt. 17:14-18.

22. "*And great multitudes followed him; and he healed them there.*"—Matt. 19:2.

23. "*And, behold, two blind men sitting by the way side, when they heard that Jesus passed by, cried out, saying, Have mercy on us, O Lord, thou son of David. And the multitude rebuked them, because they should hold their peace: but they cried the more, saying, Have mercy on us, O Lord, thou son of David. And Jesus stood still, and called them, and said, What will ye that I shall do unto you? They say unto him, Lord, that our eyes may be opened. So Jesus had compassion on them, and touched their eyes: and immediately their eyes received sight, and they followed him.*"—Matt. 20:30-34.

24. "*And the blind and the lame came to him in the temple; and he healed them.*"—Matt. 21:14.

In Gethsemane Peter struck off the ear of a high priest's servant and Jesus restored it, although Matthew does not tell of the healing as does Luke 22:51, but the event is mentioned (Matt. 26:51).

Does not God have some wonderful meaning by the impact of all these accounts of marvelous healings in the ministry of Jesus? If Jesus is the same today, having the same compassion, same power, ought not there be some such wonderful manifestations of that power sometimes among Christians?

II. REMARKABLE, CLEARLY MIRACULOUS POWER ILLUSTRATED IN THESE HEALINGS

No one here had a stomach-ache and so decided himself that he had appendicitis and was healed. No one here had a cough and decided he had tuberculosis and claimed healing. No one here had a pain in his chest and decided he had a heart attack and got healed.

No, here paralyzed men received full usage of their limbs. Leprosy was instantly cleansed. Blind eyes were opened. The daughter of Jairus was raised from the dead. A woman with an issue of blood twelve years was instantly healed.

That kind of clearly miraculous healings makes these different from the usual group of healings claimed in the divine healing meetings. God is able to do the same today.

III. HEALINGS OF THE LORD WERE RESPONSE OF COMPASSION FOR TROUBLED AND SICK

Some people have said that Jesus worked miracles to prove that He was the Son of God. That is not true. Would miracles prove that Elijah was the Son of God? Or Elisha? Would miracles prove that Paul was the Son of God in the same way as Jesus Christ? Miracles prove that God is with one but it does not prove deity. Nicodemus could say, "We know that thou art a teacher come from God: for no man can do these miracles that thou doest, except God be with him" (John 3:2). All miracles proved that Jesus was from God as a prophet which Nicodemus thought Him to be.

Those miracles were often given because of faith. Matthew 9:2 says, "And Jesus seeing their faith said unto the sick of the palsy: Son, be of good cheer; thy sins be forgiven thee." And He made him well. In Matthew 9:29, "According to your faith be it unto you." In Matthew 14:14, "And Jesus went forth, and saw a great multitude, and was moved with compassion toward them, and he healed their sick." Does not the tender heart of Jesus have compassion toward us in our sickness and trouble today?

When the leper came to Jesus and wanted to be healed, "Jesus, moved with compassion, put forth his hand, and touched him, and saith unto him, I will; be thou clean." Oh, the tender compassion of Jesus!

He wept with Mary and Martha at the grave of Lazarus. Does He not weep now with all who are grieved and troubled? If Jesus wanted to heal sick people then, He wants to heal sick people now. He did not heal everyone then and He doesn't heal everyone now. But He has the same tender heart of compassion and we are just as gladly received when we come to Him for help as were people during His earthly ministry.

IV. HEALINGS BY JESUS DURING HIS MINISTRY SURELY EMPHASIZE HIS CONCERN FOR SICK AND HIS INTENTION TO HEAL MULTITUDES

Because of the extravagant claims of some and the false doctrine of some, and an occasional fraud and deceit on this matter of healing, we have shied away from the great truth that Jesus Christ is a Healer as well as a Saviour. He is a Provider, He is a Protector, He is an Intercessor, He has constant watchcare over His own. And He promises food and raiment to those who seek first the kingdom of God (Matt. 6:33). We cannot escape the feeling that He is available to help as far as it is good for us and honors Him to heal the bodies of sick Christians, too. I am mightily impressed again as I go over that great list of healings in the book of Matthew. Did not the Lord intend us to be impressed by that galaxie, that amazing array of wonderful healings?

An honest, unlettered Christian, without any awareness of denominational doctrines and differences, reading this Gospel according to Matthew with an open and loving heart, would be expected to feel that God is glad to answer prayer for healing when it can honor His name.

When I was a fifteen-year-old boy and prayed earnestly for my father to be healed that very day when he was given up to die I did not know much about a Bible doctrine of healing but I knew that a loving Saviour wanted to help His people. It is as natural for a Christian to pray about his bodily ills as it is to pray about his daily bread, about protection from enemies, about guidance in duty.

We cannot escape the fact that the Lord Jesus used all these wonderful things as an argument when John the Baptist sent inquiring if He were really the Christ. Jesus answered, "Go and shew John again those things which ye do hear and see: The blind receive their sight, and the lame walk, the lepers are cleansed, and the deaf hear, the dead are raised up, and the poor have the gospel preached to them" (Matt. 11:4,5). Doesn't that answer indicate that the promised Messiah would heal the sick and preach the Gospel?

John had a right to expect that because he knew that in Isaiah 61:1 there was this prophecy about the Saviour:

"The Spirit of the Lord God is upon me; because the Lord hath anointed me to preach good tidings unto the meek; he hath sent me to bind up the brokenhearted, to proclaim liberty to the captives, and the opening of the prison to them that are bound."

Jesus wanted John the Baptist to be impressed with these wonderful healings as well as with the Gospel He preached. Surely He wants us to be impressed with them, too.

It is not always God's will to heal the sick, but all the thousands who have been sick and got well because of God's mercy prove it is usually God's will to heal the sick, whether by doctors and medicine and diets and treatments, or whether God does it through the natural, inbuilt, recuperative capacity of the body, or by miraculous means. Surely God usually wants to heal the sick.

CHAPTER III

We Are Invited to Pray for Sick and Expect Recovery When God Gives Faith

Because of inexperience or to excuse their own lack of faith and their own lack of power, some people say that the day of miracles is past. They like to say that at certain periods, we will say in the life of Moses and the life of Elijah and the personal ministry of Jesus and the first days after Pentecost, those were days of miracles and that now they are no longer to be expected. However, the Bible does not hint at any such thing.

I. WE ARE COMMANDED TO PRAY FOR SICK

In James 5:13-16, let's read the instructions of the Scripture.

"Is any among you afflicted? let him pray. Is any merry? let him sing psalms. Is any sick among you? let him call for the elders of the church; and let them pray over him, anointing him with oil in the name of the Lord: And the prayer of faith shall save the sick, and the Lord shall raise him up; and if he have committed sins, they shall be forgiven him. Confess your faults one to another, and pray one for another, that ye may be healed. The effectual fervent prayer of a righteous man availeth much."

Any who are afflicted in body should pray. And Christians are invited to call for the elders of the church and they are to pray over the sick, anointing them with oil in the name of the Lord.

Of course that does not mean that olive oil is a cure for every kind of disease. It means certainly that the oil is a symbol of the Holy Spirit who dwells within the Christian's body, and that we are invited to depend on the Holy Spirit of God for healing in answer to prayer if God leads us to that dependence. Oil does not heal, and baptism doesn't save, but baptism is a beautiful figure of salvation, and the olive oil is a reminder of the Holy Spirit.

Notice also that "the prayer of faith shall save the sick." That does not mean that every Christian can just arbitrarily demand that God heal the sick. "Faith" here does not mean believing a certain body of doctrine. Faith is a gift of God and we are to serve God "according as God hath dealt to every man the measure of faith" (Rom. 12:3). If God does not give the faith for healing, then we cannot expect God to heal. He sometimes answers prayer far beyond our faith, but He is not required to do so.

On some matters every person can have faith. The promise of God about salvation to everyone who puts his trust in Christ is so clear that it is a sin not to trust Christ for salvation. And the Bible is so clear that a Christian who gives and relies upon the Lord and seeks first His righteousness, shall have his need supplied (Matt. 6:33; Luke 6:38). So it would be a sin not to trust God for daily provisions, if you seek first His kingdom.

But it is not always God's will to heal the sick. Sometimes a Christian ought to die and go to Heaven. Sometimes God is nearer to one on a sickbed, and then sickness is for God's glory. How do I know that in some particular case it is certainly God's will to heal that person? I cannot know unless God puts faith in my heart about it.

Someone writes me, "Will you please pray the prayer of faith for the healing of my mother?" I cannot pray a prayer of faith unless God gives the faith.

We are always right to pray about sickness, and if God encourages us in our heart we should pray persistently. But a Christian always ought to understand that our prayers are to seek the will of God and want what God wants, and if He will let us know how to pray, we will pray aright.

But it is clearly a plan of God that Christians should pray for the sick, and that the "prayer of faith shall save the sick." It is also clear that our sickness is sometimes the result of sin, and our lack of healing is sometimes because sins stand in the way. So we should confess our sins and get them out of the way if we expect God to answer prayer for healing.

II. PROMISES OF GOD SO CLEAR THEY OBVIOUSLY, IN MANY CASES, WOULD INCLUDE MARVELOUS HEALINGS OF BODY

When the Lord Jesus said to the father of the afflicted boy, "If thou canst believe, all things are possible to him that believeth" (Mark 9:23), He was stating not simply a truth for that day but a universal truth. And when He gave us the promise in Matthew 17:20, "And Jesus said unto them, Because of your unbelief: for verily I say unto you, If ye have faith as a grain of mustard seed, ye shall say unto this mountain, Remove hence to yonder place; and it shall remove; and nothing shall be impossible unto you," He spoke for today.

Would not the promise of Mark 11:24, "Therefore I say unto you, What things soever ye desire, when ye pray, believe that ye receive them, and ye shall have them," cover the need for healing of the body when it is the will of God?

The healings of the Lord Jesus were wonderful. But in John 14:12 He said, "Verily, verily, I say unto you, He that believeth on me, the works that I do shall he do also; and greater works than these shall he do; because I go unto my Father." Then we ought to have the same kind of works as Jesus had since we represent Him and stand in His place. While He is gone we are the light of the world? Does not that mean we ought to expect the same kind of results that were manifest in the personal ministry of Jesus? This is awesome; it makes us tremble, but it is the Word of God.

III. GREAT COMMISSION IN MARK 16:15-18 INDICATES GOD WANTS TO HEAL IN ANSWER TO PRAYER ALL THROUGH THIS AGE

Note this promise of Mark 16:15-18:

"And he said unto them, Go ye into all the world, and preach the

gospel to every creature. He that believeth and is baptized shall be saved;
but he that believeth not shall be damned. And these signs shall follow
them that believe; In my name shall they cast out devils; they shall speak
with new tongues; They shall take up serpents; and if they drink any
deadly thing, it shall not hurt them; they shall lay hands on the sick, and
they shall recover."

Some have doubted whether this Scripture ought really to be a part of the Gospel of Mark. I do not doubt it. In the first place, these kinds of results did follow New Testament Christians. These things did occur as Jesus here promised. In the second place, they are in accordance with the other great promises of the Bible. Those who keep His commandments of taking the Gospel to all the world ought to expect God's blessing on them, as on New Testament Christians who met the same requirements.

If one like Paul on the Isle of Miletus accidently picks up a serpent and is bitten, would it not be proper to pray for God to intervene and save His child from death? (Acts 28:1-6). And if, unaware, one drinks deadly poison, would it not be proper to pray to Christ for deliverance? So surely New Testament Christians felt, and so we should believe.

IV. OBVIOUS THAT WONDERFUL HEALINGS IN ANSWER TO PRAYER GIVE MORE AUTHORITY AND POWER TO GOSPEL

In Acts 4:29 and 30 the apostles and others prayed, "And now, Lord, behold their threatenings: and grant unto thy servants, that with all boldness they may speak thy word, By stretching forth thine hand to heal; and that signs and wonders may be done by the name of thy holy child Jesus." And the mighty power of God came, and multitudes were saved. And verse 12 tells that "by the hands of the apostles were many signs and wonders wrought among the people. . . ." And again in verse 15, "Insomuch that they brought forth the sick into the streets, and laid them on beds and couches, that at the least the shadow of Peter passing by might overshadow some of them."

In Acts, chapter 3, we find that Peter and John went up

to the Temple at the hour of prayer. There a poor, deformed man, a beggar about forty years old who had never walked a step was wonderfully healed as Peter took him by the right hand and lifted him up. The crowd came, Peter preached, and many were saved. Yes, it is right to pray that God will stretch forth His hand to heal "that signs and wonders may be done by the name of thy holy child Jesus," as the apostle prayed.

When Elijah prayed down the power of God on Mount Carmel, it was a test and the people fell on their faces and cried out, "The Lord, he is the God" (I Kings 18:39).

One has a right to be a little skeptical about a gospel that doesn't have the power of God upon it and no manifestation of His blessing.

V. PSALMIST'S INSPIRED PRAISE GIVES HEALING GREAT IMPORTANCE

The psalmist said in Psalm 103, "Bless the Lord, O my soul: and all that is within me, bless his holy name. Bless the Lord, O my soul, and forget not all his benefits." Then he names the blessings. First of all is forgiveness—"Who forgiveth all thine iniquities." But second is healing—"Who healeth all thy diseases." Doesn't that encourage one to bring every disease to God and pray about it? Remember that the third blessing for which we are to thank God is, He redeems our life from destruction. The fourth is He crowns us with lovingkindness and tender mercies, and the fifth is that He "satisfieth thy mouth with good things; so that thy youth is renewed like the eagle's." But second only to forgiveness is the promise of healing of the body. It is not always God's will to heal the sick but certainly it is intended that a Christian should rely daily on God for strength for the body and for healing when it can please God.

CHAPTER IV

Gifts of Healing

Some claim to have "the gift of healing" and so they regularly have "healing lines," have special healing services in which they lay hands on people and pray for them to be healed. They think it is always God's will for every Christian to be healed and be perfectly well, so they think everyone has a right to claim healing. They think, therefore, they have a permanent gift of healing and are authorized to use it continually. However, the facts do not bear out their claims. We believe that does not fit with the Bible doctrine of the gifts of the Spirit.

We believe that what they had in Bible times, by God's loving plan and mercy and only those He chose for each gift, we ought to have, too. We do not believe the gifts of the Spirit are now passed away.

First Corinthians 13:9-12 says:

"For we know in part, and we prophesy in part. But when that which is perfect is come, then that which is in part shall be done away. When I was a child, I spake as a child, I understood as a child, I thought as a child: but when I became a man, I put away childish things. For now we see through a glass, darkly; but then face to face: now I know in part; but then shall I know even as also I am known."

But that does not mean that when the Bible is completed, the spiritual gifts are to pass away. It means surely that in our perfect resurrection bodies we will know perfectly what we now know only in part. Now we see through a glass, darkly; but then—in the presence of Christ and in resurrection bodies—we will see face to face. Yes, Bible Christianity is for today also.

Read what the Scripture says about gifts of healing:

"Now there are diversities of gifts, but the same Spirit. And there are differences of administrations, but the same Lord. And there are diversities of operations, but it is the same God which worketh all in all. But the manifestation of the Spirit is given to every man to profit withal. For to one is given by the Spirit the word of wisdom; to another the word of knowledge by the same Spirit; To another faith by the same Spirit; to another the gifts of healing by the same Spirit; To another the working of miracles; to another prophecy; to another discerning of spirits; to another divers kinds of tongues; to another the interpretation of tongues: But all these worketh that one and the selfsame Spirit, dividing to every man severally as he will."—I Cor. 12:4-11.

Now the close of the chapter continues:

"And God hath set some in the church, first apostles, secondarily prophets, thirdly teachers, after that miracles, then gifts of healings, helps, governments, diversities of tongues. Are all apostles? are all prophets? are all teachers? are all workers of miracles? Have all the gifts of healing? do all speak with tongues? do all interpret?"—I Cor. 12:28-30.

I. GIFTS (PLURAL) FOR SEPARATE, SPECIFIC CASES IN WILL OF GOD, NOT ONE LIFELONG GIFT!

Note the language of the Scriptures above. Note that God gives "severally as he will" these gifts. No one person has all the gifts. And not all are apostles, not all are teachers, not all have these various gifts.

But note particularly that in listing the gifts in verses 4 to 10 above, some other gifts are mentioned such as the word of wisdom, the word of knowledge, of faith—and all as if they were single gifts put permanently upon some people. Certain people had a word of wisdom and would have it still tomorrow, as necessary. One who had more faith by knowing the Word of God better or by proving it more often, would have more faith tomorrow, also. Not so with the gift of healing. There are "gifts," that is, plural, separate, single gifts of healing. (See "gifts of healing" in verse 9 and "gifts of healing"[plural] in verse 28 and "gifts of healing" in verse 30.) That is, when God gives a gift for a certain person to be healed, if another person is to be healed at a different time, it takes another gift of healing for that, too.

God does not intend for every person to be healed, so He does not give any person a single, always-present gift to heal everyone.

Paul had a gift of healing to cast out a devil in the slave girl in Acts 16. He had a gift of healing when he healed the father of Publius on the island of Melita in Acts 28:7,8. He did not have the gift of healing for Timothy's weak stomach (I Tim. 5:23). He did not have the gift of healing for Trophimus whom he left sick at Miletum (II Tim. 4:20).

The same thing is true about the gift of tongues. The gift of tongues is never given to everybody. But it is also true it was never given to anybody as a permanent gift to be exercised at will.

In Acts 2 we have one clear case where God gave the gift of tongues and for the particular purpose that people could hear the Gospel in their own tongue in which they were born. We cannot be sure that there is any other single case clearly mentioned in the Bible. Twice more, in Acts 10 and Acts 19, people "spake in tongues," but that simply means speaking in languages, probably foreign languages, and they may well have been natural languages. The Bible does not say that they spoke in tongues unknown to them nor by a miracle and, of course, we have no right to insist that it was a miracle.

But in any case, tongues is the last and least of the gifts, and there would rarely be an occasion when there is any need to talk to people in a foreign language which one had to know miraculously, not having learned it. The Bible never hints that any person in Bible times had a permanent gift of tongues and could use it for his own enjoyment daily or regularly.

We may be sure also that no one was given an ever-present permanent power to work miracles at his will. At separate times, in answer to prayer and faith, and when it was in the will of God, He would give a gift of miracles to someone.

II. GIFT OF HEALING SEEMS TO HAVE COME ONLY IN ANSWER TO EARNEST PRAYER AND GOD-GIVEN FAITH

The Lord Jesus had given the apostles power to cast out devils, but when the devil-possessed boy was brought to them (Mark 9 and Matt. 17), they could not cast out the devil. And why? Because of their unbelief. And an explanation given is, "Howbeit this kind goeth not out but by prayer and fasting." The apostles had no gift of healing that was automatic without prayer and waiting on God and being in the will of God on the matter.

Paul cast out the demon in the slave girl at Philippi but only after she cried after Paul and Silas for some days. Paul then got faith and assurance to cast the demon out!

And the Scripture in James 5:13-16 clearly indicates that God may give faith for healing and heal people any time when sick people call for the elders of the church and they pray over him, anointing him with oil in the name of the Lord. The "the prayer of faith shall save the sick, and the Lord shall raise him up; and if he have committed sins, they shall be forgiven him," we are told.

It would be expected that godly men, elders or pastors of a church, and spiritual leaders might be more effective in prayer than others. Naturally one would want his pastor or pastors to pray for him. And that is proper and right. But in any such case there is no suggestion that some particular people would have a gift of healing at will. No, in every case, as people waited on God and prayed, if God gave the faith He would give the healing.

We believe that gifts of healing and the other gifts of the Spirit are for us today, but only as God gives severally as He will and only when they will be worked in the will and plan of God. God does not casually put all the volts of Heaven's power in the hands of any man to use as he will. The gifts of the Spirit are subject to the will of God and are given as God wills to penitent, pleading people who wait on Him in faith.

CHAPTER V

Not Always God's Will to Heal the Sick

We suppose it is usually God's will to heal the sick. Nearly every Christian has had times of sickness, then recovered by the blessing of God. Sometimes people think that doctors, nurses, hospitals, medicines, treatments, exercises and diets heal the sick. Actually, the more sensible of us all think that healing is usually natural. God has put certain powers of recuperation in the body and that it is God Himself who does all healing, whether or not doctors and medicine and treatments are used. Usually it is God's will to heal the sick.

But it ought not be hard to show from the Bible that it is not always the will of God to heal sick people, either by natural means or by a miraculous intervention.

If it were always God's will to heal the sick, then why could not a Christian be healed every time he needed it and live a thousand years or more? If it were always God's will to heal the sick, surely He would not have placed Cherubims with a flaming sword at the gate of Eden to keep man out "lest he put forth his hand, and take also of the tree of life, and eat, and live for ever" (Gen. 3:22-24).

No, it is never hinted in the Bible that Christians always have the right, purchased on the cross, to be completely well. It is not always God's will to heal sick people, even the best Christians.

I. BEST BIBLE CHRISTIANS NOT ALWAYS HEALED

The Apostle Paul is a wonderful illustration of this fact. He said:

"And lest I should be exalted above measure through the abundance of

the revelations, there was given to me a thorn in the flesh, the messenger of Satan to buffet me, lest I should be exalted above measure. For this thing I besought the Lord thrice, that it might depart from me. And he said unto me, My grace is sufficient for thee: for my strength is made perfect in weakness. Most gladly therefore will I rather glory in my infirmities, that the power of Christ may rest upon me. Therefore I take pleasure in infirmities, in reproaches, in necessities, in persecutions, in distresses for Christ's sake: for when I am weak, then am I strong."—II Cor. 12:7-10.

Notice how earnestly Paul prayed: he "besought the Lord," not once but at least in three extended periods of prayer. But God refused to remove that weakness, that "thorn in the flesh." It was "in the flesh," that is, it had to do with his body. It was physical sickness and weakness. But instead of healing him, God gave him grace day by day. And Paul was content.

There was a reason for that affliction of Paul, that "thorn in the flesh." It was "lest I should be exalted above measure." Sickness is not always bad. Sometimes it is good. One good man said, "Health is the best thing in the world besides sickness." And now, continuing in his affliction, Paul took pleasure in infirmities, in reproaches, in necessities, in persecution, in distresses for Christ's sake. He says also that one of the wonderful blessings of being weak and afflicted is that now the power must be of God and He must get the glory.

Then it is obvious that it is not always God's will to heal the sick. There is much evidence that Paul was frequently weak and sickly and that God got the glory. In II Corinthians 6:4 he said, "But in all things approving ourselves as the ministers of God, in much patience, in afflictions, in necessities, in distresses." Yes, "afflictions" come from God and honor Him.

And in II Corinthians 1:8 Paul wrote of "our trouble which came to us in Asia, that we were pressed out of measure, above strength, insomuch that we despaired even of life." And he said, ". . . though our outward man perish, yet the inward man is renewed day by day" (II Cor. 4:16).

It is probable that Paul suffered all his life with weak eyes. His compassionate converts, he said, would have plucked out their own eyes for him (Gal. 4:15). He did not usually write his own letters. Tertius wrote one for him (Rom. 16:22). The epistles to the Philippians and Colossians had salutations from "Paul and Timotheus," and we suppose that Timothy did the actual writing at the words of Paul. But Paul signed the letter to the Corinthians—"The salutation of me Paul with mine own hand"—after it was written by another.

In Galatians 6:11 Paul said, "Ye see how large a letter I have written unto you with mine own hand." But Dr. Scofield says it would be better translated "with how large letters." He says:

> The apostle was, it appears from many considerations, afflicted with ophthalmia, a common disease in the East, to the point almost of total blindness (e.g. Gal. 4.13-15). Ordinarily, therefore, he dictated his letters. But now, having no amanuensis at hand, but urged by the spiritual danger of his dear Galatians, he writes, we cannot know with what pain and difficulty, with his own hand, in the 'large letters' his darkened vision compelled him to use.

We note this carefully because it is quite evident that all his days Paul suffered sickness, weakness and pain, and it may be this was the thorn in the flesh which continually grieved and troubled him.

Surely because He did not heal Paul, this makes very clear it is not always God's will to heal the sick.

Timothy also seemed to have been the victim of continual infirmity. Paul was inspired to say to him in I Timothy 5:23, "Drink no longer water, but use a little wine for thy stomach's sake and thine often infirmities." He needed unfermented wine, fruit juices with their vitamins, for the oft infirmities, the upset stomach, the indigestion that came to this earnest young man, a traveling preacher, eating all kinds of food and living in every kind of community. It is not always God's will to heal; He did not heal Timothy's "often infirmities."

In II Timothy 4:20 Paul said, "Erastus abode at Corinth: but Trophimus have I left at Miletum sick." What, could not Paul have his dear friend and fellowworker Trophimus healed? No, he could not.

IT IS NOT ALWAYS GOD'S WILL TO HEAL THE SICK. He never said so. It is presumptuous for anyone else to say so. Although healing is in the atonement in the sense of our perfect resurrected bodies, they are not yet available. And all Christ purchased for us has not yet been delivered. When Pentecostal people and others teach that it is God's will for every Christian to be well and strong, he teaches what is contrary to the Bible and contrary to facts.

II. PRESENT-DAY HEALERS ALSO ARE SICK AND DIE LIKE ALL OTHERS

There is evidence that the most fervent and active people in what they call divine healing die just as young as others, often younger.

Jack Coe, one of the most famous of the healing evangelists, died at 38 years of bulbar polio, complicated by pneumonia and lung abscess, according to newspaper reports. He operated the Dallas Revival Center and the Herald of Healing at Waxahachie, Texas. When he was taken sick he was rushed to the hospital and then to another hospital where he died. Despite all his insistence that it was God's will for everybody to be healed and his idea that doctors and medicine were wrong, he was sick, he went to the hospitals, he had doctors, and he died at age 38.

Evangelist A. A. Allen, another of the best known healing evangelists, died at the age of 59.

Dr. A. J. Gordon, eminent Baptist pastor and the founder of Gordon College, who believed it was always God's will to heal and that there was never any need for doctors and medicine, that these showed a lack of faith, yet he died at 59.

The newspaper reported last week that Kathryn Kuhlman was seriously sick and in the hospital. Yet she has said that perfect healing is the right of every Christian. It didn't work in her case. (A week later the report came that Miss Kuhlman had died.)

In Dallas, Texas, I once announced in the newspaper that I would be preaching on "Spiritism, Fortunetelling and False Prophets." A man came to see me greatly distressed. He said his wife was a fortuneteller, and handed me her card. The card announced that she was a gospel preacher, evangelist, healer who could foretell the future, could help people with problems of love, marriage and business. He protested that I ought not preach against that which his wife believed and practiced.

I asked him, "Where is she? Why didn't she come to see me?"

He answered, "She is in bed with inflammatory rheumatism."

Although she set herself up to heal others, she could not heal herself nor have herself healed.

Dr. A. B. Simpson, the distinguished founder of the Christian and Missionary Alliance, was a devout believer in divine healing. He believed it was wrong to use doctors and medicine. He believed it was always God's will to heal. Yet he had long months and years of suffering, and despite earnest, beseeching prayers of his own and those of many others, he died in pain.

God does often heal the sick. Praise the Lord that He invites us to pray over every time of trouble. He says that "the prayer of faith shall save the sick." But He does not always give faith because it is not always His will to heal the sick.

III. SICKNESS, WEAKNESS, DEATH ARE COMMON LOT OF ALL

All the disease, the weakness and death entered the world by sin. God plainly said to Adam and Eve about the tree of forbidden fruit, ". . .in the day that thou eatest thereof thou shalt surely die" (Gen. 2:17). The very day they sinned, Adam and Eve not only became dead in trespasses and in sins spiritually, but death entered into their bodies and they began to die.

This truth is borne out in Romans 5:12, "Wherefore, as

by one man sin entered into the world, and death by sin; and so death passed upon all men, for that all have sinned." Now death is passed upon all men everywhere.

Hebrews 9:27 says, ". . .it is appointed unto men once to die."

In James 1:15 the same truth is plainly stated, ". . .and sin, when it is finished, bringeth forth death."

Some people think that when men are saved, God repeals all His rules, but that is not true. Some people think that when they repent, all the curse of the past is instantly gone, and that since they are forgiven there is no penalty yet to be paid for sin. But they are mistaken. Many good and noble Christians have ignored the clear teaching of God, but it is still true that sickness, weakness, and death are the common lot of all mankind!

Some Christians learn the beautiful, marvelous truth that God answers prayer, that God has all power, and that always, in every trouble, we are invited to call upon Him for help. So they leap to the conclusion that all the inbred results of sin are gone, and that now it is always God's will to heal, that any person may believe and be completely healed of all sickness. Some men have themselves been healed wonderfully, and then, preaching largely their experience instead of the Scriptures, or making the Scriptures fit their own understanding of their experience, they ignore the clear teaching that all men are yet sinners and so under the curse of sin.

It is true that Christians are forgiven sinners. It is true that the eternal damnation which is due sinners has been removed by the atoning death of Christ. But the fact of sin and the death and disease and limitations which sin brings are still facts that must be faced.

So noble men of God taught that healing was available for the body, complete healing, instant healing, in answer to the prayer of faith. But they themselves eventually came to die. Dr. John Roach Straton of famous Calvary Baptist Church, New York City, was a most ardent advocate of complete healing for the body. But Dr. Straton sickened and died. Dr. A. B. Simpson, one of the noblest men of God, made much of divine healing. But eventually Dr. Simpson sickened and, after a long period of depression, died.

Mrs. Aimee Semple McPherson had great crowds over America, and particularly in the Angelus Temple in Los Angeles. She laid great emphasis on the healing of the body, stressing that it was always God's will to heal the sick and that only unbelief prevented healing. Yet she herself was sick, was treated in hospitals, and eventually died of an overdose of sleeping tablets, as I understand.

From all I hear, Dr. Alexander Dowie, who made much of healing and had great healing campaigns, must have been a good and sincere man. To be sure, he became fanatical and fell into disrepute and brought reproach upon the cause of Christ. But eventually he died a disappointed and disillusioned man.

As mentioned, Jack Coe died at 38 of bulbar polio. He had a lung abscess and pneumonia. His body was subject to the same weakness and sickness of other people. The congregation prayed for Coe "around the clock" hour after hour after hour, and medical science did all that it could do. But the healer could not get healing for himself. He was a comparatively young man when he died, living out only half of the life expectancy of a strong man.

There is a sense in which everybody in the world is sick already. Anyone who has a decayed tooth is sick. Anyone who has to wear glasses is sick. Anyone who has a hearing loss is sick. Any man whose hair is coming out so he becomes bald is sick. Anyone who has inflamed tonsils is sick. One who has athlete's foot is sick. No living person is perfectly well.

Why should I fool myself, deceive myself that I have perfect health. I am 80 years old, and nominally counted well and strong. But the truth is, in college football I had a broken nose. It is still crooked and one nasal passage is almost closed.

In 1956 I fell in the dark into the basement in my office

at Wheaton, Illinois, and sustained a skull fracture. The thin bony structure under the brain was evidently cracked and the olfactory nerve was cut, so I cannot smell. I don't pretend to have perfect health. I have to wear glasses to read. That means I am sick. I have now and then a touch of neuritis or arthritis in a shoulder or finger. That means I am sick.

Now I rejoice in the blessing of God and His loving care through the years, but for me to pretend that I have perfect health would be foolish; so for anybody else. Paul had a thorn in the flesh. I think every other Christian has some such thorn in the flesh, too, though it will not be the same as Paul's, or has some "often infirmities" like Timothy. It is not God's will to heal everybody.

That will come, praise God, at the resurrection, and what a glorious thing it will be! Jesus said, "In the world ye shall have tribulation: but be of good cheer; I have overcome the world" (John 16:33). We can have help in our weakness. Psalm 34:19 says, "Many are the afflictions of the righteous: but the Lord delivereth him out of them all."

There is the true picture. The best Christians in the world have afflictions, but the Lord is present to help, to comfort, to make the evil into good, to make all things work together for good. He can heal wonderfully when it is His will. He can give grace for the thorn in the flesh when it is not His will to remove it.

Paul the apostle was conscious of this great truth of God's help in suffering, so he was inspired to say in II Corinthians 4:7-12:

"But we have this treasure in earthen vessels, that the excellency of the power may be of God, and not of us. We are troubled on every side, yet not distressed; we are perplexed, but not in despair; Persecuted, but not forsaken; cast down, but not destroyed; Always bearing about in the body the dying of the Lord Jesus, that the life also of Jesus might be made manifest in our body. For we which live are alway delivered unto death for Jesus' sake, that the life also of Jesus might be made manifest in our mortal flesh. So then death worketh in us, but life in you."

IV. HEALING IN ATONEMENT, BUT NOT ALL RESULTS OF ATONEMENT AVAILABLE UNTIL RESURRECTION

Some people say that since healing is in the atonement, therefore every Christian has a right to claim perfect healing all the time. I think they are justified in saying that healing is in the atonement, from Matthew 8:16 and 17:

"When the even was come, they brought unto him many that were possessed with devils: and he cast out the spirits with his word, and healed all that were sick: That it might be fulfilled which was spoken by Esaias the prophet, saying, Himself took our infirmities, and bare our sicknesses."

But we should remember that the glorified body, which we will receive at the rapture when Jesus comes to take us to Himself, is paid for in the atonement also. But it is not immediately available. We do not have resurrected bodies. The simple truth is, Heaven is purchased for me but I have not yet entered Heaven. That wonderful time is coming when there will be no more war between the flesh and the Spirit in my soul, but it is not yet mine. And so whatever perfection in body is involved in the atonement must wait until Jesus calls us forth from the grave or changes the living to meet Him in the air.

You see, all healing of the body in this life is only temporary and partial. A person who is healed will get sick again and die, if Jesus tarries. Even though Jesus raised Lazarus from the dead, there came a time when Lazarus again sickened and died. All healing now is only partial and temporary. You see, as far as the body is concerned, the full result of the atoning death of Jesus is not ours until the resurrection.

V. HEALING OFTEN WAITS UNTIL CHRISTIANS CONFESS AND FORSAKE SIN

James 5:16 says, "Confess your faults one to another, and pray one for another, that ye may be healed." A worldly life would certainly hinder one's healing. A careless and frivolous attitude toward the Bible would certainly hinder God's answer to prayer about healing. I do not believe God is likely to show His mighty power, as He showed it in New Testament times with signs and wonders and miracles of healing, when those prayers are offered to Mary or in a jabber in tongues, or when women are put in leadership in the pulpit or church, or when they associate with modernists and infidels, and otherwise fail of strict New Testament standards.

VI. SUCH WONDERFUL HEALINGS IN ANSWER TO PRAYER SURELY ASSOCIATED WITH GREAT SOUL-WINNING POWER

Mark 16:17 says, "These signs shall follow them that believe. . . ." He has just given the command to go to all the world and preach the Gospel to every creature and then says, "these signs shall follow them that believe. . . ." There is a connection here between personal witness, soul-winning power, and wonderful healings in answer to prayer following.

It is not surprising that we read in Acts, chapter 2, of three thousand people saved, and later about five thousand and then "multitudes both of men and women" saved. And right along with these we find the mighty power of God shown in healing the sick. Peter who preached with such power could walk along the street and his shadow falling on sick people would be used of God to heal them (Acts 5:12,14).

I believe it more important to see one soul saved and kept out of Hell forever than to see many people healed of some incidental disease of the body. One who does not put soul winning first is not being true to Christ. God has wonderfully answered prayer for me in healing many sick people, but I would be foolish and untrue to Christ were I to put healing equal in importance or above the importance of winning souls. Oh, how much more important to win souls than any other activity. Christ died to save sinners. The Great Commission centers on soul winning. One is not a good Christian who doesn't win souls.

In my own poor ministry, I have found that in the times of great revival when many, many people were being saved, and in the times of persecution for Christ's sake, then there were miraculous answers to prayer, and marvelous signs and wonders.

D. L. Moody never stressed healing especially, yet there were some amazing cases of healing in answer to prayer. John V. Farwell, a layman associated with Moody, tells of some of these healings in *Early Recollections of Dwight L. Moody.*

Charles G. Finney was a soul winner mightily blessed of God. Though he put no stress on miraculous answers to prayer, yet he tells about a woman who could not read, and when she earnestly prayed, God made it so she could read the Bible.

I believe that when soul winning is made the main thing and we pay the price in tears, toil, and in waiting on God for Holy Spirit power, then we may expect God to give us souls and, when necessary and when it can honor Him, some wonderful answers to prayer.

CHAPTER VI

Should Christians Use Physicians and Medicines?

In that very valuable book, *Miraculous Healing*, by Henry W. Frost, he especially uses the examples of A. J. Gordon, famous Baptist pastor, and Dr. A. B. Simpson, the godly founder of Christian and Missionary Alliance. Both believed in divine healing, believed it was always God's will to heal, believed that the use of doctors and medicines were unnecessary and showed lack of faith. Dr. Frost sums up the teaching on this matter:

1. Sickness resulted from the sin of the fall; so that all sickness is the direct consequence of sin, and special sickness is the result of special sin.

2. Christ came into the world to save men from sin, and from the consequences of sin; and hence, among other things, He came to deliver the Christian from the present, earthly consequences of sin, including physical ill.

3. Christ went to heaven to make good for His saints on earth His redemptive purposes; and as one purpose was to deliver them from sickness and even physical weakness, to be well and strong is a redemptive right and privilege.

4. The person who brings to the saint God's purposes of grace is the Holy Spirit; and hence, if the Christian receives and holds, by faith, the Spirit in His fulness it will mean to him the fulness of Christ's indwelling, resurrection life, both spiritually and physically.

5. Such being the birthright inheritance of the saint, the Christian has no need of a doctor or medicine; and hence, it is spiritually unjustifiable for him to have recourse to the one or other.

6. These blessings were for the apostles as members of the body of Christ; and as this body is one, irrespective of place and time, what was true for the apostles is true for all other saints.

7. It is, therefore, both the privilege and duty of the Christian, in case of sickness, to send for the elders of the church, to confess every known sin, to be anointed with oil, to offer the prayer of faith, and then to rise up and remain both well and strong.

Notice the proposition five above: ". . .the Christian has no need of a doctor or medicine; and hence, it is spiritually unjustifiable for him to have recourse to the one or other."

Now it is true that physicians are human. They do not always know what is wrong, and sometimes when they do, and do all that man can do, they fail. Sensible physicians know that all healing is primarily of God. They may call it "nature" when the blood conquers an infection, or knits a broken bone, or quells a fever, or when antibodies in the blood prevent catching smallpox or measles or cholera. But nature is simply a usual means God has of working. Doctors can help nature. The antibodies may help kill germs. Laxatives help restore normal elimination.

Physicians are human. We believe sometimes tonsillectomies and appendectomies and hysterectomies are unnecessary. Doctors have great training. They are oftentimes properly proud of their learning and skill acquired at great cost. They sometimes may be more eager to operate than is justified.

Then doctors, like the rest of us, want money. Some doctors are influenced too much by money. So now since it is legal and more or less respectable, many doctors murder unborn babies in abortions and get rich with this blood money. And perhaps if it were respectable and legal and as easily done and as profitable, the same kind of doctors might also murder others for money. I say, doctors are human and subject to the same temptations as the rest of us.

But, thank God, most doctors are not of that class but are men of high ideals, honestly dedicated to healing the sick and doing good. We believe that on the whole doctors are great benefactors of mankind. And God is pleased that physicians and medicines are used for the good of the people.

I. GOD USES MEANS IN HIS MOST SPIRITUAL WORK

Is it wrong to call for a physician to help in sickness! Well, is it wrong to call for a preacher to help in spiritual matters? You see, God uses men and means in all His spiritual work. God used men to write the Bible. It is true that God provided the very words, but He used men to write it down. He uses men to translate the Bible. He uses men to publish the Bible. He uses the printed page to get the Gospel out and get people saved. God uses means.

So God uses people to preach the Gospel, or to witness and win souls. He could have sent angels. In fact, He did send an angel to Cornelius, but the angel could not tell Cornelius how to be saved. That was not his business. Cornelius must send to Joppa to get Simon Peter to tell him and his family "words, whereby thou and all thy house shall be saved." God uses men in His business. Why should He not then use them in healing as well as in building church houses, or in passing out tracts, or in preaching the Gospel, or publishing a Christian magazine, or praying with a sinner? God uses doctors and medicines.

We are told that "it pleased God by the foolishness of preaching to save them that believe" (I Cor. 1:21). Not just the Gospel but the preached Gospel. Not just the Gospel but the Gospel filtered through human understanding, compassion, experience, tears and burden; the human being filled and moved by the Spirit of God!

I remember a young preacher who preached in the church of which I was pastor, and said, as he thought in great humility, "I don't want you to see me tonight. I wish there were a curtain before me here so you couldn't even see me but could just hear the Gospel." I told Mrs. Rice that since curtains are not expensive, he could carry one around with him if he really thought that. But he did not. No, God wants a human face and voice and features and tears and laughter and wisdom and testimony and experience. God wants to use men with all their personalities.

Somebody said about a certain preacher, "He puts too much of the flesh in his preaching." And that preacher reminded us that God wants the flesh. He said, ". . .present your bodies a living sacrifice." He wants your hands and feet and voice and tears, your testimony and your love, your joy to be expressed to get the Gospel out and get people saved.

So if God uses human means and people to get out the Gospel, why should He not use means in healing people?

II. GOD SPEAKS WELL OF PHYSICIANS AND MEDICINE IN BIBLE

Is it wrong to use doctors? The Bible never hints that it is. In fact, Jesus said, "They that be whole need not a physician, but they that are sick," and it is reported three times in the Bible: Matthew 9:12; Mark 2:17; Luke 5:31. Who needs a physician? Anybody who is not "whole," that is, not well, Jesus said. That makes the role of a physician respectable and right.

Luke is called "Luke, the beloved physician" (Col. 4:14). It does not say that he was *once* a physician. He was not like Mary Magdalene who, when she was saved, had the seven devils cast out. But this godly Christian man, used of God to write the Gospel according to Luke and to write the book of Acts, was still a "beloved physician." So Dr. Luke is a good model for doctors.

Nor does the Bible ever speak slightingly of medicine. In fact, Proverbs 17:22 says, "A merry heart doeth good like a medicine." And thus He honors a merry heart. It is good physically for you to be happy and good medicine also does good. There is not any slur against medicine here.

When Hezekiah was sick and about to die, he prayed earnestly to the Lord and God promised him fifteen additional years. Then the inspired prophet Isaiah said, "Take a lump of figs," and they took it and laid it on the boil and he recovered (II Kings 20:7). And the same incident and the same remedy are mentioned in Isaiah

38:21. That was medical treatment, wasn't it?

When Paul said to Timothy, "Drink no longer water, but use a little wine for thy stomach's sake and thine often infirmities" (I Tim. 5:23), wasn't that a medical prescription? The unfermented wine or grape juice was just as useful then as fruit juice is now, and doctors often prescribe it.

Even in the heavenly Jerusalem we are told about the tree of life which bare twelve manner of fruits "and the leaves of the tree were for the healing of the nations" (Rev. 22:2).

Ah, then, even in these glorified bodies God will someway have things so prepared that perfect and continuous healing will be ours forever. That is not true now, but it is still true that God is in favor of using medicines. Bicarbonate of soda is an antacid that people need some times. It is foolish to think evil of the wonderful things God Himself provided that are used for the healing of the body. God is not against medicine.

In the book, *Miraculous Healing*, Dr. Frost uses this illustration. A man may eat figs and find them wonderfully helpful to him. They balance the diet, and have a laxative effect. That is, he thinks, natural food and he probably bought them at a health food store!

But, says Dr. Frost, if a doctor should take the figs and cook them and extract the juice and put it in a bottle and label it "syrup of figs," and then prescribe two tablespoonsful after every meal, many of these who think it is wrong to take medicine would refuse to take that "drug," although it is the same thing God Himself prepared in the figs!

Let us remember, however, that our first dependence should always be on God and not on men. God can use doctors and does use them often in healing the sick. He often heals without doctors and without medicine, in answer to prayer. But in either case, whether with or without doctors and medicine, we should rely upon God and be glad to take whatever means He has provided for the care of the body and the healing of sickness.

As a young preacher, I was afflicted with tonsillitis, accompanied with fever. Once in a revival campaign I would pray most earnestly for God to clear my throat and make it possible for me to preach that evening. He would. But the next day the pain and the fever were there again.

At last I decided to have my tonsils removed. A date was set and an appointment with the doctor made. And that morning in our devotions I read II Chronicles 16:12, 13 which says:

"And Asa in the thirty and ninth year of his reign was diseased in his feet, until his disease was exceeding great: yet in his disease he sought not to the Lord, but to the physicians. And Asa slept with his fathers, and died in the one and fortieth year of his reign."

I was shocked. "In his disease he sought not to the Lord, but to the physicians. And Asa slept with his fathers. . . ." I took it as a reminder that I must take the thing to the Lord more seriously and pray about the operation. I did. The operation was postponed indefinitely. And very soon I met with a noble Christian doctor who insisted I leave off most fats and sweets which I enjoyed. I did, and I never again had inflamed tonsils. And I found that with proper diet I did not need an operation.

Let the warning be simply this: Always we should take our need to the Lord in prayer. And sometimes then the leading will be clear that we ought to use doctors and medicine and operations; sometimes He has other means, but always dependence must be on God and our first concern to please Him and to know His will.

Let us remember, then, that doctors and medicine can be used of God, and we have great respect for dedicated men and women of the medical profession.

CHAPTER VII

Some Miraculous Healings in Answer to Prayer Clearly Attested

The psalmist said, "I sought the Lord, and he heard me, and delivered me from all my fears." Again he said, "This poor man cried, and the Lord heard him, and saved him out of all his troubles" (Ps. 34:4, 6). Then surely it is proper to tell what things God has done for us.

I must admit and with shame that I have greatly failed the Lord in manifesting His mighty power in soul winning and in other matters. I have had all too rarely divine intervention, miraculous answers to prayer. But I would be remiss if I failed to give God the glory for some particular answers to prayer.

I. HOW GOD ANSWERED THIS POOR MAN'S PRAYERS FOR HEALING

1. My Father Raised From Deathbed

When I was fifteen years old, my father became very seriously sick. He had been so broken down in health that a specialist in Fort Worth, Texas, demanded that he lay everything aside for three months to regain his health. But my father said, "I cannot do it. I have a large family, and debts to pay. I can't do it." So he continued working until finally he was completely overcome. The doctor came to wait on him, and he did his best, but my father's life seem to be ebbing away. Another doctor was called in. And those two did all that medical skill could do, but it seemed hopeless. One evening they said to my stepmother, "Mr. Rice cannot live through the night."

That night I went out into the barn and knelt in the horse's stall to pray for my father. I pleaded, not knowing any special Bible doctrine but knowing that God answered prayer. As I started to return to the house I heard a voice under the buggy shed. It was my older sister Gertrude pleading for God to spare my father. I went into the house and there my stepmother was kneeling by the bed in the front room begging God to spare her husband.

The next morning at seven o'clock my dad opened his eyes and said, "Where are my pants?" Half laughing and half crying, my stepmother said, "You don't need your pants; you are sick." But he felt he had something to do. So he dressed and walked a block or so down to the little business district.

By the time Dr. Robinson harnessed his team to the buggy and drove by to get the other doctor, Dr. King, to come with him, my father had walked back toward the house and was sitting on the front porch. The doctors scolded him. "You get to bed! You will kill yourself." But my dad said, "No, I am all right. I will take a nap this afternoon." He ate luncheon at the table and in the afternoon lay across the bed for a nap, and that was that. Then he went on about his work and as far as we could tell, was in good health.

He went to Fort Worth to see again the specialist, who was amazed that he had lived through such a trial and was now so well. He thought that the country doctors had done marvels in saving my father's life. But Dad knew, and I knew, it was not the country doctors.

2. My Daughter Healed of Diphtheria in a Day

When my older daughter Grace was five years old, one morning she had a sore and inflamed throat. We gave her Milk of Magnesia and mopped her throat with mercurochrome. But the fever mounted. When it got to 105 we took her to the doctor. He looked her over carefully, took her temperature, saw the inflamed throat and said, "I feel sure she has diphtheria but we will make certain." So he took a culture from her throat, put it on a slide and sent it down to the medical laboratory. In a few minutes the telephone call came back. Yes, she had a virulent form of diphtheria. The doctor gave her a shot and our other baby a shot, toxin and antitoxin.

We went home. The county health officer quarantined the house. Mrs. Rice and I knelt by the bed and prayed, one and then the other, and again and again, until at last I said, "I believe God has heard our prayer." My wife agreed. The fever went down and it disappeared that afternoon.

We sent for the county health nurse and she came the next morning. No fever, no inflammation of the throat! She said, "Why, this child doesn't have diphtheria!" I said, "No, but she had it yesterday."

That morning Grace had said, "Daddy, can I get up?" I told her she had better stay in bed until we were sure she was well.

She said, "Am I still sick?" I told her I thought not but we would wait until the health nurse came to check. She sait up in bed and played with her dolls. The health nurse came, found no fever, no inflammation in the throat, pulled down the quarantine sign, the matter was finished! I know God answered prayer.

3. Mrs. Jewel Duncan Miraculously Healed of T. B.

In 1931 in Fort Worth, Texas, a Mrs. Kelly came to me asking me to pray for a sick woman. Mrs. Jewel Duncan had been sent home to die from the Kerrville, Texas, State T. B. Sanitarium. She had wasted away from 140 pounds down to 90 pounds. She could only speak in a whisper. After two years' treatment in those days when there were no antibiotic drugs, the doctor said to her, "One more hemorrhage and you will die. If you want to stay here, we will give you the best care we can, but there is nothing else we can do. If you want to die at home with your husband and your two boys, you may."

She said, "Let me die at home."

She came home. The despairing husband had already sold the house but was not to give up possession until his wife died. The two boys, eight and ten years old, had been given to relatives, and were to be sent to them when their mother died.

But Mrs. Kelly asked Mrs. Duncan if I could come pray for her. She consented. I went to the home. She could only speak in a whisper. I said, "I don't claim any special power. I just know we are always right to pray. If you wish, I will pray for you." Then I said, "If God heals you, will you give Him the glory and praise?"

She whispered that she would.

I said, "Will you check up in your heart and see if there is anything there that would dishonor God, any sin unconfessed?"

She promised to confess anything that God brought to mind.

The nurse brought olive oil. I put a little oil upon her forehead and I prayed, the olive oil being simply a symbol of the Holy Spirit who lives in that body.

After I prayed for her, I went away for revival services. Three months later I was back in Fort Worth and in the midst of a great crowd when the friends filed by to shake hands, here came Mrs. Kelly and Mrs. Jewel Duncan. I didn't recognize Mrs. Duncan, of course. Mrs. Kelly said, "You know this woman, don't you?"

I did not.

She said, "Of course you know her."

I said, "Excuse me, but I meet ten thousand new people a year. I believe I do not know her."

She said, "This is Mrs. Duncan for whom you prayed."

Mrs. Duncan, in beautiful health and weighing 140 pounds, with tears running down her face and laughing for joy, said, "Brother Rice, after you prayed for me it was two weeks before I was strong enough to do all my own housework and the family washing!"

I saw her two years after that seemingly in perfect health. Twenty-two years later she wrote me she was a buyer for Belk's Department Store of Greenville, Texas. Some thirty years after her healing she was still alive and well.

Oh, God did intervene and answer prayer.

4. Pastor's Wife Wonderfully Healed of Cancer

I was with Rev. Jack Adrian, pastor in Wichita, Kansas. The doctors found Mrs. Adrian had terminal cancer, a tumor in the brain. It had so spread doctors said it was not operable. The doctors frankly said she might live three months or six, but she couldn't live long.

The three of us, Pastor Adrian, Mrs. Adrian and I, knelt in the bedroom and prayed. I put a little olive oil on her forehead as a symbol to encourage our faith. And we prayed. God removed all symptoms of cancer. Mrs. Adrian was very active in the church and soul winning. She continued better and stronger than ever. That has been now nearly seven years, and she is still well and active and with no sign of cancer. God wonderfully intervened.

I could tell again and again of barren women made fertile, of babies given after fruitless years of marriage. I could tell when God sent the rain at Peacock, Texas, in the midst of a great drouth in answer to prayer, sent it within twenty-four hours. I could tell again and again of God's miraculous intervention. Oh, we have not as much New Testament power as we ought to have, but surely it is for us today.

I lay on your heart this Scripture again:

"Is any among you afflicted? let him pray. Is any merry? let him sing psalms. Is any sick among you? let him call for the elders of the church; and let them pray over him, anointing him with oil in the name of the Lord: And the prayer of faith shall save the sick, and the Lord shall raise him up; and if he have committed sins, they shall be forgiven him. Confess your faults one to another, and pray one for another, that ye may be healed. The effectual fervent prayer of a righteous man availeth much."—Jas. 5:13-16.

II. MANY GODLY MEN REPORT MIRACULOUS HEALINGS

In my book, *Prayer—Asking and Receiving*, which God has blessed with an amazing circulation of about a quarter of a million copies in English and translations in eight foreign languages, I use some wonderful testimonies about miraculous healings. And these testimonies are from the most reputable, godly men, and are often documented so that honest people cannot well doubt them.

1. Dr. H. A. Ironside

Dr. H. A. Ironside, who was for eighteen years pastor of the famous Moody Church in Chicago, had this article in *Our Hope* magazine August, 1942:

> No instructed Christian can help acknowledging the power of the Lord to heal the body as well as to save the soul. He who credits the miracles of the New Testament, as every sincere Christian must, necessarily recognizes the healing power of God. . . .God can heal. God has healed. God does heal. He heals in answer to prayer. He heals where there is no prayer at all by the recuperative power of nature. He heals, as in Hezekiah's case, by the use of means. He has often healed in answer to the prayer of the individual who was sick, or of others who prayed for him. There are too many reputable testimonies at the present time to such healings to question them for a moment.

2. Dr. W. B. Riley

Dr. Riley was pastor of the First Baptist Church of Minneapolis, the largest Baptist church in the Northern Baptist Convention. He was the founder and president of the American Fundamentals Association, and the author of many books. And in his little book, *Saved or Lost?* he tells of the wonderful healing of Miss Hollister.

> Miss Hollister, of Minneapolis, for seven years lay on a couch on the fifth floor in Syndicate Arcade, her right lower limb shriveled and drawn; and yet one day, as she and others prayed, Jesus of Nazareth, the Physician of all physicians, passed that way and she heard Him say: "I will; be thou whole." Instantly that weariness, that waiting, that affliction was at an end!

> From that moment she walked these streets on two good feet, entered this house of prayer scores and scores of times, bore her testimony in our prayer meetings again and again, as to how, by one touch, one speech from the

Master's lips, her weariness and waiting were at an end!

3. Dr. Henry W. Frost of China Inland Mission

In the book, *Miraculous Healing*, by Dr. Henry W. Frost, bearing the special endorsement of Dr. Charles G. Trumbull, late editor of the *Sunday School Times*, Dr. Frost gives the story of six healings which he plainly marks as miraculous, since they were instantaneous and since the healings were performed without the usual natural means.

One instance was where he himself was instantly healed in answer to prayer after he had about given up to die. Another was the healing of Hudson Taylor, the founder of the China Inland Mission, which happened when only he and Mr. Taylor and Mrs. Taylor were present on a houseboat in China and Mr. Taylor was at the point of death. Another was of the marvelous healing of an insane woman. Another yet was the healing of a well-known Bible teacher who has recently gone to Glory. Another was the instant healing of Dr. Frost's own son after long prayer and after doctors had utterly failed.

4. Charles G. Finney Tells of Woman Miraculously Taught to Read

God works miracles in answer to prayer!

In his autobiography, Charles G. Finney, the great evangelist, tells of many miracles: men struck dead for opposing revivals; sinners falling in many, many cases, unable to lift themselves up; of the Holy Spirit's revealing to himself and others what God would do. But here is Finney's account of how a woman, in answer to prayer, was instantly given the ability to read the Bible, when before she did not know even the alphabet:

> I addressed another, a tall dignified looking woman, and asked her what was the state of her mind. She replied immediately that she had given her heart to God; and went on to say that the Lord had taught her to read, since she had learned how to pray. I asked her what she meant. She said she never could read, and never had known her letters. But when she gave her heart to God, she was greatly distressed that she could not read God's Word.

"But I thought," she said, "that Jesus could teach me to read; and I asked him if he would not please to teach me to read his word." She said, "I thought when I had prayed that I could read. The children have a Testament, and I went and got it; and I thought I could read what I had heard them read. But," she said, "I went over to the school ma'am, and asked her if I read right; and she said I did; and since then," said she, "I can read the word of God for myself."

I said no more; but thought there must be some mistake about this as the woman appeared to be quite in earnest, and quite intelligent in what she said. I took pains afterwards to inquire of her neighbors about her. They gave her an excellent character; and they all affirmed that it had been notorious that she could not read a syllable until after she was converted. I leave this to speak for itself; there is no use in theorizing about it. Such, I think, were the undoubted facts.

5. Dr. Alexis Carrel Says He Saw Actual Cases of Miraculous Healings

Dr. Alexis Carrel, M. D., had in the *Reader's Digest* for March, 1941, an article on "Prayer Is Power." This scientist, Dr. Carrel, takes the position that miracles are a fact, often attested by intelligent, reliable people. The footnote to his article says:

> Dr. Alexis Carrel has long been impressed by the fact that many of life's phenomena cannot be scientifically explained. He knows, for example, that miracles of healing are possible; he spent weeks at Lourdes studying them, and will never forget seeing a cancerous sore shrivel to a scar before his eyes. Dr. Carrel concluded 33 years of brilliant biological research at the Rockefeller Institute in 1939. Among his many honors are the Nordhoff-Jung medal for cancer research and the Nobel Prize for success in suturing blood vessels. His *Man, the Unknown* was a best seller in 1935.

This Nobel Prize winner, this Rockefeller Institute scientist, has seen miracles with his own eyes. "He knows, for example, that miracles of healing are possible"; saw actual miracles of healing at the Catholic shrine Lourdes, spent weeks studying them "and will never forget seeing a cancerous sore shrivel to a scar before his eyes," he said. So

God still works miracles in answer to prayer.

6. Dr. Charles A. Blanchard Tells How God Raised the Dead

Dr. Charles A. Blanchard, late president of Wheaton College, Wheaton, Illinois, was the author of a blessed book on prayer, *Getting Things From God.* The book is published by the Moody Press of Chicago. Dr. Blanchard tells the remarkable story of a railroad engineer raised from the dead in answer to his wife's prayer.

A Railroad Engineer Testifies

I was a few weeks ago in the Eighth Avenue Mission in New York. On the platform by me sat a gentleman, to whom I was introduced, but whom I had never before seen. When the meeting had progressed for an hour or so, Miss Wray, the superintendent, called upon him for a testimony. He said: "Friends, about two and a half or three years ago I was in the hospital in Philadelphia. I was an engineer on the Pennsylvania Lines, and although I had a praying wife, I had all my life been a sinful man. At this time I was very ill. I became greatly wasted. I weighed less than one hundred pounds. Finally the doctor who was attending me said to my wife that I was dead, but she said, "No, he is not dead. He cannot be dead. I have prayed for him for twenty-seven years and God has promised me that he should be saved. Do you think God would let him die now after I have prayed twenty-seven years and God has promised, and he is not saved?" "Well," the doctor replied, "I do not know anything about that, but I know that he is dead." And the screen was drawn around the cot, which in the hospital separates between the living and the dead.

"To satisfy my wife, other physicians were brought, one after another, until seven were about the cot, and each one of them as he came up and made the examination confirmed the testimony of all who had preceded.   The seven doctors said that I was dead. Meanwhile my wife was kneeling by the side of my cot, insisting that I was not dead—that if I were dead God would bring me back, for He had promised her that I should be saved and I was not yet saved. By and by her knees began to pain her, kneeling on the hard hospital floor. She asked the nurse for a pillow and the nurse brought her a pillow upon which she kneeled. One hour, two hours, three hours passed. The screen still stood by the cot. I was lying there still, apparently dead. Four hours, five hours, six hours, seven hours, thirteen hours passed, and all this while my wife was kneeling by the cotside, and when people remonstrated and wished her to go away she said: "No, he has to be saved. God will bring him back if he is dead. He is not dead. He cannot die until he is saved.

"At the end of thirteen hours I opened my eyes, and she said: 'What do you wish, my dear?' And I said: 'I wish to go home,' and she said: 'You shall go home.' But when she proposed it, the doctors raised their hands in horror. They said, 'Why, it will kill him. It will be suicide.' She said: 'You have had your turn. You said he was dead already. I am going to take him home.'

"I weigh now 246 pounds. I still run a fast train on the Pennsylvania Lines. I have been out to Minneapolis on a little vacation, telling men what Jesus can do, and I am glad to tell you what Jesus can do."

Dr. Charles Blanchard was a great educator, a man of national prominence, a scholar as well as a devout Christian. It was not hard for him to believe that God had answered the prayer of a wife for her unsaved husband, and that he was brought back in order that he might be saved. And if it is hard for you to believe, then I ask you in the words of Paul the apostle, "Why should it be thought a thing incredible with you, that God should raise the dead?" (Acts 26:8).

That is an amazing story, but no more amazing than some in the Bible. And if Jesus Christ is the same yesterday, today and forever, He will not be raising the dead every day, nor did He do it every day in His own ministry on earth, but He can do it. And in this case it appears that He did. Either the man was in a coma and thought to be dead or he was actually dead. In either case, God miraculously healed him. The simple truth is that if you are going to have a miracle, God is not limited in what He can do.

And let us remember Jesus Christ is "the same yesterday, and to day, and for ever" (Heb. 13:8). It is not always His will to heal the sick. The normal way of healing people is through doctors, medicine, diet, exercise and such matters. He does sometimes miraculously heal in a moment. But let no one be arrogant and claim it is always God's will to heal the sick. Let no one set himself up as a miracle worker. Let no one set out to make a fortune out of the healing business. But, oh, let us leave the door open to call on God for what we need in every time of trouble and distress. And when God gives the faith for healing, He will give the healing.

An Honest Appraisal of Divine Healers' Healing Meetings and Their False Teaching

If someone quotes to me the verse, "Jesus Christ the same yesterday, and to day, and for ever," I will say Amen to that. If someone says that God is just as able and willing to heal now as He has been in ages past, I will agree to that. God is able, He has loving compassion, and He loves to heal people.

I know usually God's healing is done through natural causes and with medicine, doctors, nurses, exercises, diet and such matters. But I believe He also heals miraculously when it is His will. God can work miracles in answer to prayer when it pleases Him to do so. I also know that it is not usually God's will to use miracles instead of natural means in healing the sick. But I thank God that I have known some wonderful cases of healing in answer to prayer.

I. WHEN GOD GIVES FAITH AND LEADS PEOPLE TO PRAY, HE OFTEN HEALS THE SICK

In a preceding chapter I have given case after case where I know that God healed people in answer to prayer.

However, I do not believe that all who claim to be healed in healing meetings are really healed of serious diseases. I believe that some of the so-called healers are well-meaning but ignorant people. And some of them willingly stay ignorant because they have a good racket. I believe some are deliberate frauds. But some who trust the Lord to heal them are healed.

It is still true as James 5:14-16 says that "the prayer of faith shall save the sick." And the psalmist praises the Lord "who healeth all thy diseases" (Ps. 103:3).

Does God heal people in healing campaigns? Yes, if in His mercy someone is led to trust in Him and God gives him faith. Are people healed outside healing campaigns? Oh, yes. Sometimes people are healed in answer to their own prayers and in answer to prayer by others, but only as it is the will of God and as He gives faith.

But many times the most spiritual, godly people are not healed. God has a better plan. Very ignorant and poor people and poor Christians are often healed. Praise His name that He is a God of mercy! So I believe that some are healed when the doctrine proclaimed is not altogether scriptural, though it is probable in the healing campaigns that many who claim to be healed are not healed and that usually there are no miraculous incontestable cases of healing of terminal cancer and of other such killing diseases. We believe that the disappointments are more than the fulfillment people hope for and that more harm is done than good in public healing campaigns, with false doctrine and false claims. But we are glad to concede that when God gives a sufferer faith, God can and does heal.

II. DIVINE HEALERS, CLAIMING IT ALWAYS GOD'S WILL TO HEAL THE SICK, HAVE SICKNESS, NEED GLASSES, OPERATIONS AND DO DIE

Those who are known as divine healers or healing evangelists, those who hold large healing meetings, regularly teach that it is always God's will to heal the sick, that when one is not healed, it is simply because of sin and unbelief. They often teach also that the use of doctors and medicine is a sign of unbelief and dishonors the Lord. Yet these who make a lifetime work of divine healing and often have great financial income from healing meetings, get sick, have decayed teeth, wear glasses, have infirmities, and die like other people.

It is no sign of special wickedness that the healers are sick or die like others, but it is a sign that their teaching is false. When a healer is sick and cannot get healing, then he proves that what he has been saying—that everybody ought to be healed and could be healed—is not true.

1. Healing Evangelist Jack Coe Died at 38

But Evangelist Jack Coe, who taught that it was God's will to heal everybody and that only lack of faith prevented healing, was soon dead. We quote the following from the *Good News Broadcaster* magazine.

> A news report from Dallas, Texas, states that Evangelist Jack Coe, Texas faith healer, died there of bulbar polio at the age of 38.
>
> Earlier news releases indicated that Coe's condition was complicated by pneumonia and a lung abscess.
>
> He was brought home in a very serious condition from a meeting in Hot Springs, Arkansas. A few hours later he became unconscious. When he gave no sign of rallying but symptoms indicated that his condition was worsening, his wife had him taken to a hospital. After the doctors had diagnosed his case as bulbar polio, they had him transferred to another hospital.
>
> Prayer was made for Coe around the clock by members of his congregation, and medical science did what it could for him; but the disease proved fatal.
>
> He operated the Dallas Revival Center and the Herald of Healing at Waxahachie, Texas, about thirty miles south of Dallas, and preached extensively throughout the South.

When even the average person, saved or lost, lives beyond the age of 38, God must have intended to discredit Jack Coe's testimony that it was always God's will to heal the sick, that healing was in the atonement for everybody, and only lack of faith prevented every one from having perfect health.

Note that despite his teaching he went to the hospital, had doctors, but died.

2. A. A. Allen, Prominent Healing Evangelist, Died at 59 in San Francisco Hospital

A newspaper clipping is before me with a heading, "Evangelist's Death: Acute Alcoholism." The Associated Press from San Francisco says:

> The Rev. Asa A. Allen, noted evangelist who was found dead in his San Francisco hotel room June 11, died from acute alcoholism, Coroner Henry W. Turkel's office said Wednesday.
>
> "He was drinking heavily when he died," Turkel's assistant reported. "The cause of death was acute alcoholism and fatty infiltration of the liver."
>
> At first, the coroner's office said it appeared Allen had died of a heart attack.
>
> The body of the 59-year-old faith healer, whose headquarters were at Miracle Valley, Arizona, was found in his room at the Jack Tar Hotel here by his longtime associate Bernard Schwartz. The time of death was set at 11:15 p.m.
>
> Allen was in his underwear, slumped at a table. Schwartz reported Allen's brother, Jamee Allen, had telephoned him from Oregon to ask him to check on the evangelist's welfare as he was suffering from arthritis. Schwartz discovered the stricken minister.
>
> Allen's wallet contained $2,809, police said.
>
> He was known throughout the country for his evangelical revival meetings, which were frequently televised.

You will note that although he made much of divine healings, he himself had arthritis. We do not excuse his drinking liquor, but it may well have been that to somewhat deaden the pain, he drank. We don't know. At any rate, his death belied his teaching that it was always God's will to heal the sick, and it also indicated that there are great temptations to healing evangelists and the danger of immorality.

3. Miss Kathryn Kuhlman

From Los Angeles United Press International is a brief article with a headline: "Faith Healer Kathryn Kuhlman

Hospitalized." It says:

> Kathryn Kuhlman, the evangelist whose fundamentalist faith-healing sessions are broadcast by television stations across the nation, has been hospitalized in Los Angeles.
>
> A spokesman said Miss Kuhlman was suffering from "physical exhaustion and a minor heart flareup" and needed "complete rest" for at least a week.

More recent news reports say that Kathryn Kuhlman died at, I think, the age of 60.

I have no doubt that Miss Kuhlman had tremendous burdens, that she had tried to help many, many people. She did help many. But it is still true that what she preached and taught, that healing was in the atonement, that it is God's will to give everybody perfect health, did not work in her case. She had heart trouble and eventually died at 60.

But is not "threescore and ten" the more or less normal life span according to the Scriptures? And if she believed that perfect healing was for everybody, why did not she live longer? Why should she have heart attacks and other frailties that other people have? The simple truth is, however sincere and devoted Miss Kathryn Kuhlman was, she still died and had the frailties and sicknesses that other people have. Her doctrine on healing did not work for her. In fact, it is not true to the Scriptures.

4. Many Examples Illustrate It Is Not Always God's Will to Heal

In Dallas years ago was a godly, earnest Christian man. He preached divine healing, had healing services, thought it always God's will to heal the sick. Despite his teaching, he had an extended period of sickness and died at a moderately early age.

A prominent healer who insisted it was always God's will to heal the sick needed to continually wear glasses. It seemed not to enter his mind that if he could not get his eyes healed, then it was not always God's will to heal the sick.

This author preached in a united revival campaign in

Phoenix, Arizona. We rented a great tent without poles, sustained only by heated air pumped into it continually. We rented that tent from a healing evangelist. He did not need it for he had fallen and broken his leg and was in the hospital! However good a man he was, he could not get his leg healed except through the normal process of nature. He may not have thought about it, but surely that meant that his doctrine that it is always God's will to heal the sick was wrong.

In Dallas, Texas, I announced in the daily papers that I would preach on fortunetellers, spiritualistic mediums, etc. One woman healer who widely advertized herself that she could get people healed, that she advised in love, marriage and business and could tell fortunes—was distressed at my announcement. She sent her husband to see me saying that I ought not preach against any other Christian.

"Why did not your wife come herself to see me?" I asked.

The husband answered, "She is sick in bed with inflammatory rheumatism."

Yet on her personal card she openly announced that she was a divine healer.

Some great and noble men, misled on this healing matter, died early and died in great distress.

Dr. John Roach Straton thought it was always God's will to heal the sick. But it did not prevent his getting sick and eventually dying.

Dr. A. J. Gordon, a Baptist pastor of Boston, founder of Gordon College, has a book, *The Ministry of Healing*, and he thought it was always God's will to heal the sick and that use of doctors and medicine showed a lack of faith. Yet he died after extensive sickness, died after a great period of darkness and trouble and disillusionment, wondering why he could not be healed and what was between him and God. He was a good man but his doctrine was wrong.

Dr. A. B. Simpson, founder of the Christian and Missionary Alliance, a noble good man, great preacher, believed that divine healing was always the will of God for Christians. Yet he had a lingering illness, hardening of the arteries and was in great distress because, despite all the prayers of many, he could not be healed. His continued illness and lack of healing proved that his doctrine was wrong. It is not always God's will to heal the sick.

Healers die like other people die. They have decayed teeth, they have arthritis, they need eye glasses, they go to hospitals, and eventually they die. They die as young on the average as other people do. That discredits the whole doctrine of healers that it is always God's will to heal.

III. MANY CONVINCED THEY ARE HEALED AND ARE HAPPIER

1. Any Healing Method Will Have Fifty Percent Success, Doctor Says

Dr. William A. Nolen, a Fellow of the American College of Surgeons, Chief of Surgery at the Meeker County Hospital in Minnesota, and on the board of editors of the Minnesota state medical journal, says:

> So let us admit that healers do relieve symptoms and may even, as I've already mentioned, cure some functional diseases. They use hypnosis, suggestion if you prefer, just as we M.D.s, to one degree or another, use it. They also encourage patients to think positively and may, by so doing, correct a malfunction of the autonomic nervous system.
>
> I know I've said this before, but it's worth repeating: half the patients who go to the office of a general practitioner have diseases or complaints that are self-limited, e.g., the common cold. No matter what anyone does for these people, they are going to get better. So the healers are going to achieve at least a 50 percent cure rate, even if they do nothing. Add to that 50 percent those patients whom the healers cure of functional disabilities—tension headaches, for example—and they are going to achieve an overall cure rate of 70 percent. We may as well admit this; it's a fact. (*HEALING, A Doctor in Search of a Miracle*, p. 307.)

Of course doctors know this. The state of mind has a lot to do with one's health. Often, simply to make the patient comfortable is to allow him to get well. In other cases, to make the patient happy and optimistic, take away his fears and worries, means that nature can more readily do its work.

2. A Cheerful Attitude Has Healing Power, Actually Helps Nature Heal

That is a Bible principle clearly stated in Proverbs 17:22, "A merry heart doeth good like a medicine." Then a merry heart oftentimes has the same effect on health as a medicine, the Bible says and doctors know. One of the main things people seek from a doctor is assurance that they are in good hands, that they are on the way to recovery, that they will be well. That is why a doctor's "bedside manner" is rated so important.

The truth is, very often doctors give "placebos," that is, some kind of medicine that will do no harm but will leave the patient knowing he is cared for and, depending on that medicine (which is no medicine at all), he has more tendency to get well.

When I was a boy, it was well known that doctors made bread pills by simply taking bits of bread, rolling them up in little balls, putting them in a box or bottle, with instructions to take one after every meal, or something of the kind, to help people get well. It was not a fraud. It did no harm. It was a psychological medicine they needed, not a physical medicine. It is surprising how many diseases are caused by the mind. Worry may bring migraine headaches. Tension may lead to a heart condition or cause a heart attack or a stroke.

Distress of mind can lead to a severe case of hives or shingles and a breaking out on the body. One man with an incurable breaking out on his body was finally relieved when it was found that the presence of his mother-in-law brought him such distress! When the mother-in-law moved away, he got well!

A woman's mental condition may bring on prematurely menstruation or may stop it altogether for a time. An attitude of mind may result in a headache, a backache, indigestion or sleeplessness. So if a doctor or a divine healer can make one feel better, can make one think he will now be healed, he may accept it and may for a time at least have the symptoms of his trouble removed.

That is one reason thousands of people have, at a healing meeting, thrown away their crutches and then found they had to take them up again, or thrown away their braces on deformed legs and found they must wear them again. They honestly thought they had been healed. They felt like they had been healed. Their feelings affected the symptoms and in some cases the symptoms were the main trouble. But where there was serious physiological sickness, it was usually not cured. The man who felt he was cured of cancer might soon die of cancer, as many, many have.

3. Natural Healing May Sometimes Be Credited to Healing Service

I have been a very active evangelist for many years. Some years ago I had a very painful attack of sciatica in my left hip and thigh. I was in citywide revival campaigns, and I can remember going on crutches to meals and then to the big Textile Hall auditorium in Greenville, South Carolina. I would leave my crutches in an anteroom, hobble to the platform, stand on one foot and preach.

Doctors gave me cortisone. I had chiropractic treatments. I had massage and careful diet. None of these, however, helped this very painful inflammation of the sciatic nerve until I took three weeks at home and rested. Then the pain and inflammation disappeared!

Now, had I gone to a public healing meeting and had them pray for me, I might well have thought that the healing was due to prayer. I know God did answer prayer, but I think He did that through normal means of rest.

Tuberculosis used to be called the "great white plague." There was no specific remedy for the infected lungs then. Now there are antibiotics. If the body could get enough rest, good food, sunshine and peace of mind, it often would heal itself. So people were simply put to bed with plenty of fresh air, given milk and eggs, and sometimes the body healed itself; perhaps more often it did not.

My younger brother Joe for a brief period worked in a mine in Colorado in the midst of a great deal of dust. His lungs were soon affected. He came back to Decatur, Texas, had a careful examination and diagnosis. The lung had developed TB.

A good doctor told him that examination of his lungs showed scars where he probably had had TB in the past and had conquered it and now it had flared up again. What should he do? Should he go to bed?

In this case that wise doctor told him no, that he should get plenty of rest every night, and correct his diet, but he should go ahead in his vigorous work with a dairy herd loading the trucks to go to creamery, etc. He did. With peace of mind, better diet, and stimulation of activity and plenty of rest, the tuberculosis was cured after a bit. The body tends to cure itself when it has a chance. Let us say God wonderfully has equipped nature; and how much He has given us in these marvelous bodies of ours! But had Joe gone to a healing meeting, he might well have supposed that in answer to the healer's prayer he was now made well.

I was surprised to read the other day a statement by Dr. Oral Roberts, famous Pentecostal and healing preacher, who has often said that God healed him in answer to prayer. I believe He did. But his book says that it took a year for him to be healed of TB. It may well be that there was a progress in healing by the forces of nature. God did the healing, but He did it through natural means, I would suppose, and in answer to prayer.

Don't misunderstand me. I know God can instantly, miraculously change the body and overcome a disease. I told elsewhere about a woman at the point of death with tuberculosis who was miraculously raised up, who lived for thirty-odd years more with not a touch of TB. But most of those who claim healing in healing meetings simply feel better. Maybe their feeling of good health (and that is a part of health itself) came because they were miraculously healed in a healing meeting.

Many are healed of arthritis or bursitis or neuritis, they say, in healing meetings. Well, I have sometimes had very serious painful arthritis in my right shoulder, sometimes in my right hand. Sometimes that comes and goes. I do not feel it right now. But when one says he was healed of arthritis in a healing meeting, then the arthritis may have simply disappeared normally but may return.

IV. APPARENT HEALINGS OFTEN THE RESULT OF AUTOSUGGESTION, HYPNOTISM, BRAINWASHING

There are many details of the healing meetings which are evidently planned to provide the psychological factors in convincing people that they can be healed, they will be healed, they are healed.

Remember, the healings are always in public services, along with singing, a great deal of emotion, with the insistence it is the power of God, always God's will to heal, etc. All the successful healers are great showmen.

It is not the quiet business as pictured in James 5:14-16 where people call the elders of the church to come to the home or the hospital bed to pray for the sick. No, there is a need for excitement, for the psychology of the crowd, for building up sentiment and expectation.

1. People Who Expect to "Fall Under the Power" Usually Fall Under Self-Suggestion

When people are touched by the "healer" publicly and fall to the floor "under the power," as it is called—is that the power of God? We think not. There is neither example nor teaching of the Bible to justify it. Nobody in Bible times fell when Jesus or Peter or Paul or others prayed for them.

Is it the power of Satan? Well, all we do or think wrongly must be in some sense evil, but I think in this case the regular, inevitable crumpling on the floor is simply the reaction of a mind somewhat hypnotized to expect it. It is a tradition long cultivated among "divine healers" and not from the Word of God. But people expect it and are taught to expect it.

In the healing meetings and talking in tongues, which go together, there is carefully built up an expectation, a desire, a feeling that this is the way to be a "super" Christian, so one longs to talk in tongues, earnestly seeks it, because that is called "the baptism of the Holy Ghost" and supposedly puts him in a class far ahead of all the Baptists, Methodists, Presbyterians and others. Also people are taught to think that if they did not fall to the floor, the Holy Spirit did not come upon them in power to heal, perhaps.

So, whether you call it autosuggestion, which is encouraged by others and in a sense a kind of hypnotism or brainwashing, people in healing services are taught to believe that now they are healed. Did not the healer insist that anybody could be healed and it is only unbelief to deny it or question it? Did not the healer insist that these are signs that we are in the last days and so there is a great pouring out of "the latter rain" and you can be one of that elite group who have the blessing of healing?

So because they have been told so many, many times that when a person is healed the part of the body affected feels very warm and that must be evidence that they are healed, they felt warm! If their need was mainly psychological and emotional, they are satisfied. If their trouble was primarily in the mind and now they have a settled, happy heart, they are less likely to have an upset stomach, less likely to have migraine headaches, and the body is more likely to carry on a normal healing function.

Healing services may ease the mind of many whose sickness is imagined or give a peaceful, happy attitude that does really help to heal many ills. But that is not the same as miraculous healing in answer to prayer such as is portrayed in the New Testament.

My wife felt greatly bereft when our six married daughters and their husbands moved away from us. Now gone were the big Sunday dinners with all the chattering, happy group together!

We soon moved to Murfreesboro and she said, "I don't like Murfreesboro! I am not happy here!"

I said to her, "You will not be happy anywhere until you get accustomed to being without your daughters."

Once she said to me seriously, "My back hurts! The doctor says there is nothing wrong with me but I know there is! What shall I do?"

Her distress was real but I knew the problem. I said, "Go visit one of the girls and it will be well!"

She made the visit and was well and happy as a result.

But any honest dealing with this problem of divine healing must make a distinction between that mental healing and actual miraculous intervention of God to make people well in answer to prayer.

Many who claim miraculous healings are mistaken, but if the trouble was the sort that a contented mind and assurance could heal, many have been healed. Or if they had a backache or arthritis or other ailments which alternately come and go, it is easy for them to believe they are healed. If it was an unseen cancer, then they may feel it is healed. They may refuse to go to the doctor for the examinations, refuse the surgery or cobalt treatments necessary. But because they are convinced they are healed does not prove they are healed in such a case.

2. "Healing Evangelists" Carefully Screen Those to Be Healed

Those who are selected to be healed (and all divine healers have one way or another of selecting people), those who are obviously the most "healable" are urged to come forward for healing. But those who have totally blind eyes, have a limb removed, or have a disease which has been clearly pronounced terminal, are usually shunted aside.

Sometimes they are required to meet three days in the services to see what is going on before they can enter the healing line. Sometimes they may not have enough faith, they are told, so they are put aside for another time.

My brother Dr. Bill Rice had a revival campaign on the island of Barbados. A healing evangelist had rented the big auditorium preceding my brother's engagement there. But the healing evangelist wanted to continue. So the authorities suggested that since both men were evangelists, that the healing evangelist and my brother should combine in the auditorium and the evangelist could have a healing meeting each night and then my brother Dr. Bill could preach to the unsaved!

My brother agreed to that heartily—with one condition. With him was the blind singer, Dr. Billy Renstrom. The condition was that the first person to be healed the first night that the healing evangelist was in the service would be Dr. Billy Renstrom. After he was healed of his blindness, then they would continue their healing service. The healing evangelist refused that condition, of course.

It would be hard to convince a man that his blindness is cured if he cannot see. Happily since that time an operation has greatly improved the sight in Dr. Renstrom's one eye in which his sight was not totally gone.

3. Many Heathen Witch Doctors Clearly Claim to Heal the Same Way

Reader, do not be insulted nor angry that we speak of those who claim healing as often being under hypnotic suggestion or being brainwashed to expect they will be healed and so thinking that they are, when many times they are not. The same thing happens with psychic surgeons in the Philippine Islands where thousands of Americans fly each year to be treated. The same thing happens with Norbu Chen in Houston, Texas, a profane man claiming to be a Tibetan healer. And the surprising thing is that these people have many, many friends in important places who are convinced that they can heal! (Incidentally, the psychic surgeons in the Philippine Islands also have talking in tongues in the services. But careful investigation for weeks by a physician, Dr. William

A. Nolen, and others have proved that the healings there are fake, except such as are psychological.)

In Africa missionaries have found a startling fact. Some people may pay a witch doctor to put a curse on a certain person they hate. That person then finds a little doll effigy representing him or her put in the home by the enemy, and pierced through with a pin to picture death. And many, many people are so convinced that when the witch doctor pronounces a curse they must die, some actually do die without any known reason except their fear and the fact they are convinced!

The truth is, when witch doctors or anybody else encourage people to believe they are healed, some people are healed. Every quack doctor in the world has some healings, enough to gain the confidence of some people. You see, the truth is that nature is on the side of healing. And those who expect to get well often do, whatever the medicine or treatment.

4. "Do Some Pentecostalist Preachers Intentionally Use Hypnotic Methods?"

That is a heading of Rev. Enoch Coppin's in his book, *The Charismatic Renewal and Pentecostalist Spirit-Baptism?*

Mr. Coppin speaks with more expertise on this question than many, since he himself had practiced hypnotism. He said:

> When 18 years of age in a territorial camp, I saw a young soldier hypnotise a group of men. I was convinced that any person bold enough could possibly do the same thing. When I suggested it the soldiers laughed at the idea but invited me to try. Immediately I was able to do the very things that the other man had done. That was the commencement for me of a two years' experience in the use of hypnotism during which period I made such headway as to be able to give public demonstrations.

On a strange occasion he hypnotized two soldiers on a train, was offered a booking in theaters as a hypnotist, then became conscious that Satan was in the matter and dropped it. Now he says on this question of whether Pentecostal preachers intentionally use hypnotic methods:

It would not be possible to say how many of them do, but when the writer was in Sydney, Australia, in 1956—_____,(name deleted, famous American preacher)—one of the best known Pentecostalist preachers, was conducting a huge mission in the Show Grounds. Most may remember that things became so hot for him that he fled the country. A man wrote to the paper and said he believed Franquin the Hypnotist who was also in Sydney at the time, could do any of the so-called healing miracles _____ was doing, and apparently Franquin felt he should have something to say in reply.

The following is an exact copy of his letter which appeared in the *Daily Telegraph,* January 26, 1956.

As a matter of interest I first heard of U. S. Evangelist Valdez, mentioned in another story on the same page as a "Miracle Healer" when I went to Honolulu initially. I had hired the Civic Auditorium which holds 5,500 people, for our show for ten nights. The operators of the Auditorium told me that Mr. Valdez had hired their building for two weeks day and night, just before our revival, and had then wanted to extend his tenancy.

They refused him on the ground he was taking too much money out of the town. His attempts to get the other large buildings and the football stadium were baulked by the Honolulu Chamber of Commerce. Valdez left Honolulu with what the Auditorium operators estimated was around $250,000. In America this is tax-free, and no accounting to anybody. This was my first introduction to Hot-Gospelling.

In Jacksonville, Florida, I was approached by a group of men who sounded me out on my religious beliefs or otherwise. Although my beliefs didn't conform with the leanings these gentlemen claimed to have, they soon came to the point and stated bluntly what they wanted with me. Briefly it was, they had seen my show 22 times. They were impressed with my abilities to control an audience, and handle people both individually and en masse, and after a lot of backing and billing they came out with a bold proposition. They would back me, provide me with a large Press and Public Relations Staff, give my wife and me a Cadillac car each, and after several months training in their ideas of the accepted usage of the Bible, they proposed to exploit my abilities.

I was to be an Evangelist and Healer. They even promised me the biggest tent in the world, triple-skinned and fully air-conditioned. In return for my services, my share was to be 25% of the gross, or a minimum of $100,000 a year tax-free.

My wife, who has somewhat orthodox religious views, was appalled. So was I, from different reasons, because even with my agnostic outlook, I have a certain code by which I try to live. To demonstrate their bona fides, and doubtless to impress me, the committee handed me a cheque for $40,000 which they told me I could cash as soon as I liked. All they wanted was my assurance that I would go along with them.

That afternoon I took the cheque to the bank to see if it would be met. The manager left me in his office for less than half a minute, then he came back saying, "How would you like it? In large bills or small?" I tore the cheque up and left the bank.

The writer still has preserved the actual papers. No doubt the 100 kinds of Pentecostalists would each deny it was their kind who acted as above, but the hypnotic element is the strongest factor in all Pentecostalist groups, and to escape being exposed, they loudly denounce hypnotism as of the devil, *while doing it religiously.* (pp. 86-88.)

We have no doubt that some people use hypnotism and autosuggestion more or less ignorantly. Some certainly do it intentionally.

And the tremendous amount of money raised in healing meetings is enough to tempt men to continue, even when they may doubt whether their work is usually authentic or not. Probably many prefer not to investigate that but not to lose a good thing.

V. MANY WHO COULD BE HELPED OR HEALED BY INTELLIGENT MEDICAL AND SURGICAL REMEDIES, DIE OR SUFFER NEEDLESSLY

However sincere those are who have healing meetings, it is still true that the doctrine they preach (that it is always God's will to heal the sick and that doctors and medicine are wrong) is unscriptural. Evil doctrine is wrong. It dishonors God, it is always hurtful in its effect. And so it is with this false doctrine.

1. Evangelist Sued for Injury of Boy Who Was Told He Was Healed, Threw Away Braces Still Needed

In 1956 this writer was in Miami, Florida, where Evangelist Jack Coe had just been arrested and was on trial. Doctors accused him of dangerously pretending to heal people who were not healed. One particular case concerned a little boy who had been brought to the Coe healing meetings, had been prayed for, and had been pronounced healed. Coe had insisted the braces be taken off his legs. However, the boy still was not healed. Doctors said that going without braces would have injured him permanently and the family brought suit for damages. That was a case where the healer did harm, and but for the intervention of those parents who insisted the boy put back on the braces, he would probably have been injured even more permanently.

That kind of story has come to me from hundreds of sources. How many people, thinking they were healed, threw away their crutches, then in pain and disability found they must buy other crutches, and aside from the shock and grief and disappointment, some were injured permanently.

2. Two Elderly Women Told to Throw Away Crutches: Both Fell and Broke Hips

Rev. Enoch Coppin of New Zealand, well-known author and Bible teacher, tells of meetings at Launceston, Tasmania.

> About two months later I was myself conducting special divine services in Launceston, so I made it my business to investigate the nature of that man's so-called miraculous "healings." This is a little of what I found. Two different elderly women on crutches attended the healing meetings and both, with others, accepted the invitation to come forward for healing by the laying on of hands. They were hypnotically convinced God had certainly healed them, and as was told them to do, they left their crutches behind while the hypnotic deceiver led

the congregation in loud praises to his "God." However as the congregation was leaving and the two elderly women were going down the front steps of the public hall, each one of them fell over and broke her hip. Friends sent for the Pentecostalist preacher but he would not come to their aid this time! You see, mental suggestion even of the religious kind would not heal broken hips, and the dishonest fraudulent Pentecostalist "healer" shrewdly but cruelly kept away. Nor did he even see them in the hospital. (From *The Charismatic Renewal and Pentecostalist Spirit-Baptism?* p. 41, by Enoch Coppin.)

3. Dr. Price's Healing Campaign in Vancouver

Mr. Coppin quotes the following:

Mr. A. Pollock states from an authoritative source that "after Dr. Price's four square campaign in Vancouver that there were 350 cases of healing claimed." Christian forces amalgamated to investigate the reality of the work. The findings were:

39 cases died within six months of the diseases they were supposed to be cured of;

5 of the cases went insane;

301 cases were found at the end of six months to have received no benefit; many frankly admitted it was so;

5 were reported to be actually cured but they suffered from functional ailments that responded to mental treatment.

At least in some cases, Pentecostalist "healers" ask for testimonials from those supposedly healed, before any doubts arise as to the permanence of the work. These are used for publicity and they state the name and church as well as the complaint. Though the supposed cure fails, the case is still quoted as if genuine, in tracts and books, together with photos. (From page 94 of Rev. Coppin's book.)

Dr. T. T. Shields of Toronto, Canada, published in his paper "the case of a young woman who was a diabetic kept alive by insulin injections until she came under control of a Pentecostalist. She refused to have the needle again believing God would heal her. But she died."

VI. REPUTABLE, SCHOLARLY SURGEON STUDIES KATHRYN KUHLMAN'S HEALINGS

One very careful study on this matter will give us more

light, perhaps, than many separate illustrations.

Dr. William A. Nolen, a physician and surgeon from Litchfield, Minnesota, graduate of the Holy Cross and Tufts Medical School, with a surgical internship at Bellevue Hospital, is author of the book, *HEALING: A Doctor in Search of a Miracle*. He is a Fellow of the American College of Surgeons and is Chief of Surgery at the Meeker County Hospital. He was formerly an attending surgeon at the Hennepin General Hospital in Minneapolis, a teaching hospital associated with the University of Minnesota. He is on the board of editors of the Minnesota state medical journal.

Some time ago he took two years to study the whole matter of divine healing. For example, he took extended trips to the Philippine Islands to see it first-hand and even live among the psychic surgeons of the Philippine Islands where thousands of Americans fly to be treated. He spent some time with Norbu Chen in Houston, a Tibetan healer, he claims, widely commended by many in important places. And he spent weeks and then months in careful investigation and study of Kathryn Kuhlman's healing meetings and following up the results in people who were healed or were told they were healed.

1. A Scholarly, Kindly, Thorough Study of Kathryn Kuhlman

Kathryn Kuhlman went regularly to Minneapolis for healing services in the giant auditorium, and it was always filled to the doors. Dr. Nolen was appointed an usher of the wheelchair division with the approval of Miss Kuhlman. And he interviewed many of those coming for healing then, visited and talked with Miss Kuhlman personally in detail, had legal secretaries take down the names and addresses of those who said they were healed, even had Miss Kuhlman's permission to visit them and follow them up personally, which he did.

Dr. Nolen's book is titled, *HEALING: A Doctor in Search of a Miracle*, and that is an honest title. Spending thousands of dollars and traveling many thousands of miles, taking up to two years' time, Dr. Nolen honestly tried to find cases of miraculous healing. On pages 64 to 68 he says:

> Occasionally Miss Kuhlman would turn and say, "Someone with a brace. . .a brace on your leg. . .you don't need that brace any more. Take it off, come to the stage, and claim your cure."
>
> The first time she called for a brace there was a delay in the proceedings. No one came forth. The audience began to grow restive; you could sense that they all felt this was most embarrassing for Miss Kuhlman. Finally, after what was probably a minute but seemed an hour, a very pretty young girl limped up to the stage. She waved her leg brace in the air and stood, with her pelvis tilted badly, on one good leg and one short, withered leg. Kathryn Kuhlman questioned her.
>
> "How old are you?"
>
> "Twenty."
>
> "How long have you worn the brace?"
>
> "Thirteen years. Since I had polio at seven."
>
> "And now you've taken it off."
>
> "Yes," she said, "I believe so much in the Lord. I've prayed and He's curing me."
>
> Everyone applauded. The girl cried.
>
> This scene was, to my mind, utterly revolting. This young girl had a withered leg, the result of polio. It was just as withered now as it had been ten minutes earlier, before Kathryn Kuhlman called for someone to remove her brace. Now she stood in front of ten thousand people giving praise to the Lord—and indirectly to Kathryn Kuhlman—for a cure that hadn't occurred and wasn't going to occur. I could imagine how she'd feel the next morning, or even an hour later, when the hysteria of the moment had left her and she'd have to again put on the brace that had been her constant companion for thirteen years and would be with her the rest of her life. She was emotionally high right now; soon she'd be emotionally low, possibly despondent.
>
> This case shook severely what little hope I had left that Kathryn Kuhlman was, truly, a "miracle worker."
>
> I had accepted as a misunderstanding the deception that went with "Not yours surely?"—referring to the wheelchair—even though I knew the man hadn't been in a wheelchair until that afternoon; I had chalked it up to

innocent error when the ability to take a deep breath was passed off as evidence of a lung-cancer cure (even though I knew most patients with lung cancer can breathe deeply); I had assumed that it was simple overenthusiasm that enabled Kathryn Kuhlman to call a multiple-sclerosis patient "cured," even though she obviously still walked with the multiple-sclerosis gait; but this episode involving the girl with the brace was pure, unadulterated, flagrant nonsense. For Kathryn Kuhlman to really believe that the Holy Spirit had worked a miracle with this girl, it seemed to me that Kathryn Kuhlman would have had to be either blind or incredibly stupid, and she was obviously neither. Was she, then, a hypocrite or a hysteric? I didn't know, but I had begun to seriously question her credibility and that of her organization.

Not once, in the hour and a half that Kathryn Kuhlman spent healing, did I see a patient with an obvious organic disease healed (i.e., a disease in which there is a structural alteration). At one point the young man with liver cancer staggered down the aisle in a vain attempt to claim a "cure." He was turned away, gently, by Maggie. When he collapsed into a chair I could see his bulging abdomen—as tumor-laden as it had been earlier.

One desperate mother managed to work her child's wheelchair down to the front of the auditorium. The little girl in the chair, about five years old, glassy-eyed, hydrocephalic, could barely sit upright. The mother, weeping, lifted her daughter out of the chair and attempted to get her to walk to the stage. The child, with the mother holding her, made two pitiful attempts to walk, both times nearly collapsing on the floor before the mother could catch her. Finally, weeping, the mother put her imbecilic child back in the wheelchair and pushed her away down the aisle. . . .

Before going back to talk to Miss Kuhlman I spent a few minutes watching the wheelchair patients leave. All the desperately ill patients who had been in wheelchairs were still in wheelchairs. In fact, the man with the kidney cancer in his spine and hip, the man whom I had helped to the auditorium and who had his borrowed wheelchair brought to the stage and shown to the audience when he had claimed a cure, was now back in the wheelchair. His "cure," even if only a hysterical one, had been extremely short-lived.

As I stood in the corridor watching the hopeless cases leave, seeing the tears of the parents as they pushed their crippled children to the elevators, I wished Miss Kuhlman had been with me. She had complained a couple of times during the service of "the responsibility, the enormous responsibility," and of how her "heart aches for those that weren't cured," but I wondered how often she had really looked at them. I wondered whether she sincerely felt that the joy of those "cured" of bursitis and arthritis compensated for the anguish of those left with their withered legs, their imbecilic children, their cancers of the liver.

I wondered if she really knew what damage she was doing. I couldn't believe that she did.

2. Serious Follow-Up of Those "Healed" in Kuhlman Meetings

Dr. Nolen got eighty-two names of people claiming to be healed in that service, all the names the secretaries could get down in the limited time in talking to people in person.

On page 85 he speaks about Rita Swanson who had a seriously scarred face from a skin problem, had been treated by dermatologists off and on for years. Miss Kuhlman, in the service, pointed in her direction and said,

"Someone there—someone in Section Six—is suffering from a skin problem. I rebuke that problem. In three days that skin problem will be cured." Rita looked around, saw no one else in her section with an obvious skin problem, and knew then that she would be cured.

Then on page 85 Dr. Nolen says:

There are two other points worth mentioning here, both having to do with skin diseases.

The first is that Kathryn Kuhlman did not say, and as far as I've been able to determine, never says, "Someone with a skin disease has just been cured." At her services there are instant cures of cancer, bursitis, hearing loss—all ailments that no one can see—but skin defects, which are obvious, take three days or more to cure. Kathryn Kuhlman wouldn't want Rita or anyone else coming up on the stage to claim a cure of a skin disease when it would be perfectly obvious to everyone that it was still there. It wouldn't be honest—and Kathryn Kuhlman is, at least in her own mind, honest—to plant in the audience someone with an unblemished face and have her come up on the stage and claim a cure. Besides, all those sitting next to that person would know the claim was false. Much better to promise skin cures for three days later, when the audience is dispersed and Kathryn Kuhlman is many miles away.

Then Dr. Nolen says that if a skin disease is from nerves, it may clear up when one is happy. But Miss Kuhlman never presented an obvious, visible case of disease as cured then. It was always to be cured later!

Dr. Nolen checked up on many of the cases and he gives this report:

Did the Kuhlman service even offer a remote chance that a patient with a malignant disease might be cured? Even though none of those who had claimed a cancer cure at the time of the service returned to Minneapolis to reaffirm their cure, I was anxious to find out what had happened to them. I wrote to everyone on my list who at the time of the meeting had claimed a cure of a malignant disease. I called or visited those who didn't respond. This is what I learned.

Case A—Richard Whalen, the twenty-one-year-old boy with what appeared to be cancer of the liver. He had tried to claim a cure, but Maggie had prevented him from getting to the stage. The legal secretaries had gotten his address.

Richard had died of his cancer twelve days after Kathryn Kuhlman's visit.

Case B—Leona Flores, the woman who had "claimed a cure" of lung cancer, and who had, on the stage, at Kathryn Kuhlman's suggestion, "proved" her cure by taking deep breaths without any pain.

Leona, it turned out when I contacted her, did not have lung cancer at all. "I have Hodgkin's disease," she said, "and some of the glands in my chest are involved. But since no one else got up when Miss Kuhlman said, 'Someone with lung cancer is being cured,' I figured it had to be me.

"I've been back to my doctor and he says he can't see any change in my X-ray. I think I breathe better than I did before the miracle service, but it's hard to tell, since I never had much trouble with my breathing anyway. I've had Hodgkin's disease for almost four years now. I still take my drugs regularly and my doctor says I'm doing nicely."

. . .Leona Flores, who had breathed deeply to a loud ovation at the miracle service, had definitely not been cured of lung cancer, Hodgkin's disease or anything else by Kathryn Kuhlman.

Case C—Peter Warren, the sixty-three-year-old man with kidney cancer which had spread to the bone. He is the man I helped to walk into the auditorium and for whom I found a wheelchair. He went to the stage to claim a cure of bone cancer. The wheelchair I had found for his temporary use was carried to the stage by an usher and put beside him as evidence of his cure. He was one of the many to whom Kathryn Kuhlman addressed the question, "Is that *your* wheelchair?" in a voice full of amazement; and when he answered yes she said, to a rousing ovation, "Praise the Lord."

On the stage Mr. Warren had performed, at Kathryn Kuhlman's suggestion, a number of deep knee bends to demonstrate his cure. I asked Mr. Warren's daughter, when I reached her two months later, about Mr. Warren's subsequent course.

"After the miracle service he felt real good for about three or four days," she said. "Then he began to get weak again and we took him back to the doctor. The doctor took some more X-rays and told us that the tumor had grown some more, and that was making Dad's blood drop. So he gave him a transfusion and changed his medicines around.

"Since then he's had to go back once a week for shots. He's losing weight and he needs pain pills now for his back.

"I guess Dad was wrong when he thought Kathryn Kuhlman had cured him."

. . .Case E—Mrs. Helen Sullivan, a fifty-year-old woman with cancer of the stomach which had spread to both her liver and vertebrae in her back.

At the miracle service Mrs. Sullivan had, at Kathryn Kuhlman's suggestion, taken off her back brace and run back and forth across the stage several times. Finally she walked back down the aisle to her wheelchair, waving her brace as she went, while the audience applauded and Kathryn Kuhlman gave thanks to the Lord.

Two months after the miracle I talked to Mrs. Sullivan. At that time she was confined to her bed, which had been moved into the living room of her farm home. Her husband was at work in the fields and Mrs. Sullivan's eighteen-year-old daughter, the youngest of her three children (the other two are married), had just arrived home from school and was busy cleaning the house.

Mrs. Sullivan was not thin; she was emaciated. Her arms weren't much thicker than a broom handle and her cheekbones were barely covered with flesh. Despite this wasting away, when she smiled you could tell that she had once been a pretty woman. Her eyes, though they were sunk far back in her head, still radiated a feeling of warmth. I liked her immediately.

"In September of 1971," she told me, "I began to have trouble with swallowing. Food would stick in my throat, but when I started to lose weight I thought I'd better see a doctor. He took some X-rays and told me I had a growth in my upper stomach and esophagus. They operated on me and found a cancer. They took out the part of the stomach and esophagus where the tumor was, but they couldn't cure me with the operation; the tumor had already spread to the liver.

"After the operation I could swallow pretty well, but I didn't have much appetite and I kept losing weight. The doctor gave me treatment with 5-F.U. [5-fluorouacil, a relatively new anti-cancer drug] and after I got over the nausea that the treatment caused, I felt better for about three months. Then I began to lose weight again. My doctor gave me another course of treatment with 5-F.U., but this time it didn't do any good.

"I knew about Kathryn Kuhlman from watching her television show, and when I read that she was coming to Minneapolis I got pretty excited. My husband tried to calm me down—he kept telling me not to get my hopes too high—but when you're awfully sick and someone tells you that you may be cured, it's impossible not to get excited. By the time Kathryn Kuhlman came to the auditorium I was just about sure I was going to get better.

"At the service, as soon as she said, 'Someone with cancer is being cured,' I knew she meant me. I could just feel this burning sensation all over my body and I was convinced the Holy Spirit was at work. I went right up on the stage and when she asked me about the brace I just took it right off, though I hadn't had it off for over four months, I had so much back pain.

"While I was up on that stage, bending over, touching my toes and running up and down as she asked me to, I felt just wonderful. I didn't have a pain anywhere. Even when we were riding back home [Mrs. Sullivan lives 130 miles from Minneapolis] I refused to wear the brace. I was sure I was cured. That night I said a prayer of thanksgiving to the Lord and Kathryn Kuhlman and went to bed, happier than I'd been in a long time.

"At four o'clock the next morning I woke up with a horrible pain in my back. It was so bad that I broke out in a cold sweat. I didn't dare move. I called to Ralph and he got up and brought me some pain pills. They helped, but not enough so I could sleep. In the morning we called the doctor. He took me to the hospital and got some X-rays that showed one of my vertebrae had partially collapsed. He said it was probably from the bending and running I had done. I stayed in the hospital, in traction, for a week. When I went home I was back in my brace.

"Since then, as you can probably guess by looking at me, I've gotten a lot weaker. I can't make it upstairs any more; that's why we've got the bed down here. Sometimes I can sit up to eat, but not often.

"I was awfully depressed for about a month after Kathryn Kuhlman's visit. I cried a lot. Our minister finally convinced me to forget about her and just put my faith in God.

"I know I'm going to die soon but I've learned to accept the idea of death. I've had a pleasant life. . .nothing out of the ordinary, I suppose, but I've had a loving husband and three children I'm proud of. A lot of women haven't had as much.

"I still pray a lot—not to be cured and not even to be free of pain; just to have less pain, so that I can bear it. And God answers my prayers. He never gives me more pain than I can stand. I'm very grateful to Him."

Mrs. Sullivan died of cancer four months after she had been "cured" at Kathryn Kuhlman's miracle service. (*HEALING: A Doctor in Search of a Miracle*, pp. 93,94,95,97,98,99.)

3. A Doctor's Diagnosis

Then Dr. Nolen gives his estimate, his kindly and considerate estimate of Kathryn Kuhlman and her work:

Which brings me back to Kathryn Kuhlman's lack of medical sophistication—a point that is, in her case, critical. I don't believe Miss Kuhlman is a liar; I don't believe she is a charlatan; I don't believe she is, consciously, dishonest. I think (and this is, of course, only my opinion, based on a rather brief acquaintance with her) that she honestly believes the Holy Spirit works through her to perform miraculous cures. I think that she sincerely believes that the thousands of patients who come to her services every year and claim cures are, through her ministrations, being cured of organic diseases. I also think—and my investigations confirm this—that she is wrong.

The problem is, and I'm sorry this has to be so blunt, one of ignorance. Miss Kuhlman doesn't know the difference between psychogenic and organic diseases; she doesn't know anything about hypnotism and the power of suggestion; she doesn't know anything about the autonomic nervous system. If she does know something about any or all of these things, she has certainly learned to hide her knowledge.

There is one other possibility. It may be that Miss Kuhlman doesn't want to learn that her ministry is not as miraculous as it seems. If so, she had trained herself to deny, emotionally and intellectually, anything that might threaten the validity of her ministry.

. . .I find it difficult to believe that all those who surround her are true believers. I know, for example, from talking to people who have attended many services, that one of Maggie's main functions is to find reluctant patients and encourage them to stand, claim cures and start the flow toward the stage—hardly an honest or honorable assignment.

I don't have anything more to say about Kathryn Kuhlman as a person. Having finished my report, I'm inclined to rest my case on the axiom, often used by the prosecutor in malpractice cases when a sponge has been found in an abdomen, that *res ipsa loquitur*—"the thing speaks for itself" (pp. 101,102).

I do not believe that the matter of cases of divine healing was ever studied any more carefully with scientific honesty than Dr. Nolen studied the work of Miss Kathryn Kuhlman and those who claimed healing in her services. I think her services were typical, and I think her case is typical. I think she meant well. She deliberately kept things in the background of her mind and did not want to know all that happened. Besides that, as she took in offerings of thousands of people and many of them were urged to give $25, $50, $100, we can see she had a bias in favor of that ministry.

The Scripture says, "For the love of money is the root of all evil" (I Tim. 6:10). That is, of every kind of evil. And "they that will be rich fall into temptation and a snare" (I Tim. 6:9).

VII. THE DISILLUSIONMENT, HURT AND HEART-BREAK OF DECEIVED PEOPLE IS TRAGIC

I can understand how grieved Dr. Nolen must have been to see people come so hopefully to the Kathryn Kuhlman healing meeting and saw the thousands of people who came hoping to be healed go away without healing. That was heartbreak often for them and for their loved ones.

1. Because Her Mother Died, She Said God Failed Her

A woman wrote me from San Antonio some years ago, urging me to pray for her mother who had terminal cancer. I wrote back and said I would pray but that I had no impression from God whether it was His will to heal the mother or not and that she must pray that the will of God would be done. If God encouraged her to pray, then pray earnestly, but that it is not always God's will to heal the sick.

She wrote back insistently. "Mother is all I have; God must heal her." She said she had prayed the prayer of faith and she knew God was going to heal her mother. She had been taught that in certain healing meetings and believed it.

Later she wrote back sadly disillusioned. Her mother had died and she said, "God didn't treat me right. God didn't honor His word. God took my mother, the dearest thing in the world to me, when in my heart I had trusted Him to heal her!" She might have been confident that her mother was going to be healed, but it was not faith based on a clear promise of God. It was not faith given by God. She had no right to claim except as God put faith in her heart. But the heartbreak and trouble were there.

Sometimes one who now loses all confidence in a divine healer who failed him then loses all confidence in God. Their hero or heroine, the one who seemed like an angel of light, had promised them they could be healed or a loved one would be healed. It didn't work out. So, was the healer a fraud? It may be the gospel they preach is fraudulent also. Maybe God doesn't really love people and care about them. And how much worse is the spiritual atmosphere of one who has been so seriously disappointed and feels that God has not kept His promise in healing. Their confidence was a false confidence and not based on what God had said but on what the healer said. The spiritual results are tragic. Sometimes such brokenhearted people have become mentally unbalanced and sometimes a lifetime of bitterness follows.

2. Dr. Torrey Tells of Man Who Claimed Healing Died a Few Days Later Insane

Dr. R. A. Torrey, in his pamphlet, *Divine Healing*, now published by Baker Book House, tells of many wonderful healings in answer to prayer. Expounding James 5:14,16 he says about the sick man:

> No, he is to "call for *the elders*," the word is always masculine. He is not to "attend meetings for three days" (or three hours, or three minutes) to get under the spell of psychological influences, that are akin to Coueistic autosuggestively therapeutic influences. He is not to be brought into the mesmeric atmosphere of a meeting where there is skilfully-planned, highly emotional music and swaying of the body and passings of the hand and shouts of hallelujahs, that excite the imagination and thrill the body. No, he is to "call for the elders of the church, and let them pray over him" in the calm and quiet of the home, and *"the prayer"* of (Spirit-given) *faith* is to "*save* him that is sick," and not *intense carnal excitement* temporarily *galvanize* him into brief activities, from which there is an appalling reaction, often leaving the poor victim of the religious charlatan worse than ever, and not infrequently sending him to the insane asylum or the cemetery.*

On that matter of the harmful effect and distress of the

public healing meetings and healing evangelists he continues:

> *The writer knows personally of some heart-breaking incidents of this kind under two of the most widely advertised healers of the present day, who have been drawing thousands to their weird and hypnotic gatherings. Listening to a story of a friend, a brokenhearted sister, whose brother, a consecrated Baptist minister, had been lured to these meetings and had been "healed," and whose healing had been loudly heralded, but who died in a sanitarium a few days later, a raving maniac, was one of the factors that led to the publishing of this book (pp. 13,14).

There are terrible results in teaching people to claim what God did not give and a false kind of pretended healing where people go away with false expectations and drink the bitter myrrh of disillusionment and failure.

3. Disillusionment and Heartbreak of Two Famous Men

The disappointment, heartache and sense of failure that comes to Christian people who expected to be healed and were not, is well illustrated in the book, *Miraculous Healing*, by Frost of the China Inland Mission. Dr. Frost has one chapter on two great men of God, Dr. A. J. Gordon and Dr. A. B. Simpson. Both were distinguished godly men: Dr. Gordon, a Baptist pastor and founder of Gordon College; Dr. Simpson, founder of the Christian and Missionary Alliance, a preacher at the tabernacle in New York.

Both of these men believed that healing was in the atonement for everybody. They believed to use doctors and medicine was a lack of faith and unnecessary. Yet it turned out that both of them had extensive illness and great times of trouble of heart over this matter because they were not healed.

Ernest B. Gordon, writing about his father, Dr. A. J. Gordon, says:

> "The physician was called and the disease pronounced

to be grippe, with tendencies to bronchitis. Then for days did he struggle on as in a blinding storm. The fever became violent and was accompanied with intermittent delirium. Night after night he lay in the agonies of a prolonged insomnia. He complained of 'the ceaseless storm, the incessant noise as of great raindrops on a window-pane,' though all the while the air outside was as still as an Indian summer. He would groan at 'the sudden bursts of blackness' which overwhelmed him 'as if he were felled with a club to the ground.' Often in those night hours could we hear him whispering John Angelus' hymn:

> " 'Jesus, Jesus, visit me;
> How my soul longs after thee!
> When, my best, my dearest friend,
> Shall our separation end?'

"For with all the intense physical suffering there went along a sense of isolation and of destruction. On the Wednesday night before his death this feeling seemed to be overpowering. He asked that every one might leave the room that he might be alone and face to face with Jesus. Then followed such a heart-rending confession of unworthiness, such an appeal for the presence and companionship of the Saviour, such promises, with strong crying and tears, of renewed consecration, of greater diligence and devotion in God's service, as are rarely heard. It was as if the Gethsemane prayer were again ascending.

"The next morning it was clear that he was worse. The long period of sleeplessness was fast wearing him out. Toward evening the doctor, coming in, said in a cheery voice, to rouse him from his lethargy, 'Dr. Gordon, have you a good word for us to-night?' With a clear, full voice he answered, 'Victory!' It was as if, after the typhoon-like sickness, he had passed the last range of breakers and had been given a glimpse of the Eternal City gleaming beyond.

"This was his last audible utterance. Between nine and ten in the evening the nurse motioned to his wife that she was wanted. As she bent over him he whispered, 'Maria, pray.' She led in prayer; he scarce followed sentence by sentence, trying at the close to utter a petition for himself; but his strength was not sufficient for articulation. Five minutes after midnight on the morning of February 2nd he fell asleep in Jesus." *(Miraculous Healing,* pp. 62,63).

Note the pitiful concern, almost despair, as, "He complained of 'the ceaseless storm, the incessant noise as of great raindrops on a window-pane,' " and, "He would groan at 'the sudden bursts of blackness' which overwhelmed him." It was like a Gethsemane. That is part of the disillusionment and heartbreak of those who believe it is always the will of God to heal and do not get healed.

A. E. Thompson tells of some of the final sickness of Dr. Simpson:

> "He attempted to continue to meet the pressure that was upon him during the early months of his physical decline as he had always done. The great adversary, against whose kingdom he had so valiantly warred, attacked him in his weakness and succeeded in casting a cloud over his spirit."

He and his friends battled in prayer with the sickness. He lamented to two friends, "Boys, I do not seem to be able to take quite all that you have asked." And he sent word to the Annual Council of the Christian and Missionary Alliance, "I hope soon to meet you all again as He will. My text to-day is John 11:4—'This sickness is not unto death, but for the glory of God.' " But the sickness *was* unto death. He who had had a cloud over his spirit because of the failure to be healed when he thought everyone ought to have faith to be healed, that illustrates the tragic suffering and heartbreak and disillusionment of people who expect more than God has promised and think it is always God's will to heal the sick.

Dr. Frost sums up the matter in these words:

> 1. Dr. Gordon and Dr. Simpson were, at various times, healed of serious diseases; and, beyond doubt, they lived and worked through many years by reason of the physical empowering of Christ.
> 2. But at times sickness overcame them, and at last final diseases laid hold upon them, grippe, bronchitis and pneumonia, in the case of Dr. Gordon, and hardening of the arteries and paralysis of the body and brain in the case of Dr. Simpson.
> 3. Both were attended, at the last, by physicians, Dr. Gordon taking medicine, Dr. Simpson taking none, this

last because the physician said that there was nothing to be done, which meant that he believed that the disease (arteriosclerosis) was not subject to medical treatment and was incurable, this proving to be true.

4. In both cases, much prayer, by the patients themselves and by hundreds of believing Christians, was offered for immediate and entire healing, scriptural promises being reverently claimed and spiritual and physical deliverance being trustingly anticipated.

5. Neither one sent for the elders of the church and neither was anointed with oil, Dr. Simpson never having been so anointed.

6. Each one, for a considerable time, fell under a spiritual cloud, each concluding that he had lost fellowship with God and was suffering from His displeasure and chastisement. But each one was finally delivered from spiritual darkness and was brought back into the light, though this did not result in prayer for healing being answered and healing being given.

7. In spite of prayer and faith and the ministry of physicians, nurses and friends, both died.

I shall not comment upon the above findings beyond making one remark: While no blame is to be attached to these men of God because of their sickness, suffering and death, yet it is a fact there is a wide discrepancy between their final experiences and what they had taught concerning the Christian's privilege of momentarily and continually deriving his physical life from the life of the resurrected Christ" (*Miraculous Healing*, pp. 67,68).

They do great harm who teach falsehood about anything. And they play with griefs and broken hearts of people in trouble when they teach people to expect what God did not promise and when they claim what God does not give, that is, He does not give always healing to everyone who calls upon Him the best he can. It is not always God's will to heal the sick. And those who so teach do great harm and cause great suffering.

VIII.   GREAT TEMPTATIONS COME TO
DIVINE HEALERS

Divine healers usually claim to be "baptized with the Holy Ghost." Most of them claim the "gift of tongues." Many also claim to have attained "entire sanctification."

Yet there are many temptations that go with claiming the power of God to get people healed. So we find, with grief, Pentecostal leaders are often money-minded, sometimes drunken, sometimes immoral, and they seem to gravitate to companionship with heretics, Catholics, Episcopalians, Mormons and anybody who talks in tongues or believes in healing.

1. The Money Temptation

We do not deny that many healing evangelists are devoted Christians. But do you think they are not tempted and influenced largely by the great financial rewards that come to them? For example, Miss Kathryn Kuhlman was so popular she was almost regarded as apostolic, nearly divine. She always said, of course, that it was the Holy Ghost who did the healing, if some were healed. Thus, of course, any failure in a healing could not be blamed on her. It must be the responsibility of the seeker or the Holy Spirit. But still it was Miss Kuhlman who was idolized.

Miss Kuhlman, speaking as she said for the Holy Spirit, would tell the people, "I feel that several here should give $250. Others should give $100. Some should give $50." And some did, of course, in those giant meetings, with every auditorium she used packed to the doors from, say, 5,000 or 6,000 to 18,000 people. Her income was enormous, of course. She was said to have many beautiful jewels and a million dollars or more. We do not say that the money was not given freely nor that many agree she earned it.

Likely she thought that success proved God's favor on her. She would not be likely to consider the heartbreak of those who failed to be healed or those who were led to claim healing and then didn't have it. She would not be likely to think her doctrine wrong that healing for everybody was offered freely, as long as there was so much money in the campaign, and so she carried it on. It is hard for a divine healer to stop and consider the deception, sometimes the fraud, the false doctrines and the companionship with heretics involved in the healing and tongues meetings, since so much money is involved.

We believe Dr. Oral Roberts is a saved man and a good Christian, but with millions of dollars at hand and more coming in, we can see why Mr. Roberts would continue his course. He has had the fanatical support of multiplied thousands in his healing and tongues ministry.

It would be foolish to suppose that the enormous wealth often amassed by these healing evangelists does not influence them and sometimes corrupt them.

2. Immorality Is Too Often Observed Among Pentecostal Leaders

A newspaper report tells how A. A. Allen, one of the most famous of the healing evangelists, died drunk in a hotel in San Francisco.

A famous woman evangelist, wife of the healing evangelist who died, later announced that she was to have a baby by miraculous conception and birth. The baby was illegitimate, of course.

It was a shocking experience to me, in dealing with many Pentecostal women preachers, to find that usually the woman's husband would be unsaved and often her children unsaved and they had no confidence in her profession. I decided that of all the Pentecostal women I had ever met, a big majority of them had unsaved husbands. That speaks poorly for their influence.

One young man wrote me a few weeks ago telling how he and his wife had been involved in the tongues movement. His wife had talked in tongues, but he found himself coming under possession of an evil spirit and was definitely convinced that the program in that particular case was of Satan.

Is it not strange that the most prominent leaders in the Full Gospel Christian Business Men's Association brazenly pass around misinformation that D. L. Moody talked in tongues, that Charles G. Finney talked in tongues? And they have said the same thing about the principal

Christian leaders today whom I know personally. There is a strange irresponsibility, a lack of reliability in Pentecostal people.

And thousands of ignorant followers, from time to time, openly charge that those of us who do not talk in tongues are devil-possessed, that we blaspheme the Holy Ghost, etc. There is something wrong with the heresies of the Pentecostal movement that tend to break down character.

3. Association With Heretics and Unsaved People in Pentecostal Movement

I lived near a big Episcopal church that had big dances on Saturday night and healing services Sunday night. Why no conviction about that?

Why would Pentecostal leaders rejoice that 4,000 Catholics at Notre Dame talked in tongues and believed in healing, yet they did not know to personally trust Christ for salvation and are depending on confessions to a priest, prayers to Mary, etc.? What kind of doctrine is this that puts one in the company of unconverted Catholics, of unconverted cultists and even in some cases in the company of liberals who do not believe the Bible, the deity of Christ, the virgin birth?

Why is it that Dr. Oral Roberts felt so free to come into the Methodist denomination and so sought and had the company of the most blatant modernists? Dr. George Buttrick, Bishop Oxnam, Bishop Kennedy and others who denied all the fundamentals of the Christian faith—their fellowship and their kind of program did not repel him. What is this lack of fundamental, basic Bible knowledge and conviction that makes a Pentecostalist feel perfectly free with a Mormon, a Catholic or anyone else who has healing meetings or talks in tongues? Heresy always has a moral implication and always is a way downhill.

Why is it that among divine healers and Pentecostal people there is such a great percentage of women preachers? The Scriptures say plainly, "But I suffer not a woman to teach, nor to usurp authority over the man, but to be in silence" (I Tim. 2:12). The Scripture plainly says, "Let your women keep silence in the churches: for it is not permitted unto them to speak; but they are commanded to be under obedience, as also saith the law. And if they will learn any thing, let them ask their husbands at home: for it is a shame for women to speak in the church" (I Cor. 14:34,35).

Why this unconcern about the plain teaching of the Bible? I am saying that the whole Pentecostal movement, with its tongues and healing services, is not based upon the Scriptures and thus leaves people open to every kind of temptation.

4. But Failure of Some Men Does Not Change Heart of God Who So Often Heals the Sick

And we would not leave this discussion of healing without reminding you that God wonderfully answers prayer many, many times for the healing of the sick. He answers prayer in helping doctors and nurses in making clear diets and exercises and medicine that are needed. I have elsewhere described many answers to prayer for healing. I am comforted to remind the reader of another.

At a family reunion, my daughter went into labor and in the hospital had a little boy prematurely. He was so small and weak he was left in the hospital for care for some weeks. They could find no formula that would be retained on his stomach. For several days this went on and the little fellow dwindled to four pounds or less. One day, in deep concern of heart, I got into my car and drove round and round the block in which the hospital was. I pleaded with God that day to help doctors and nurses to know what to do, and to heal this little one. When I was satisfied in my mind that God had heard me, I drove home. That day they tried a new formula. It was just what the baby needed. He began to gain an ounce a day and he prospered and is now a vigorous, fine young fellow in school. God does answer prayer in the matter of doctors and medicine, too.

And God wonderfully answers prayer sometimes without

doctors and contrary to all they think they know. How wonderfully I have seen that again and again—with my father, with my daughter Grace, with Mrs. Jewel Duncan, with a pastor's wife scheduled to die with cancer. God does answer prayer wonderfully, and often He does miraculous healings in answer to prayer.

Let us remember that God's ways are good ways and His will is good. It is not always God's will to heal the sick. It is not very often God's will to work a miracle. Only once, perhaps, in the life of Peter did God raise one like Dorcas from the dead. Only once, we think, in the life of Paul did God raise anyone from the dead—the young man who fell out of the third-loft window and died. God multiplied the meal and the oil for the widow at Zarephath in the case of Elijah, but she was the only widow so treated then.

So miracles are to be unusual, a matter above all, clearly miraculous and wonderful. I leave that door open and when I need a miracle I will plead for one. But miracles were never playthings, never given at the casual desire nor for a show. So, "Is any sick among you? let him call for the elders of the church; and let them pray over him, anointing him with oil in the name of the Lord: And the prayer of faith shall save the sick, and the Lord shall raise him up; and if he have committed sins, they shall be forgiven him. Confess your faults one to another, and pray one for another, that ye may be healed" (Jas. 5:15,16).

That is a wonderful Scripture. I believe it. I have tried to obey it in calling on the Lord for the sick. When God gives the faith, God gives healing. He does not always give the faith.

Index